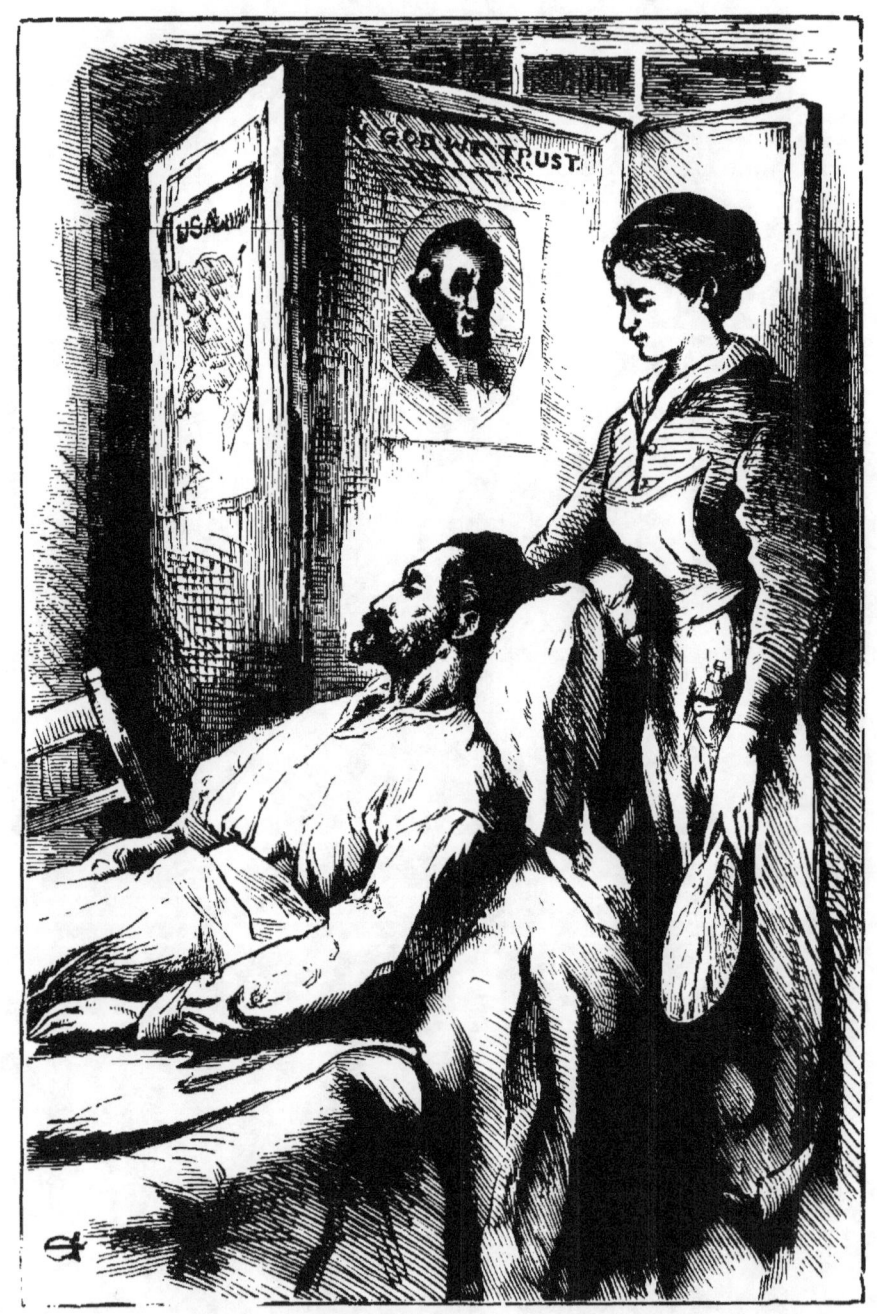

"JOHN."
The manliest man among my forty. — PAGE 53.

Hospital Sketches

AND

Camp and Fireside Stories.

BY

LOUISA M. ALCOTT,

AUTHOR OF "LITTLE WOMEN," "AN OLD-FASHIONED GIRL," "LITTLE MEN," "EIGHT COUSINS," "ROSE IN BLOOM," "UNDER THE LILACS," "JACK AND JILL," "WORK," "SILVER PITCHERS," "AUNT JO'S SCRAP-BAG."

With Illustrations.

BOSTON:
ROBERTS BROTHERS.
1885.

Entered according to Act of Congress, in the year 1869, by
ROBERTS BROTHERS,
In the Clerk's Office of the District Court of the District of Massachusetts.

UNIVERSITY PRESS: JOHN WILSON & SON,
CAMBRIDGE.

PREFACE TO HOSPITAL SKETCHES.

THESE sketches, taken from letters hastily written in the few leisure moments of a very busy life, make no pretension to literary merit, but are simply a brief record of one person's hospital experience. As such, they are republished, with their many faults but partially amended, lest in retouching they should lose whatever force or freshness the inspiration of the time may have given them.

To those who have objected to a "tone of levity" in some portions of the sketches, I desire to say that the wish to make the best of every thing, and send home cheerful reports even from that saddest of scenes, an army hospital, probably produced the impression of levity upon those who have never known the sharp contrasts of the tragic and comic in such a life.

That Nurse Periwinkle gave no account of her religious services, thereby showing a "sad want of Christian experience," can only be explained by the fact, that it would have as soon occurred to her to print the letters written for the men, their penitent confidences, or their dying messages, as to mention the prayers she prayed, the hymns she sung, the sacred words she read; while the "*Christian experience*" she was receiving then and there was far too deep and earnest to be recorded in a newspaper.

The unexpected favor with which the little book was greeted, and the desire for a new edition, increase the author's regret that it is not more worthy such a kind reception. **L. M. A.**

CONCORD, March, 1869.

CONTENTS.

HOSPITAL SKETCHES.

CHAP.		PAGE
I.	Obtaining Supplies	3
II.	A Forward Movement	15
III.	A Day	25
IV.	A Night	40
V.	Off Duty	60
VI.	A Postscript	80

CAMP AND FIRESIDE STORIES.

	PAGE
The King of Clubs and the Queen of Hearts	99
Mrs. Podgers' Teapot	143
My Contraband	169
Love and Loyalty	198
A Modern Cinderella	257
The Blue and the Gray	295
A Hospital Christmas	317
An Hour	345

LOUISA M. ALCOTT'S WRITINGS

"Miss Alcott is really a benefactor of households." — H. H.

"Miss Alcott has a faculty of entering into the lives and feelings of children that is conspicuously wanting in most writers who address them, and to this cause, to the consciousness among her readers that they are hearing about people like themselves, instead of abstract qualities labelled with names, the popularity of her books is due." — Mrs. SARAH J. HALE.

"Dear Aunt Jo! You are embalmed in the thoughts and loves of thousands of little men and little women." — EXCHANGE.

Little Women; or, Meg, Jo, Beth, and Amy. With illustrations. Two volumes. 16mo . . $3.00
The same, complete in one volume. With illustrations. 16mo 1.50
Hospital Sketches, and Camp and Fireside Stories. With illustrations. 16mo 1.50
An Old-Fashioned Girl. With illustrations. 16mo 1.50
Little Men: Life at Plumfield with Jo's Boys. With illustrations. 16mo 1.50
Eight Cousins; or, The Aunt-Hill. With illustrations. 16mo . . . 1.50
Rose in Bloom. A sequel to "Eight Cousins." 16mo . . . 1.50
Under the Lilacs. With illustrations. 16mo 1.50
Jack and Jill. A Village Story. With illustrations. 16mo . . . 1.50
Work: A Story of Experience. With character illustrations by Sol Eytinge. 16mo 1.50
Moods. A Novel. New edition, revised and enlarged. 16mo . . 1.50
Silver Pitchers and Independence. A Centennial Love Story. 16mo 1.25
Proverb Stories. New edition, revised and enlarged. 16mo . . . 1.25
Spinning-Wheel Stories. With illustrations. 16mo 1.25
My Boys, &c. First volume of Aunt Jo's Scrap-Bag. 16mo . . 1.00

Shawl-Straps. Second volume of Aunt Jo's Scrap-Bag. 16mo . . $1.00
Cupid and Chow-Chow, &c. Third volume of Aunt Jo's Scrap-Bag. 16mo 1.00
My Girls, &c. Fourth volume of Aunt Jo's Scrap-Bag. 16mo . . 1.00
Jimmy's Cruise in the Pinafore, &c. Fifth volume of Aunt Jo's Scrap-Bag. 16mo 1.00
An Old-Fashioned Thanksgiving, &c. Sixth volume of Aunt Jo's Scrap-Bag. 16mo . . . 1.00
Little Women. Illustrated. Embellished with nearly 200 characteristic illustrations from original designs drawn expressly for this edition of this noted American Classic. One small quarto, bound in cloth, with emblematic designs 3.50
Little Women Series. Printed on large paper, with new illustrations, and in uniform bindings of new and tasteful design, printed in black, red, and gold. Each volume is complete in itself. The books comprising this set are as follows, viz.: —

Little Women; Little Men; Eight Cousins; Under the Lilacs; An Old-Fashioned Girl; Hospital Sketches; Rose in Bloom; Jack and Jill. 8 large 16mo volumes in a handsome box 12.00

These books are for sale at all bookstores, or will be mailed, post-paid, on receipt of price, to any address.

ROBERTS BROTHERS, PUBLISHERS.

HOSPITAL SKETCHES.

CHAPTER I.

OBTAINING SUPPLIES.

"I want something to do."

This remark being addressed to the world in general, no one in particular felt it their duty to reply; so I repeated it to the smaller world about me, received the following suggestions, and settled the matter by answering my own inquiry, as people are apt to do when very much in earnest.

"Write a book," quoth the author of my being.

"Don't know enough, sir. First live, then write."

"Try teaching again," suggested my mother.

"No thank you, ma'am, ten years of that is enough."

"Take a husband like my Darby, and fulfill your mission," said sister Joan, home on a visit.

"Can't afford expensive luxuries, Mrs. Coobiddy."

"Turn actress, and immortalize your name," said sister Vashti, striking an attitude.

"I won't."

"Go nurse the soldiers," said my young neighbor, Tom, panting for "the tented field."

"I will!"

So far, very good. Here was the will, and plenty of it; now for the way. At first sight not a foot of it appeared; but that didn't matter, for the Periwinkles are a hopeful race. Their crest is an anchor, with three cock-a-doodles crowing atop. They all wear rose-colored spectacles, and are lineal descendants of the inventor of aerial architecture. An hour's conversation on the subject set the whole family in a blaze of enthusiasm. A model hospital was erected, and each member had accepted an honorable post therein. The paternal P. was chaplain, the maternal P. was matron, and all the youthful P.'s filled the pod of futurity with achievements whose brilliancy eclipsed the glories of the present and the past. Arriving at this satisfactory conclusion, the meeting adjourned; and the fact that Miss Tribulation was available as army nurse went abroad on the wings of the wind.

In a few days a townswoman heard of my desire, approved of it, and brought about an interview with one of the sisterhood which I wished to join, who was at home on a furlough, and able and willing to satisfy all inquiries. A morning chat with Miss General S.—we hear no end of Mrs. Generals, why not a Miss?—produced three results: I felt that I could do the work, was offered a place, and accepted it, promising not to desert, but stand ready to march on Washington at an hour's notice.

A few days were necessary for the letter containing my request and recommendation to reach headquarters, and another, containing my commission, to return; therefore no time was to be lost; and heartily thanking my pair of friends, I tore home through the December slush as if the rebels were after me, and like many another recruit, burst in upon my family with the announcement—

"I've enlisted!"

An impressive silence followed. Tom, the irrepressible, broke it with a slap on the shoulder and the graceful compliment—

"Old Trib, you're a trump!"

"Thank you; then I'll *take* something:" which I did, in the shape of dinner, reeling off my news at the rate of three dozen words to a mouthful; and as every one else talked equally fast, and all together, the scene was most inspiring.

As boys going to sea immediately become nautical in speech, walk as if they already had their "sea legs" on, and shiver their timbers on all possible occasions, so I turned military at once, called my dinner my rations, saluted all new comers, and ordered a dress parade that very afternoon. Having reviewed every rag I possessed, I detailed some for picket duty while airing over the fence; some to the sanitary influences of the wash-tub; others to mount guard in the trunk; while the weak and wounded went to the Work-basket Hospital, to be made ready for active service again. To this squad I devoted myself for a week; but all was done, and I had time to get powerfully impatient before the letter came. It did arrive however, and brought a disappointment along with its good will and friendliness, for it told me that the place in the Armory Hospital that I supposed I was to take, was already filled, and a much less desirable one at Hurly-burly House was offered instead.

"That's just your luck, Trib. I'll take your trunk up garret for you again; for of course you won't go," Tom remarked, with the disdainful pity which small boys affect when they get into their teens. I was wavering in my secret soul, but that settled the matter, and I crushed him on the spot with martial brevity—

"It is now one; I shall march at six"

I have a confused recollection of spending the afternoon in pervading the house like an executive whirlwind, with my family swarming after me, all working, talking, prophesying and lamenting, while I packed my " go-abroady " possessions, tumbled the rest into two big boxes, danced on the lids till they shut, and gave them in charge, with the direction,—

" If I never come back, make a bonfire of them."

Then I choked down a cup of tea, generously salted instead of sugared, by some agitated relative, shouldered my knapsack—it was only a traveling bag, but do let me preserve the unities—hugged my family three times all round without a vestige of unmanly emotion, till a certain dear old lady broke down upon my neck, with a despairing sort of wail—

" Oh, my dear, my dear, how can I let you go ?"

" I'll stay if you say so, mother."

" But I don't ; go, and the Lord will take care of you."

Much of the Roman matron's courage had gone into the Yankee matron's composition, and, in spite of her tears, she would have sent ten sons to the war, had she possessed them, as freely as she sent one daughter, smiling and flapping on the door-step till I vanished, though the eyes that followed me were very dim, and the handkerchief she waved was very wet.

My transit from The Gables to the village depot was a funny mixture of good wishes and good byes, mud-puddles and shopping. A December twilight is not the most cheering time to enter upon a somewhat perilous enterprise, and, but for the presence of Vashti and neighbor Tom, I fear that I might have added a drop of the briny to the native moisture of—

" The town I left behind me ;"

though I'd no thought of giving out: oh, bless you, no ! When the engine screeched " Here we are," I clutched my escort in a fervent embrace, and skipped into the car with as blithe a farewell as if going on a bridal tour—though I believe brides don't usually wear cavernous black bonnets and fuzzy brown coats, with a hair-brush, a pair of rubbers, two books, and a bag of ginger-bread distorting the pockets of the same. If I thought that any one would believe it, I'd boldly state that I slept from C. to B., which would simplify matters immensely; but as I know they wouldn't, I'll confess that the head under the funereal coal-hod fermented with all manner of high thoughts and heroic purposes "to do or die,"— perhaps both; and the heart under the fuzzy brown coat felt very tender with the memory of the dear old lady, probably sobbing over her army socks and the loss of her topsy-turvy Trib. At this juncture I took the veil, and what I did behind it is nobody's business; but I maintain that the soldier who cries when his mother says "Good bye," is the boy to fight best, and die bravest, when the time comes, or go back to her better than he went.

Till nine o'clock I trotted about the city streets, doing those last errands which no woman would even go to heaven without attempting, if she could. Then I went to my usual refuge, and, fully intending to keep awake, as a sort of vigil appropriate to the occasion, fell fast asleep and dreamed propitious dreams till my rosy-faced cousin waked me with a kiss.

A bright day smiled upon my enterprise, and at ten I reported myself to my General, received last instructions and no end of the sympathetic encouragement which women give, in look, touch, and tone more effectually than in words. The next step was to get a free pass to Washington, for I'd no desire to waste my substance on railroad companies when "the boys" needed even a spinster's mite. A friend of mine had procured such a pass, and I was bent on doing likewise, though I had to face the president of the railroad to accomplish it. I'm a bashful individual, though I can't get any one to believe it; so it cost me a great effort to poke about the Worcester depot till the right door appeared, then walk into a room containing several gentlemen, and blunder out my request in a high state of stammer and blush. Nothing could have been more courteous than this dreaded President, but it was evident that I had made as absurd a demand as if I had asked for the nose off his respectable face. He referred me to the Governor at the State House, and I backed out, leaving him no doubt to regret that such mild maniacs were left at large. Here was a Scylla and Charybdis business: as if a President wasn't trying enough, without the Governor of Massachusetts and the Hub of the Hub on top of that.

"I never can do it," thought I. "Tom will hoot at you if you don't," whispered the inconvenient little voice that is always goading people to the performance of disagreeable duties, and always appeals to the most effective agent to produce the proper result. The idea of allowing any boy that ever wore a felt basin and a shoddy jacket with a microscopic tail, to crow over me, was preposterous, so giving myself a mental slap for such faint-heartedness, I streamed away across the Common, wondering if I ought to say "your Honor," or simply "Sir," and decided upon the latter, fortifying myself with recollections of an evening in a charming green library, where I beheld the Governor placidly consuming oysters, and laughing as if Massachusetts was a myth, and he had no heavier burden on his shoulders than his host's handsome hands.

Like an energetic fly in a very large cobweb, I struggled through the State House, getting into all the wrong rooms and none of the right, till I turned desperate, and went into one, resolving not to come out till I'd made somebody hear and answer me. I suspect that of all the wrong places I had blundered into, this was the most so. But I didn't care; and, though the apartment was full of soldiers, surgeons, starers, and spittoons, I cornered a perfectly incapable person, and proceeded to pump for information with the following result:

"Was the Governor anywhere about?"

No, he wasn't.

"Could he tell me where to look?"

No, he couldn't.

"Did he know anything about free passes?"

No, he didn't.

"Was there any one there of whom I could inquire?"

Not a person.

"Did he know of any place where information could be obtained?"

Not a place.

"Could he throw the smallest gleam of light upon the matter, in any way?"

Not a ray.

I am naturally irascible, and if I could have shaken this negative gentleman vigorously, the relief would have been immense. The prejudices of society forbidding this mode of redress, I merely glowered at him; and, before my wrath found vent in words, my General appeared, having seen me from an opposite window, and come to know what I was about. At her command the languid gentleman woke up, and troubled himself to remember that Major or Sergeant or something Mc K. knew all about the tickets, and his office was in Milk Street. I perked up instanter, and then, as if the exertion was too much for him, what did this animated wet blanket do but add—

"I think Mc K. may have left Milk Street, now, and I don't know where he has gone."

"Never mind; the new comers will know where he has moved to, my dear, so don't be discouraged; and if you don't succeed, come to me, and we will see what to do next," said my General.

I blessed her in a fervent manner and a cool hall, fluttered round the corner, and bore down upon Milk street, bent on discovering Mc K. if such a being was to be found. He wasn't, and the ignorance of the neighborhood was really pitiable. Nobody knew anything, and after tumbling over bundles of leather, bumping against big boxes, being nearly annihilated by descending bales, and sworn at by aggravated truckmen, I finally elicited the advice to look for Mc K. in Haymarket Square. Who my informant was I've really forgotten; for, having hailed several busy gentlemen, some one of them fabricated this delusive quietus for the perturbed spirit, who instantly departed to the sequestered locality he named. If I had been in search of the Koh-i-noor diamond I should have been as likely to find it there as any vestige of Mc K. I stared at signs, inquired in shops, invaded an eating house, visited the recruiting tent in the middle of the Square, made myself a nuisance generally, and accumulated fine samples of mud from every gutter I fell into. All in vain; and I mournfully turned my face toward the General's, feeling that I should be forced to enrich the railroad company after all, when, suddenly, I beheld that admirable young man, brother-in-law Darby Coobiddy, Esq. I arrested him with a burst of news, and wants, and woes, which caused his manly countenance to lose its usual repose.

"Oh, my dear boy, I'm going to Washington at five, and I can't find the free ticket man, and there won't be time to see

Joan, and I'm so tired and cross I don't know what to do; and will you help me, like a cherub as you are?"

"Oh, yes, of course. I know a fellow who will set us right," responded Darby, mildly excited, and darting into some kind of an office, held counsel with an invisible angel, who sent him out radiant. "All serene. I've got him. I'll see you through the business, and then get Joan from the Dove Cote in time to see you off."

I'm a woman's rights woman, and if any man had offered help in the morning, I should have condescendingly refused it, sure that I could do everything as well, if not better, myself. My strong-mindedness had rather abated since then, and I was now quite ready to be a "timid trembler," if necessary. Dear me! how easily Darby did it all: he just asked one question, received an answer, tucked me under his arm, and in ten minutes I stood in the presence of Mc K., the Desired.

"Now my troubles are over," thought I, and as usual was direfully mistaken.

"You will have to get a pass from Dr. H., in Temple Place, before I can give you a pass, madam," answered Mc K., as blandly as if he wasn't carrying desolation to my soul. Oh, indeed! why didn't he send me to Dorchester Heights, India Wharf, or Bunker Hill Monument, and done with it? Here I was, after a morning's tramp, down in some place about Dock Square, and was told to step to Temple Place. Nor was that all; he might as well have asked me to catch a humming-bird, toast a salamander, or call on the man in the moon, as find a Doctor at home at the busiest hour of the day. It was a blow; but weariness had extinguished enthusiasm, and resignation clothed me as a garment. I sent Darby for Joan, and doggedly paddled off, feeling that mud was my native element, and quite sure that the evening papers would announce the appearance of the Wandering Jew, in feminine habiliments.

"Is Dr. H. in?"

"No, mum, he aint."

Of course he wasn't; I knew that before I asked: and, considering it all in the light of a hollow mockery, added:

"When will he probably return?"

If the damsel had said, "ten to-night," I should have felt a grim satisfaction, in the fulfillment of my own dark prophecy; but she said, "At two, mum;" and I felt it a personal insult.

"I'll call, then. Tell him my business is important:" with which mysteriously delivered message I departed, hoping that I left her consumed with curiosity; for mud rendered me an object of interest.

By way of resting myself, I crossed the Common, for the third time, bespoke the carriage, got some lunch, packed my purchases, smoothed my plumage, and was back again, as the clock struck two. The Doctor hadn't come yet; and I was morally certain that he would not, till, having waited till the last minute, I was driven to buy a ticket, and, five minutes after the irrevocable deed was done, he would be at my service, with all manner of helpful documents and directions. Everything goes by contraries with me; so, having made up my mind to be disappointed, of course I wasn't; for, presently, in walked Dr. H., and no sooner had he heard my errand, and glanced at my credentials, than he said, with the most engaging readiness:

"I will give you the order, with pleasure, madam."

Words cannot express how soothing and delightful it was to find, at last, somebody who could do what I wanted, without sending me from Dan to Beersheba, for a dozen other bodies to do something else first. Peace descended, like oil, upon the ruffled waters of my being, as I sat listening to the busy scratch of his pen; and, when he turned about, giving me not only the order, but a paper of directions wherewith to smooth away all difficulties between Boston and Washington, I felt as did poor Christian when the Evangelist gave him the scroll, on the safe side of the Slough of Despond. I've no doubt many dismal nurses have inflicted themselves upon the worthy gentleman since then; but I am sure none have been more kindly helped, or are more grateful, than T. P.; for that short interview added another to the many pleasant associations that already surround his name.

Feeling myself no longer a "Martha Struggles," but a comfortable young woman, with plain sailing before her, and the worst of the voyage well over, I once more presented myself to the valuable Mc K. The order was read, and certain printed papers, necessary to be filled out, were given a young gentleman—no, I prefer to say Boy, with a scornful emphasis upon the word, as the only means of revenge now left me. This Boy, instead of doing his duty with the diligence so charming in the young, loitered and lounged, in a manner which proved his education to have been sadly neglected in the—

"How doth the little busy bee,"

direction. He stared at me, gaped out of the window, ate peanuts, and gossiped with his neighbors—Boys, like himself, and all penned in a row, like colts at a Cattle Show. I don't imagine he knew the anguish he was inflicting; for it was nearly three, the train left at five, and I had my ticket to get, my dinner to eat, my blessed sister to see, and the depot to reach, if I didn't die of apoplexy. Meanwhile Patience certainly had her perfect work that day, and I hope she enjoyed the job more than I did. Having waited some twenty minutes, it pleased this reprehensible Boy to make various marks and blots on my documents, toss them to a venerable creature of sixteen, who delivered them to me with such paternal directions, that it only needed a pat on the head and an encouraging—" Now run home to your Ma, little girl, and mind the crossings, my dear," to make the illusion quite perfect.

Why I was sent to a steamboat office for car tickets, is not for me to say, though I went as meekly as I should have gone to the Probate Court, if sent. A fat, easy gentleman gave me several bits of paper, with coupons attached, with a warning not to separate them, which instantly inspired me with a yearning to pluck them apart, and see what came of it. But, remembering through what fear and tribulation I had obtained them, I curbed Satan's promptings, and, clutching my prize, as if it were my pass to the Elysian Fields, I hurried home. Dinner was rapidly consumed; Joan enlightened, comforted, and kissed; the dearest of apple-faced cousins hugged; the kindest of apple-faced cousins' fathers subjected to the same process; and I mounted the ambulance, baggage-wagon, or anything you please but hack, and drove away, too tired to feel excited, sorry, or glad.

CHAPTER II.

A FORWARD MOVEMENT.

As travelers like to give their own impressions of a journey, though every inch of the road may have been described a half a dozen times before, I add some of the notes made by the way, hoping that they will amuse the reader, and convince the skeptical that such a being as Nurse Periwinkle does exist, that she really did go to Washington, and that these Sketches are not romance.

New York Train—Seven P. M.—Spinning along to take the boat at New London. Very comfortable; munch gingerbread, and Mrs. C.'s fine pear, which deserves honorable mention, because my first loneliness was comforted by it, and pleasant recollections of both kindly sender and bearer. Look much at Dr. H.'s paper of directions—put my tickets in every conceivable place, that they may be get-at-able, and finish by losing them entirely. Suffer agonies till a compassionate neighbor pokes them out of a crack with his pen-knife. Put them in the inmost corner of my purse, that in the deepest recesses of my pocket, pile a collection of miscellaneous articles atop, and pin up the whole. Just get composed, feeling that I've done my best to keep them safely, when the Conductor appears, and I'm forced to rout them all out again, exposing my precautions, and getting into a flutter at keeping the man waiting. Finally, fasten them on the seat before me, and keep one eye steadily upon the yellow torments, till I forget all about them, in chat with the gentleman who shares my seat. Having heard complaints of the absurd way in which American women become images of petrified propriety, if addressed by strangers, when traveling alone, the inborn perversity of my nature causes me to assume an entirely opposite style of deportment; and, finding my companion hails from Little Athens, is acquainted with several of my three hundred and sixty-five cousins, and in every way a respectable and respectful member of society, I put my bashfulness in my pocket, and plunge into a long conversation on the war, the weather, music, Carlyle, skating, genius, hoops, and the immortality of the soul.

Ten, P. M.—Very sleepy. Nothing to be seen outside, but darkness made visible; nothing inside but every variety of bunch into which the human form can be twisted, rolled, or "massed," as Miss Prescott says of her jewels. Every man's legs sprawl drowsily, every woman's head (but mine,) nods, till it finally settles on somebody's shoulder, a new proof of the truth of the everlasting oak and vine simile; children fret; lovers whisper; old folks snore, and somebody privately imbibes brandy, when the lamps go out. The penetrating perfume rouses the multitude, causing some to start up, like war horses at the smell of powder. When the lamps are relighted, every one laughs, sniffs, and looks inquiringly at his neighbor—every one but a stout gentleman, who, with well-gloved hands folded upon his broad-cloth rotundity, sleeps on impressively. Had he been innocent, he would have waked up; for, to slumber in that babe-like manner, with a car full of giggling, staring, sniffing humanity, was simply preposterous. Public suspicion was down upon him at once. I doubt if the appearance of a flat black bottle with a label would have settled the matter more effectually than did the over dignified and profound repose of this short-sighted being. His moral neck-cloth, virtuous boots, and pious attitude availed him nothing, and it was well he kept his eyes shut, for " Humbug !" twinkled at him from every window-pane, brass nail and human eye around him.

Eleven, P. M.—In the boat "City of Boston," escorted thither by my car acquaintance, and deposited in the cabin. Trying to look as if the greater portion of my life had been passed on board boats, but painfully conscious that I don't know the first thing; so sit bolt upright, and stare about me till I hear one lady say to another—"We must secure our berths at once;" whereupon I dart at one, and, while leisurely taking off my cloak, wait to discover what the second move may be. Several ladies draw the curtains that hang in a semi-circle before each nest—instantly I whisk mine smartly together, and then peep out to see what next. Gradually, on hooks above the blue and yellow drapery, appear the coats and bonnets of my neighbors, while their boots and shoes, in every imaginable attitude, assert themselves below, as if their owners had committed suicide in a body. A violent creaking, scrambling, and fussing, causes the fact that people are going regularly to bed to dawn upon my mind. Of course they are; and so am I—but pause at the seventh pin, remembering that, as I was born to be drowned, an eligible opportunity now presents itself; and, having twice escaped a watery grave, the third immersion will certainly extinguish my vital spark. The boat is new, but if it ever intends to blow up, spring a leak, catch afire, or be run into, it will do the deed to-night, because I'm here to fulfill my destiny. With tragic calmness I resign myself, replace my pins, lash my purse and papers together, with my handkerchief, examine the saving circumference of my hoop, and look about me for any means of deliverance when the moist moment shall arrive; for I've no intention of folding my hands and bubbling to death without an energetic splashing first. Barrels, hen-coops, portable settees, and life-preservers do not adorn the cabin, as they should; and, roving wildly to and fro, my eye sees no ray of hope till it falls upon a plump old lady, devoutly reading in the cabin Bible, and a voluminous night-cap. I remember that, at the swimming school, fat girls always floated best, and in an instant my plan is laid. At the first alarm I firmly attach myself to the plump lady, and cling to her through fire and water; for I feel that my old enemy, the cramp, will seize me by the foot, if I attempt to swim; and, though I can hardly expect to reach Jersey City with myself and my baggage in as good condition as I hoped, I might manage to get picked up by holding to my fat friend; if not it will be a comfort to feel that I've made an effort and shall die in good society. Poor dear woman! how little she dreamed, as she read and rocked, with her cap in a high state of starch, and her feet comfortably cooking at the register, what fell designs were hovering about her, and how intently a small but determined eye watched her, till it suddenly closed.

Sleep got the better of fear to such an extent that my boots appeared to gape, and my bonnet nodded on its peg, before I gave in. Having piled my cloak, bag, rubbers, books and umbrella on the lower shelf, I drowsily swarmed on to the upper one, tumbling down a few times, and excoriating the knobby portions of my frame in the act. A very brief nap on the upper roost was enough to set me gasping as if a dozen feather beds and the whole boat were laid over me. Out I turned; and, after a series of convulsions, which caused my neighbor to ask if I wanted the stewardess, I managed to get my luggage up and myself down. But even in the lower berth, my rest was not unbroken, for various articles kept dropping off the little shelf at the bottom of the bed, and every time I flew up, thinking my hour had come, I bumped my head severely against the little shelf at the top, evidently put there for that express purpose. At last, after listening to the swash of the waves outside, wondering if the machinery usually creaked in that way, and watching a knot-hole in the side of my berth, sure that death would creep in there as soon as I took my eye from it, I dropped asleep, and dreamed of muffins.

Five, *A. M.*—On deck, trying to wake up and enjoy an east wind and a morning fog, and a twilight sort of view of something on the shore. Rapidly achieve my purpose, and do enjoy every moment, as we go rushing through the Sound, with steamboats passing up and down, lights dancing on the shore, mist wreaths slowly furling off, and a pale pink sky above us, as the sun comes up.

Seven, *A. M.*—In the cars, at Jersey City. Much fuss with tickets, which one man scribbles over, another snips, and a third "makes note on." Partake of refreshment, in the gloom of a very large and dirty depot. Think that my sandwiches would be more relishing without so strong a flavor of napkin, and my gingerbread more easy of consumption if it had not been pulverized by being sat upon. People act as if early traveling didn't agree with them. Children scream and scamper; men smoke and growl; women shiver and fret; porters swear; great truck horses pace up and down with loads of baggage; and every one seems to get into the wrong car, and come tumbling out again. One man, with three children, a dog, a bird-cage, and several bundles, puts himself and his possessions into every possible place where a man, three children, dog, bird-cage and bundles could be got, and is satisfied with none of them. I follow their movements, with an interest that is really exhausting, and, as they vanish, hope for rest, but don't get it. A strong-minded woman, with a tumbler in her hand, and no cloak or shawl on, comes rushing through the car, talking loudly to a small porter, who lugs a folding bed after her, and looks as if life were a burden to him.

"You promised to have it ready. It is not ready. It must be a car with a water jar, the windows must be shut, the fire must be kept up, the blinds must be down. No, this won't do. I shall go through the whole train, and suit myself, for you promised to have it ready. It is not ready," &c., all through again, like a hand-organ. She haunted the cars, the depot, the office and baggage-room, with her bed, her tumbler, and her tongue, till the train started; and a sense of fervent gratitude filled my soul, when I found that she and her unknown invalid were not to share our car.

Philadelphia.—An old place, full of Dutch women, in "bellus top" bonnets, selling vegetables, in long, open markets. Every one seems to be scrubbing their white steps. All the houses look like tidy jails, with their outside shutters. Several have crape on the door-handles, and many have flags flying from roof or balcony. Few men appear, and the women seem to do the business, which, perhaps, accounts for its being so well done. Pass fine buildings, but don't know what they are. Would like to stop and see my native city;

for, having left it at the tender age of two, my recollections are not vivid.

Baltimore.—A big, dirty, shippy, shiftless place, full of goats, geese, colored people, and coal, at least the part of it I see. Pass near the spot where the riot took place, and feel as if I should enjoy throwing a stone at somebody, hard. Find a guard at the ferry, the depot, and here and there, along the road. A camp whitens one hill-side, and a cavalry training school, or whatever it should be called, is a very interesting sight, with quantities of horses and riders galloping, marching, leaping, and skirmishing, over all manner of break-neck places. A party of English people get in—the men, with sandy hair and red whiskers, all trimmed alike, to a hair; rough grey coats, very rosy, clean faces, and a fine, full way of speaking, which is particularly agreeable, after our slipshod American gabble. The two ladies wear funny velvet fur-trimmed hoods; are done up, like compact bundles, in tartan shawls; and look as if bent on seeing everything thoroughly. The devotion of one elderly John Bull to his red-nosed spouse was really beautiful to behold. She was plain and cross, and fussy and stupid, but J. B., Esq., read no papers when she was awake, turned no cold shoulder when she wished to sleep, and cheerfully said, "Yes, me dear," to every wish or want the wife of his bosom expressed. I quite warmed to the excellent man, and asked a question or two, as the only means of expressing my good will. He answered very civilly, but evidently hadn't been used to being addressed by strange women in public conveyances; and Mrs. B. fixed her green eyes upon me, as if she thought me a forward huzzy, or whatever is good English for a presuming young woman. The pair left their friends before we reached Washington; and the last I saw of them was a vision of a large plaid lady, stalking grimly away, on the arm of a rosy, stout gentleman, loaded with rugs, bags, and books, but still devoted, still smiling, and waving a hearty " Fare ye well ! We'll meet ye at Willard's on Chusday."

Soon after their departure we had an accident; for no long journey in America would be complete without one. A coupling iron broke; and, after leaving the last car behind us, we waited for it to come up, which it did, with a crash that knocked every one forward on their faces, and caused several old ladies to screech dismally. Hats flew off, bonnets were flattened, the stove skipped, the lamps fell down, the water jar turned a somersault, and the wheel just over which I sat received some damage. Of course, it became necessary for all the men to get out, and stand about in everybody's way, while repairs were made; and for the women to wrestle their heads out of the windows, asking ninety-nine foolish questions to one sensible one. A few wise females seized this favorable moment to better their seats, well knowing that few men can face the wooden stare with which they regard the former possessors of the places they have invaded.

The country through which we passed did not seem so very unlike that which I had left, except that it was more level and less wintry. In summer time the wide fields would have shown me new sights, and the way-side hedges blossomed with new flowers; now, everything was sere and sodden, and a general air of shiftlessness prevailed, which would have caused a New England farmer much disgust, and a strong desire to " buckle to," and " right up " things. Dreary little houses, with chimneys built outside, with clay and rough sticks piled crosswise, as we used to build cob towers, stood in barren looking fields, with cow, pig, or mule lounging about the door. We often passed colored people, looking as if they had come out of a picture book, or off the stage, but not at all the sort of people I'd been accustomed to see at the North.

Way-side encampments made the fields and lanes gay with blue coats and the glitter of buttons. Military washes flapped and fluttered on the fences; pots were steaming in the open air; all sorts of tableaux seen through the openings of tents, and everywhere the boys threw up their caps and cut capers as we passed.

Washington.—It was dark when we arrived; and, but for the presence of another friendly gentleman, I should have yielded myself a helpless prey to the first overpowering hackman, who insisted that I wanted to go just where I didn't. Putting me into the conveyance I belonged in, my escort added to the obligation by pointing out the objects of interest which we passed in our long drive. Though I'd often been told that Washington was a spacious place, its visible magnitude quite took my breath away, and of course I quoted Randolph's expression, "a city of magnificent distances," as I suppose every one does when they see it. The Capitol was so like the pictures that hang opposite the staring Father of his Country, in boarding-houses and hotels, that it did not impress me, except to recall the time when I was sure that Cinderella went to housekeeping in just such a place, after she had married the inflammable Prince; though, even at that early period, I had my doubts as to the wisdom of a match whose foundation was of glass.

The White House was lighted up, and carriages were rolling in and out of the great gate. I stared hard at the famous East Room, and would have liked a peep through the crack of the door. My old gentleman was indefatigable in his attentions, and I said "Splendid!" to everything he pointed out, though I suspect I often admired the wrong place, and missed the right. Pennsylvania Avenue, with its bustle, lights, music, and military, made me feel as if I'd crossed the water and landed somewhere in Carnival time. Coming to less noticeable parts of the city, my companion fell silent, and I meditated upon the perfection which Art had attained in America—having just passed a bronze statue of some hero, who looked like a black Methodist minister, in a cocked hat, above the waist, and a tipsy squire below; while his horse stood like an opera dancer, on one leg, in a high, but somewhat remarkable wind, which blew his mane one way and his massive tail the other.

"Hurly-burly House, ma'am!" called a voice, startling me from my reverie, as we stopped before a great pile of buildings, with a flag flying before it, sentinels at the door, and a very trying quantity of men lounging about. My heart beat rather faster than usual, and it suddenly struck me that I was very far from home; but I descended with dignity, wondering whether I should be stopped for want of a countersign, and forced to pass the night in the street. Marching boldly up the steps, I found that no form was necessary, for the men fell back, the guard touched their caps, a boy opened the door, and, as it closed behind me, I felt that I was **fairly started, and Nurse Periwinkle's Mission was begun.**

CHAPTER III.

A DAY.

"THEY'VE come! they've come! hurry up, ladies—you're wanted."

"Who have come? the rebels?"

This sudden summons in the gray dawn was somewhat startling to a three days' nurse like myself, and, as the thundering knock came at our door, I sprang up in my bed, prepared

> "To gird my woman's form,
> And on the ramparts die,"

if necessary; but my room-mate took it more coolly, and, as she began a rapid toilet, answered my bewildered question,—

"Bless you, no child; it's the wounded from Fredericksburg; forty ambulances are at the door, and we shall have our hands full in fifteen minutes."

"What shall we have to do?"

"Wash, dress, feed, warm and nurse them for the next three months, I dare say. Eighty beds are ready, and we were getting impatient for the men to come. Now you will begin to see hospital life in earnest, for you won't probably find time to sit down all day, and may think yourself fortunate if you get to bed by midnight. Come to me in the ball-room when you are ready; the worst cases are always carried there, and I shall need your help."

So saying, the energetic little woman twirled her hair into a button at the back of her head, in a " cleared for action " sort of style, and vanished, wrestling her way into a feminine kind of pea-jacket as she went.

I am free to confess that I had a realizing sense of the fact that my hospital bed was not a bed of roses just then, or the prospect before me one of unmingled rapture. My three days' experiences had begun with a death, and, owing to the defalcation of another nurse, a somewhat abrupt plunge into the superintendence of a ward containing forty beds, where I spent my shining hours washing faces, serving rations, giving medicine, and sitting in a very hard chair, with pneumonia on one side, diptheria on the other, two typhoids opposite, and a dozen dilapidated patriots, hopping, lying, and lounging about, all staring more or less at the new " nuss," who suffered untold agonies, but concealed them under as matronly an aspect as a spinster could assume, and blundered through her trying labors with a Spartan firmness, which I hope they appreciated, but am afraid they didn't. Having a taste for " ghastliness," I had rather longed for the wounded to arrive, for rheumatism wasn't heroic, neither was liver complaint, or measles; even fever had lost its charms since " bathing burning brows " had been used up in romances, real and ideal. But when I peeped into the dusky street lined with what I at first had innocently called market carts, now unloading their sad freight at our door, I recalled sundry reminiscences I had heard from nurses of longer standing, my ardor experienced a sudden chill, and I indulged in a most unpatriotic wish that I was safe at home again, with a quiet day before me, and no necessity for being hustled up, as if I were a hen and had only to hop off my roost, give my plumage a peck, and be ready for action. A second bang at the door sent this recreant desire to the right about, as a little woolly head popped in, and Joey, (a six years' old contraband,) announced—

"Miss Blank is jes' wild fer ye, and says fly round right away. They's comin' in, I tell yer, heaps on 'em—one was took out dead, and I see him,—hi! warn't he a goner!"

With which cheerful intelligence the imp scuttled away, singing like a blackbird, and I followed, feeling that Richard was *not* himself again, and wouldn't be for a long time to come.

The first thing I met was a regiment of the vilest odors that ever assaulted the human nose, and took it by storm. Cologne, with its seven and seventy evil savors, was a posy-bed to it; and the worst of this affliction was, every one had assured me that it was a chronic weakness of all hospitals, and I must bear it. I did, armed with lavender water, with which I so besprinkled myself and premises, that I was soon known among my patients as "the nurse with the bottle." Having been run over by three excited surgeons, bumped against by migratory coal-hods, water-pails, and small boys, nearly scalded by an avalanche of newly-filled tea-pots, and hopelessly entangled in a knot of colored sisters coming to wash, I progressed by slow stages up stairs and down, till the main hall was reached, and I paused to take breath and a survey. There they were! "our brave boys," as the papers justly call them, for cowards could hardly have been so riddled with shot and shell, so torn and shattered, nor have borne suffering for which we have no name, with an uncomplaining fortitude, which made one glad to cherish each like a brother. In they came, some on stretchers, some in men's arms, some feebly staggering along propped on rude crutches, and one lay stark and still with covered face, as a comrade gave his name to be recorded before they carried him away to the dead house. All was hurry and confusion; the hall was full of these wrecks of humanity, for the most exhausted could not reach a bed till duly ticketed and registered; the walls were lined with rows of such as could sit, the floor covered with the more disabled, the steps and doorways filled with helpers and lookers on; the sound of many feet and voices made that usually quiet hour as noisy as noon; and, in the midst of it all, the matron's motherly face brought more comfort to many a poor soul, than the cordial draughts she administered, or the cheery words that welcomed all, making of the hospital a home.

The sight of several stretchers, each with its legless, armless, or desperately wounded occupant, entering my ward, admonished me that I was there to work, not to wonder or weep; so I corked up my feelings, and returned to the path of duty, which was rather " a hard road to travel " just then. The house had been a hotel before hospitals were needed, and many of the doors still bore their old names; some not so inappropriate as might be imagined, for that ward was in truth a *ball-room*, if gun-shot wounds could christen it. Forty beds were prepared, many already tenanted by tired men who fell down anywhere, and drowsed till the smell of food roused them. Round the great stove was gathered the dreariest group I ever saw—ragged, gaunt and pale, mud to the knees, with bloody bandages untouched since put on days before; many bundled up in blankets, coats being lost or useless; and all wearing that disheartened look which proclaimed defeat, more plainly than any telegram of the Burnside blunder. I pitied them so much, I dared not speak to them, though, remembering all they had been through since the fight at Fredericksburg, I yearned to serve the dreariest of them all. Presently, Miss Blank tore me from my refuge behind piles of one-sleeved shirts, odd socks, bandages and lint; put basin, sponge, towels, and a block of brown soap into my hands, with these appalling directions:

"Come, my dear, begin to wash as fast as you can. Tell them to take off socks, coats and shirts, scrub them well, put on clean shirts, and the attendants will finish them off, and lay them in bed."

If she had requested me to shave them all, or dance a hornpipe on the stove funnel, I should have been less staggered; but to scrub some dozen lords of creation at a moment's notice, was really—really——. However, there was no time for nonsense. and, having resolved when I came to do everything I was bid, I drowned my scruples in my washbowl, clutched my soap manfully, and, assuming a businesslike air, made a dab at the first dirty specimen I saw, bent on performing my task *vi et armis* if necessary. I chanced to light on a withered old Irishman, wounded in the head, which caused that portion of his frame to be tastefully laid out like a garden, the bandages being the walks, his hair the shrubbery. He was so overpowered by the honor of having a lady wash him, as he expressed it, that he did nothing but roll up his eyes, and bless me, in an irresistible style which was too much for my sense of the ludicrous; so we laughed together, and when I knelt down to take off his shoes, he "flopped" also, and wouldn't hear of my touching "them dirty craters. May your bed above be aisy darlin', for the day's work ye are doon! —Whoosh! there ye are, and bedad, it's hard tellin' which is the dirtiest, the fut or the shoe." It was; and if he hadn't been to the fore, I should have gone on pulling, under the impression that the "fut" was a boot, for trousers, socks, shoes and legs were a mass of mud. This comical tableau produced a general grin, at which propitious beginning I took heart and scrubbed away like any tidy parent on a Saturday night. Some of them took the performance like sleepy children, leaning their tired heads against me as I worked, others looked grimly scandalized, and several of the roughest colored like bashful girls. One wore a soiled little bag about his neck, and, as I moved it, to bathe his wounded breast, I said,

"Your talisman didn't save you, did it?"

"Well, I reckon it did, marm, for that shot would a gone a couple a inches deeper but for my old mammy's camphor bag," answered the cheerful philosopher.

Another, with a gun-shot wound through the cheek, asked for a looking-glass, and when I brought one, regarded his swollen face with a dolorous expression, as he muttered—

"I vow to gosh, that's too bad! I warn't a bad looking chap before, and now I'm done for; won't there be a thunderin' scar? and what on earth will Josephine Skinner say?"

He looked up at me with his one eye so appealingly, that I controlled my risibles, and assured him that if Josephine was a girl of sense, she would admire the honorable scar, as a lasting proof that he had faced the enemy, for all women thought a wound the best decoration a brave soldier could wear. I hope Miss Skinner verified the good opinion I so rashly expressed of her, but I shall never know.

The next scrubbee was a nice-looking lad, with a curly brown mane, honest blue eyes, and a merry mouth. He lay on a bed, with one leg gone, and the right arm so shattered that it must evidently follow: yet the little sergeant was as merry as if his afflictions were not worth lamenting over; and when a drop or two of salt water mingled with my suds at the sight of this strong young body, so marred and maimed, the boy looked up, with a brave smile, though there was a little quiver of the lips, as he said,

"Now don't you fret yourself about me, miss; I'm first rate here, for it's nuts to lie still on this bed, after knocking about in those confounded ambulances, that shake what there is left of a fellow to jelly. I never was in one of these places before, and think this cleaning up a jolly thing for us, though I'm afraid it isn't for you ladies."

"Is this your first battle, Sergeant?"

"No, miss; I've been in six scrimmages, and never got a scratch till this last one; but it's done the business pretty thoroughly for me, I should say. Lord! what a scramble there'll be for arms and legs, when we old boys come out of our graves, on the Judgment Day: wonder if we shall get our own again? If we do, my leg will have to tramp from Fredericksburg, my arm from here, I suppose, and meet my body, wherever it may be."

The fancy seemed to tickle him mightily, for he laughed blithely, and so did I; which, no doubt, caused the new nurse to be regarded as a light-minded sinner by the Chaplain, who roamed vaguely about, with his hands in his pockets, preaching resignation to cold, hungry, wounded men, and evidently feeling himself, what he certainly was, the wrong man in the wrong place.

"I say, Mrs.!" called a voice behind me; and, turning, I saw a rough Michigander, with an arm blown off at the shoulder, and two or three bullets still in him — as he afterwards mentioned, as carelessly as if gentlemen were in the habit of carrying such trifles about with them. I went to him, and, while administering a dose of soap and water, he whispered, irefully:

"That red-headed devil, over yonder, is a reb, hang him! He's got shet of a foot, or he'd a cut like the rest of the lot. Don't you wash him, nor feed him, but jest let him holler till he's tired. It's a blasted shame to fetch them fellers in here, along side of us; and so I'll tell the chap that bosses this concern; cuss me if I don't."

I regret to say that I did not deliver a moral sermon upon the duty of forgiving our enemies, and the sin of profanity, then and there; but, being a red-hot Abolitionist, stared fixedly at the tall rebel, who was a copperhead, in every sense of the word, and privately resolved to put soap in his eyes, rub his nose the wrong way, and excoriate his cuticle generally, if I had the washing of him.

My amiable intentions, however, were frustrated; for, when I approached, with as Christian an expression as my principles would allow, and asked the question—"Shall I try to make you more comfortable, sir?" all I got for my pains was a gruff—

"No; I'll do it myself."

"Here's your Southern chivalry, with a witness," thought I, dumping the basin down before him, thereby quenching a strong desire to give him a summary baptism, in return for his ungraciousness; for my angry passions rose, at this rebuff, in a way that would have scandalized good Dr. Watts. He was a disappointment in all respects, (the rebel, not the blessed Doctor,) for he was neither fiendish, romantic, pathetic, or anything interesting; but a long, fat man, with a head like a burning bush, and a perfectly expressionless face: so I could dislike him without the slightest drawback, and ignored his existence from that day forth. One redeeming trait he certainly did possess, as the floor speedily testified; for his ablutions were so vigorously performed, that his bed soon stood like an isolated island, in a sea of soap-suds, and he resembled a dripping merman, suffering from the loss of a fin. If cleanliness is a near neighbor to godliness, then was the big rebel the godliest man in my ward that day.

Having done up our human wash, and laid it out to dry, the second syllable of our version of the word War-fare was enacted with much success. Great trays of bread, meat, soup and coffee appeared; and both nurses and attendants turned waiters, serving bountiful rations to all who could eat. I can call my pinafore to testify to my good will in the work, for in ten minutes it was reduced to a perambulating bill of fare, presenting samples of all the refreshments going or gone. It was a lively scene; the long room lined with rows of beds, each filled by an occupant, whom water, shears, and clean raiment, had transformed from a dismal ragamuffin into a recumbent hero, with a cropped head. To and fro rushed matrons, maids, and convalescent "boys," skirmishing with knives and forks; retreating with empty plates; marching and counter-marching, with unvaried success, while the clash of busy spoons made most inspiring music for the charge of our Light Brigade:

"Beds to the front of them,
Beds to the right of them,
Beds o the left of them,
　Nobody blundered.
Beamed at by hungry souls,
Screamed at with brimming bowls,
Steamed at by army rolls,
　Buttered and sundered.
With coffee not cannon plied,
Each must be satisfied,
Whether they lived or died;
　All the men wondered."

Very welcome seemed the generous meal, after a week of suffering, exposure, and short commons; soon the brown faces began to smile, as food, warmth, and rest, did their pleasant work; and the grateful "Thankee's" were followed by more graphic accounts of the battle and retreat, than any paid reporter could have given us. Curious contrasts of the tragic and comic met one everywhere; and some touching as well as ludicrous episodes, might have been recorded that day. A six foot New Hampshire man, with a leg broken and perforated by a piece of shell, so large that, had I not seen the wound, I should have regarded the story as a Munchausenism, beckoned me to come and help him, as he could not sit up, and both his bed and beard were getting plentifully anointed with soup. As I fed my big nestling with corresponding mouthfuls, I asked him how he felt during the battle.

"Well, 'twas my fust, you see, so I aint ashamed to say I was a trifle flustered in the beginnin', there was such an allfired racket; for ef there's anything I do spleen agin, it's noise. But when my mate, Eph Sylvester, fell, with a bullet through his head, I got mad, and pitched in, licketty cut. Our part of the fight didn't last long; so a lot of us larked round Fredericksburg, and give some of them houses a pretty consid'able of a rummage, till we was ordered out of the mess. Some of our fellows cut like time; but I warn't a-goin to run for nobody; and, fust thing I knew, a shell bust, right in front of us, and I keeled over, feelin' as if I was blowed higher'n a kite. I sung out, and the boys come back for me, double quick; but the way they chucked me over them fences was a caution, I tell you. Next day I was most as black as that darkey yonder, lickin' plates on the sly. This is bully coffee, ain't it? Give us another pull at it, and I'll be obleeged to you."

I did; and, as the last gulp subsided, he said, with a rub of his old handkerchief over eyes as well as mouth:

"Look a here; I've got a pair a earbobs and a handkercher pin I'm a goin' to give you, if you'll have them; for you're the very moral o' Lizy Sylvester, poor Eph's wife: that's why I signalled you to come over here. They aint much, I guess, but they'll do to memorize the rebs by."

Burrowing under his pillow, he produced a little bundle of what he called "truck," and gallantly presented me with a pair of earrings, each representing a cluster of corpulent grapes, and the pin a basket of astonishing fruit, the whole large and coppery enough for a small warming-pan. Feeling delicate about depriving him of such valuable relics, I accepted the earrings alone, and was obliged to depart, somewhat abruptly, when my friend stuck the warming-pan in the bosom of his night-gown, viewing it with much complacency, and, perhaps, some tender memory, in that rough heart of his, for the comrade he had lost.

Observing that the man next him had left his meal untouched, I offered the same service I had performed for his neighbor, but he shook his head.

"Thank you, ma'am; I don't think I'll ever eat again, for I'm shot in the stomach. But I'd like a drink of water, if you aint too busy."

I rushed away, but the water-pails were gone to be refilled, and it was some time before they reappeared. I did not forget my patient patient, meanwhile, and, with the first mugful, hurried back to him. He seemed asleep; but something in the tired white face caused me to listen at his lips for a breath. None came. I touched his forehead; it was cold: and then I knew that, while he waited, a better nurse than I had given him a cooler draught, and healed him with a touch. I laid the sheet over the quiet sleeper, whom no noise could now disturb; and, half an hour later, the bed was empty. It seemed a poor requital for all he had sacrificed and suffered,—that hospital bed, lonely even in a crowd; for there was no familiar face for him to look his last upon; no friendly voice to say, Good bye; no hand to lead him gently down into the Valley of the Shadow; and he vanished, like a drop in that red sea upon whose shores so many women stand lamenting. For a moment I felt bitterly indignant at this seeming carelessness of the value of life, the sanctity of death; then consoled myself with the thought that, when the great muster roll was called, these nameless men might be promoted above many whose tall monuments record the barren honors they have won.

All having eaten, drank, and rested, the surgeons began their rounds; and I took my first lesson in the art of dressing wounds. It wasn't a festive scene, by any means; for Dr P., whose Aid I constituted myself, fell to work with a vigor which soon convinced me that I was a weaker vessel, though nothing would have induced me to confess it then. He had served in the Crimea, and seemed to regard a dilapidated body very much as I should have regarded a damaged garment; and, turning up his cuffs, whipped out a very unpleasant looking housewife, cutting, sawing, patching and piecing, with the enthusiasm of an accomplished surgical seamstress; explaining the process, in scientific terms, to the patient, meantime; which, of course, was immensely cheering and comfortable. There was an uncanny sort of fascination in watching him, as he peered and probed into the mechanism of those wonderful bodies, whose mysteries he understood so well. The more intricate the wound, the better he liked it. A poor private, with both legs off, and shot through the lungs, possessed more attractions for him than a dozen generals, slightly scratched in some " masterly retreat ;" and had any one appeared in small pieces, requesting to be put together again, he would have considered it a special dispensation.

The amputations were reserved till the morrow, and the merciful magic of ether was not thought necessary that day, so the poor souls had to bear their pains as best they might. It is all very well to talk of the patience of woman; and far be it from me to pluck that feather from her cap, for, heaven knows, she isn't allowed to wear many; but the patient endurance of these men, under trials of the flesh, was truly wonderful. Their fortitude seemed contagious, and scarcely a cry escaped them, though I often longed to groan for them, when pride kept their white lips shut, while great drops stood upon their foreheads, and the bed shook with the irrepressible tremor of their tortured bodies. One or two Irishmen anathematized the doctors with the frankness of their nation, and ordered the Virgin to stand by them, as if she had been the wedded Biddy to whom they could administer the poker, if she didn't; but, as a general thing, the work went on in silence, broken only by some quiet request for roller, instruments, or plaster, a sigh from the patient, or a sympathizing murmur from the nurse.

It was long past noon before these repairs were even partially made; and, having got the bodies of my boys into something like order, the next task was to minister to their minds, by writing letters to the anxious souls at home; answering questions, reading papers, taking possession of money and valuables; for the eighth commandmnnt was reduced to a very fragmentary condition, both by the blacks and whites, who ornamented our hospital with their presence. Pocket books, purses, miniatures, and watches, were sealed up, labelled, and handed over to the matron, till such times as the owners thereof were ready to depart homeward or campward again. The letters dictated to me, and revised by me, that afternoon, would have made an excellent chapter for some future history of the war; for, like that which Thackeray's "Ensign Spooney" wrote his mother just before Waterloo, they were "full of affection, pluck, and bad spelling;" nearly all giving lively accounts of the battle, and ending with a somewhat sudden plunge from patriotism to provender, desiring "Marm," "Mary Ann," or "Aunt Peters," to send along some pies, pickles, sweet stuff, and apples, "to yourn in haste," Joe, Sam, or Ned, as the case might be.

My little Sergeant insisted on trying to scribble something with his left hand, and patiently accomplished some half dozen lines of hieroglyphics, which he gave me to fold and direct, with a boyish blush, that rendered a glimpse of "My Dearest Jane," unnecessary, to assure me that the heroic lad had been more successful in the service of Commander-in-Chief Cupid than that of Gen. Mars; and a charming little romance blossomed instanter in Nurse Periwinkle's romantic fancy, though no further confidences were made that day, for Sergeant fell asleep, and, judging from his tranquil face, visited his absent sweetheart in the pleasant land of dreams.

At five o'clock a great bell rang, and the attendants flew, not to arms, but to their trays, to bring up supper, when a second uproar announced that it was ready. The new comers woke at the sound; and I presently discovered that it took a very bad wound to incapacitate the defenders of the faith for the consumption of their rations; the amount that some of them sequestered was amazing; but when I suggested the probability of a famine hereafter, to the matron, that motherly lady cried out: "Bless their hearts, why shouldn't they eat?

It's their only amusement; so fill every one, and, if there's not enough ready to-night, I'll lend my share to the Lord by giving it to the boys." And, whipping up her coffee-pot and plate of toast, she gladdened the eyes and stomachs of two or three dissatisfied heroes, by serving them with a liberal hand; and I haven't the slightest doubt that, having cast her bread upon the waters, it came back buttered, as another large-hearted old lady was wont to say.

Then came the doctor's evening visit; the administration of medicines; washing feverish faces; smoothing tumbled beds; wetting wounds; singing lullabies; and preparations for the night. By twelve, the last labor of love was done; the last " good night " spoken; and, if any needed a reward for that day's work, they surely received it, in the silent eloquence of those long lines of faces, showing pale and peaceful in the shaded rooms, as we quitted them, followed by grateful glances that lighted us to bed, where rest, the sweetest, made our pillows soft, while Night and Nature took our places, filling that great house of pain with the **healing miracles of Sleep, and his diviner brother, Death.**

CHAPTER IV.

A NIGHT.

Being fond of the night side of nature, I was soon promoted to the post of night nurse, with every facility for indulging in my favorite pastime of "owling." My colleague, a black eyed widow, relieved me at dawn, we two taking care of the ward between us, like regular nurses, turn and turn about. I usually found my boys in the jolliest state of mind their condition allowed; for it was a known fact that Nurse Periwinkle objected to blue devils, and entertained a belief that he who laughed most was surest of recovery. At the beginning of my reign, dumps and dismals prevailed; the nurses looked anxious and tired, the men gloomy or sad; and a general "Hark!-from-the-tombs-a-doleful-sound" style of conversation seemed to be the fashion: a state of things which caused one coming from a merry, social New England town, to feel as if she had got into an exhausted receiver; and the instinct of self-preservation, to say nothing of a philanthropic desire to serve the race, caused a speedy change in Ward No. 1

More flattering than the most gracefully turned compliment, more grateful than the most admiring glance, was the sight of those rows of faces, all strange to me a little while ago, now lighting up, with smiles of welcome, as I came among them, enjoying that moment heartily, with a womanly pride in their regard, a motherly affection for them all. The evenings were spent in reading aloud, writing letters, waiting on and amusing the men, going the rounds with Dr. P., as he made his second daily survey, dressing my dozen wounds afresh, giving last doses, and making them cozy for the long hours to come, till the nine o'clock bell rang, the gas was turned down, the day nurses went off duty, the night watch came on, and my nocturnal adventures began.

My ward was now divided into three rooms; and, under favor of the matron, I had managed to sort out the patients in such a way that I had what I called, "my duty room," my "pleasure room," and my "pathetic room," and worked for each in a different way. One, I visited, armed with a dressing tray, full of rollers, plasters, and pins; another, with books, flowers, games, and gossip; a third, with teapots, lullabies, consolation, and, sometimes, a shroud.

Wherever the sickest or most helpless man chanced to be, there I held my watch, often visiting the other rooms, to see that the general watchman of the ward did his duty by the fires and the wounds, the latter needing constant wetting. Not only on this account did I meander, but also to get fresher air than the close rooms afforded; for, owing to the stupidity of that mysterious "somebody" who does all the damage in the world, the windows had been carefully nailed down above, and the lower sashes could only be raised in the mildest weather, for the men lay just below. I had suggested a summary smashing of a few panes here and there, when frequent appeals to headquarters had proved unavailing, and daily orders to lazy attendants had come to nothing. No one seconded the motion, however, and the nails were far beyond my reach; for, though belonging to the sisterhood of "ministering angels," I had no wings, and might as well have asked for a suspension bridge, as a pair of steps, in that charitable chaos.

One of the harmless ghosts who bore me company during the haunted hours, was Dan, the watchman, whom I regarded with a certain awe; for, though so much together, I never fairly saw his face, and, but for his legs, should never have recognized him, as we seldom met by day. These legs were remarkable, as was his whole figure, for his body was short, rotund, and done up in a big jacket, and muffler; his beard hid the lower part of his face, his hat-brim the upper; and all I ever discovered was a pair of sleepy eyes, and a very mild voice. But the legs!—very long, very thin, very crooked and feeble, looking like gray sausages in their tight coverings, and finished off with a pair of expansive, green cloth shoes, very like Chinese junks with the sails down. This figure, gliding noiselessly about the dimly-lighted rooms, was strongly suggestive of the spirit of a beer-barrel mounted on cork-screws, haunting the old hotel in search of its lost mates, emptied and staved in long ago.

Another goblin who frequently appeared to me, was the attendant of "the pathetic room," who, being a faithful soul, was often up to tend two or three men, weak and wandering as babies, after the fever had gone. The amiable creature beguiled the watches of the night by brewing jorums of a fearful beverage, which he called coffee, and insisted on sharing with me; coming in with a great bowl of something like mud soup, scalding hot, guiltless of cream, rich in an all-pervading flavor of molasses, scorch and tin pot. Such an amount of good will and neighborly kindness also went into the mess, that I never could find the heart to refuse, but always received it with thanks, sipped it with hypocritical relish while he remained, and whipped it into the slop-jar the instant he departed; thereby gratifying him, securing one rousing laugh in the dreariest hour of the night, and no one was the worse for the transaction but the pigs. Whether they were " cut off untimely in their sins," or not, I carefully abstained from inquiring.

It was a strange life — asleep half the day, exploring Washington the other half, and all night hovering, like a massive cherubim, in a red rigolette, over the slumbering sons of man. I liked it, and found many things to amuse, instruct, and interest me. The snores alone were quite a study, varying from the mild sniff to the stentorian snort, which startled the echoes and hoisted the performer erect to accuse his neighbor of the deed, magnanimously forgive him, and, wrapping the drapery of his couch about him, lie down to vocal slumber. After listening for a week to this band of wind instruments, I indulged in the belief that I could recognize each by the snore alone, and was tempted to join the chorus by breaking out with John Brown's favorite hymn:

"Blow ye the trumpet, blow!"

I would have given much to have possessed the art of sketching, for many of the faces became wonderfully interesting when unconscious. Some grew stern and grim, the men evidently dreaming of war, as they gave orders, groaned over their wounds, or damned the rebels vigorously; some grew sad and infinitely pathetic, as if the pain borne silently all day, revenged itself by now betraying what the man's pride had concealed so well. Often the roughest grew young and pleasant when sleep smoothed the hard lines away, letting the real nature assert itself; many almost seemed to speak, and I learned to know these men better by night than through any intercourse by day. Sometimes they disappointed me, for faces that looked merry and good in the light, grew bad and sly when the shadows came; and though they made no confidences in words, I read their lives, leaving them to wonder at the change of manner this midnight magic wrought in their nurse. A few talked busily; one drummer boy sang sweetly, though no persuasions could win a note from him by day; and several depended on being told what they had talked of in the morning. Even my constitutionals in the chilly halls, possessed a certain charm, for the house was never still. Sentinels tramped round it all night long, their muskets glittering in the wintry moonlight as they walked, or stood before the doors, straight and silent, as figures of stone, causing one to conjure up romantic visions of guarded forts, sudden surprises, and daring deeds; for in these war times the hum drum life of Yankeedom has vanished, and the most prosaic feel some thrill of that excitement which stirs the nation's heart, and makes its capital a camp of hospitals. Wandering up and down these lower halls, I often heard cries from above, steps hurrying to and fro, saw surgeons passing up, or men coming down carrying a stretcher, where lay a long white figure, whose face was shrouded and whose fight was done. Sometimes I stopped to watch the passers in the street, the moonlight shining on the spire opposite, or the gleam of some vessel floating, like a white-winged sea-gull, down the broad Potomac, whose fullest flow can never wash away the red stain of the land.

The night whose events I have a fancy to record, opened with a little comedy, and closed with a great tragedy; for a virtuous and useful life untimely ended is always tragical to those who see not as God sees. My headquarters were beside the bed of a New Jersey boy, crazed by the horrors of that dreadful Saturday. A slight wound in the knee brought him there; but his mind had suffered more than his body; some string of that delicate machine was over strained, and, for days, he had been re-living in imagination, the scenes he could not forget, till his distress broke out in incoherent ravings, pitiful to hear. As I sat by him, endeavoring to soothe his poor distracted brain by the constant touch of wet hands over his hot forehead, he lay cheering his comrades on, hurrying them back, then counting them as they fell around him, often clutching my arm, to drag me from the vicinity of a bursting shell, or covering up his head to screen himself from a shower of shot; his face brilliant with fever; his eyes restless; his head never still; every muscle strained and rigid; while an incessant stream of defiant shouts, whispered warnings, and broken laments, poured from his lips with that forceful bewilderment which makes such wanderings so hard to overhear.

It was past eleven, and my patient was slowly wearying himself into fitful intervals of quietude, when, in one of these pauses, a curious sound arrested my attention. Looking over my shoulder, I saw a one-legged phantom hopping nimbly down the room; and, going to meet it, recognized a certain Pennsylvania gentleman, whose wound-fever had taken a turn for the worse, and, depriving him of the few wits a drunken campaign had left him, set him literally tripping on the light, fantastic toe "toward home," as he blandly informed me, touching the military cap which formed a striking contrast to the severe simplicity of the rest of his *undress* uniform. When sane, the least movement produced a roar of pain or a volley of oaths; but the departure of reason seemed to have wrought an agreeable change, both in the man and his manners; for, balancing himself on one leg, like a meditative stork, he plunged into an animated discussion of the war, the President, lager beer, and Enfield rifles, regardless of any suggestions of mine as to the propriety of returning to bed, lest he be court-martialed for desertion.

Any thing more supremely ridiculous can hardly be imagined than this figure, all draped in white, its one foot covered with a big blue sock, a dingy cap set rakingly askew on its shaven head, and placid satisfaction beaming in its broad red face, as it flourished a mug in one hand, an old boot in the other, calling them canteen and knapsack, while it skipped and fluttered in the most unearthly fashion. What to do with the creature I didn't know; Dan was absent, and if I went to find him, the perambulator might festoon himself out of the window, set his toga on fire, or do some of his neighbors a mischief. The attendant of the room was sleeping like a near relative of the celebrated Seven, and nothing short of pins would rouse him; for he had been out that day, and whiskey asserted its supremacy in balmy whiffs. Still declaiming, in a fine flow of eloquence, the demented gentleman hopped on, blind and deaf to my graspings and entreaties; and I was about to slam the door in his face, and run for help, when a second and saner phantom came to the rescue, in the likeness of a big Prussian who spoke no English, but divined the crisis, and put an end to it, by bundling the lively monoped into his bed, like a baby, with an authoritative command to "stay put," which received added weight from being delivered in an odd conglomeration of French and German, accompanied by warning wags of a head decorated with a yellow cotton night cap, rendered most imposing by a tassel like a bell-pull. Rather exhausted by his excursion, the member from Pennsylvania subsided; and, after an irrepressible laugh together, my Prussian ally and myself were returning to our places, when the echo of a sob caused us to glance along the beds. It came from one in the corner — such a little bed! — and such a tearful little face looked up at us, as we stopped beside it! The twelve years old drummer boy was not singing now, but sobbing, with a manly effort all the while to stifle the distressful sounds that would break out.

"What is it, Billy?" I asked, as he rubbed the tears away, and checked himself in the middle of a great sob to answer plaintively:

"I've got a chill, ma'am, but I aint cryin' for that, 'cause I'm used to it. I dreamed Kit was here, and when I waked up he wasn't, and I couldn't help it, then."

The boy came in with the rest, and the man who was taken dead from the ambulance was the Kit he mourned. Well he might; for, when the wounded were brought from Fredericksburg, the child lay in one of the camps thereabout, and this good friend, though sorely hurt himself, would not leave him to the exposure and neglect of such a time and place; but, wrapping him in his own blanket, carried him in his arms to the transport, tended him during the passage, and only yielded up his charge when Death met him at the door of the hospital which promised care and comfort for the boy. For ten days, Billy had burned or shivered with fever and ague, pining the while for Kit, and refusing to be comforted, because he had not been able to thank him for the generous protection, which, perhaps, had cost the giver's life. The vivid dream had wrung the childish heart with a fresh pang, and when I tried the solace fitted for his years, the remorseful fear that haunted him found vent in a fresh burst of tears, as he looked at the wasted hands I was endeavoring to warm:

' Oh! if I'd only been as thin when Kit carried me as I am

now, maybe he wouldn't have died; but I was heavy, he was hurt worser than we knew, and so it killed him; and I didn't see him, to say good bye."

This thought had troubled him in secret; and my assurances that his friend would probably have died at all events, hardly assuaged the bitterness of his regretful grief.

At this juncture, the delirious man began to shout; the one-legged rose up in his bed, as if preparing for another dart, Billy bewailed himself more piteously than before: and if ever a woman was at her wit's end, that distracted female was Nurse Periwinkle, during the space of two or three minutes, as she vibrated between the three beds, like an agitated pendulum. Like a most opportune reinforcement, Dan, the bandy, appeared, and devoted himself to the lively party, leaving me free to return to my post; for the Prussian, with a nod and a smile, took the lad away to his own bed, and lulled him to sleep with a soothing murmur, like a mammoth bumble bee I liked that in Fritz, and if he ever wondered afterward at the dainties which sometimes found their way into his rations, or the extra comforts of his bed, he might have found a solution of the mystery in sundry persons' knowledge of the fatherly action of that night.

Hardly was I settled again, when the inevitable bowl appeared, and its bearer delivered a message I had expected, yet dreaded to receive:

"John is going, ma'am, and wants to see you, if you can come."

"The moment this boy is asleep; tell him so, and let me know if I am in danger of being too late."

My Ganymede departed, and while I quieted poor Shaw, I thought of John. He came in a day or two after the others; and, one evening, when I entered my "pathetic room," I found a lately emptied bed occupied by a large, fair man, with a fine face, and the serenest eyes I ever met. One of the earlier comers had often spoken of a friend, who had remained behind, that those apparently worse wounded than himself might reach a shelter first. It seemed a David and Jonathan sort of friendship. The man fretted for his mate, and was never tired of praising John—his courage, sobriety, self-denial, and unfailing kindliness of heart; always winding up with: "He's an out an' out fine feller, ma'am; you see if he aint."

I had some curiosity to behold this piece of excellence, and when he came, watched him for a night or two, before I made friends with him; for, to tell the truth, I was a little afraid of the stately looking man, whose bed had to be lengthened to accommodate his commanding stature; who seldom spoke, uttered no complaint, asked no sympathy, but tranquilly observed what went on about him; and, as he lay high upon his pillows, no picture of dying statesman or warrior was ever fuller of real dignity than this Virginia blacksmith. A most attractive face he had, framed in brown hair and beard, comely featured and full of vigor, as yet unsubdued by pain; thoughtful and often beautifully mild while watching the afflictions of others, as if entirely forgetful of his own. His mouth was grave and firm, with plenty of will and courage in its lines, but a smile could make it as sweet as any woman's; and his eyes were child's eyes, looking one fairly in the face, with a clear, straightforward glance, which promised well for such as placed their faith in him. He seemed to cling to life, as if it were rich in duties and delights, and he had learned the secret of content. The only time I saw his composure disturbed, was when my surgeon brought another to examine John, who scrutinized their faces with an anxious look, asking of the elder: "Do you think I shall pull through, sir?" "I hope so, my man." And, as the two passed on John's eye still followed them, with an intentness which would have won a truer answer from them, had they seen it. A momentary shadow flitted over his face; then came the usual serenity, as if, in that brief eclipse, he had acknowledged the existence of some hard possibility, and, asking nothing yet hoping all things, left the issue in God's hands, with that submission which is true piety.

The next night, as I went my rounds with Dr. P., I happened to ask which man in the room probably suffered most; and, to my great surprise, he glanced at John:

"Every breath he draws is like a stab; for the ball pierced the left lung, broke a rib, and did no end of damage here and there; so the poor lad can find neither forgetfulness nor ease, because he must lie on his wounded back or suffocate. It will be a hard struggle, and a long one, for he possesses great vitality; but even his temperate life can't save him; I wish it could."

"You don't mean he must die, Doctor?"

"Bless you, there's not the slightest hope for him; and you'd better tell him so before long; women have a way of doing such things comfortably, so I leave it to you. He won't last more than a day or two, at furthest."

I could have sat down on the spot and cried heartily, if I had not learned the wisdom of bottling up one's tears for leisure moments. Such an end seemed very hard for such a man, when half a dozen worn out, worthless bodies round him, were gathering up the remnants of wasted lives, to linger on for years perhaps, burdens to others, daily reproaches to themselves. The army needed men like John, earnest, brave, and faithful; fighting for liberty and justice with both heart and hand, true soldiers of the Lord. I could not give him up so soon, or think with any patience of so excellent a nature robbed of its fulfilment, and blundered into eternity by the rashness or stupidity of those at whose hands so many lives may be required. It was an easy thing for Dr. P. to say: "Tell him he must die," but a cruelly hard thing to do, and by no means as "comfortable" as he politely suggested. I had not the heart to do it then, and privately indulged the hope that some change for the better might take place, in spite of gloomy prophesies; so, rendering my task unnecessary.

A few minutes later, as I came in again, with fresh rollers, I saw John sitting erect, with no one to support him, while the surgeon dressed his back. I had never hitherto seen it done; for, having simpler wounds to attend to, and knowing the fidelity of the attendant, I had left John to him, thinking it might be more agreeable and safe; for both strength and experience were needed in his case. I had forgotten that the strong man might long for the gentle tendance of a woman's hands, the sympathetic magnetism of a woman's presence, as well as the feebler souls about him. The Doctor's words caused me to reproach myself with neglect, not of any real duty perhaps, but of those little cares and kindnesses that solace homesick spirits, and make the heavy hours pass easier. John looked lonely and forsaken just then, as he sat with bent head, hands folded on his knee, and no outward sign of suffering, till, looking nearer, I saw great tears roll down and drop upon the floor. It was a new sight there; for, though I had seen many suffer, some swore, some groaned, most endured silently, but none wept. Yet it did not seem weak, only very touching, and straightway my fear vanished, my heart opened wide and took him in, as, gathering the bent head in my arms, as freely as if he had been a little child, I said, "Let me help you bear it, John."

Never, on any human countenance, have I seen so swift and beautiful a look of gratitude, surprise and comfort, as that which answered me more eloquently than the whispered —

"Thank you, ma'am, this is right good! this is what I wanted!"

"Then why not ask for it before?"

"I didn't like to be a trouble; you seemed so busy, and I could manage to get on alone."

"You shall not want it any more, John."

Nor did he; for now I understood the wistful look that sometimes followed me, as I went out, after a brief pause beside his bed, or merely a passing nod, while busied with those who seemed to need me more than he, because more urgent in their demands. Now I knew that to him, as to so many, I was the poor substitute for mother, wife, or sister, and in his eyes no stranger, but a friend who hitherto had seemed neglectful; for, in his modesty, he had never guessed the truth. This was changed now; and, through the tedious operation of probing, bathing, and dressing his wounds, he leaned against me, holding my hand fast, and, if pain wrung further tears from him, no one saw them fall but me. When he was laid down again, I hovered about him, in a remorseful state of mind that would not let me rest, till I had bathed his face, brushed his bonny brown hair, set all things smooth about him, and laid a knot of heath and heliotrope on his clean pillow. While doing this, he watched me with the satisfied expression I so liked to see; and when I offered the little nosegay, held it carefully in his great hand, smoothed a ruffled leaf or two, surveyed and smelt it with an air of genuine delight, and lay contentedly regarding the glimmer of the sunshine on the green. Although the manliest man among my forty, he said, " Yes, ma'am," like a little boy; received suggestions for his comfort with the quick smile that brightened his whole face; and now and then, as I stood tidying the table by his bed, I felt him softly touch my gown, as if to assure himself that I was there. Anything more natural and frank I never saw, and found this brave John as bashful as brave, yet full of excellencies and fine aspirations, which, having no power to express themselves in words, seemed to have bloomed into his character and made him what he was.

After that night, an hour of each evening that remained to him was devoted to his ease or pleasure. He could not talk much, for breath was precious, and he spoke in whispers; but from occasional conversations, I gleaned scraps of private history which only added to the affection and respect I felt for him. Once he asked me to write a letter, and as I settled pen and paper, I said, with an irrepressible glimmer of feminine curiosity, "Shall it be addressed to wife, or mother, John?"

"Neither, ma'am; I've got no wife, and will write to mother myself when I get better. Did you think I was married because of this?" he asked, touching a plain ring he wore, and often turned thoughtfully on his finger when he lay alone.

"Partly that, but more from a settled sort of look you have; a look which young men seldom get until they marry."

"I didn't know that; but I'm not so very young, ma'am, thirty in May, and have been what you might call settled this ten years. Mother's a widow, I'm the oldest child she has, and it wouldn't do for me to marry until Lizzy has a home of her own, and Jack's learned his trade; for we're not rich, and I must be father to the children and husband to the dear old woman, if I can."

"No doubt but you are both, John; yet how came you to go to war, if you felt so? Wasn't enlisting as bad as marrying?"

"No, ma'am, not as I see it, for one is helping my neighbor, the other pleasing myself. I went because I couldn't help it. I didn't want the glory or the pay; I wanted the right thing done, and people kept saying the men who were in earnest ought to fight. I was in earnest, the Lord knows! but I held off as long as I could, not knowing which was my duty. Mother saw the case, gave me her ring to keep me steady, and said 'Go:' so I went."

A short story and a simple one, but the man and the mother were portrayed better than pages of fine writing could have done it.

"Do you ever regret that you came, when you lie here suffering so much?"

"Never, ma'am; I haven't helped a great deal, but I've shown I was willing to give my life, and perhaps I've got to; but I don't blame anybody, and if it was to do over again, I'd do it. I'm a little sorry I wasn't wounded in front; it looks cowardly to be hit in the back, but I obeyed orders, and it don't matter in the end, I know."

Poor John! it did not matter now, except that a shot in front might have spared the long agony in store for him. He seemed to read the thought that troubled me, as he spoke so hopefully when there was no hope, for he suddenly added:

"This is my first battle; do they think it's going to be my last?"

"I'm afraid they do, John."

It was the hardest question I had ever been called upon to answer; doubly hard with those clear eyes fixed on mine, forcing a truthful answer by their own truth. He seemed a little startled at first, pondered over the fateful fact a moment, then shook his head, with a glance at the broad chest and muscular limbs stretched out before him:

"I'm not afraid, but it's difficult to believe all at once. I'm so strong it don't seem possible for such a little wound to kill me."

Merry Mercutio's dying words glanced through my memory as he spoke: "'Tis not so deep as a well, nor so wide as a church door, but 'tis enough." And John would have said the same could he have seen the ominous black holes between his shoulders; he never had, but, seeing the ghastly sights about him, could not believe his own wound more fatal than these, for all the suffering it caused him.

"Shall I write to your mother, now?" I asked, thinking that these sudden tidings might change all plans and purposes. But they did not; for the man received the order of the Divine Commander to march with the same unquestioning obedience with which the soldier had received that of the human one; doubtless remembering that the first led him to life, and the last to death.

"No, ma'am; to Jack just the same; he'll break it to her best, and I'll add a line to her myself when you get done."

So I wrote the letter which he dictated, finding it better than any I had sent; for, though here and there a little ungrammatical or inelegant, each sentence came to me briefly worded, but most expressive; full of excellent counsel to the boy, tenderly bequeathing "mother and Lizzie" to his care, and bidding him good bye in words the sadder for their simplicity. He added a few lines, with steady hand, and, as I sealed it, said, with a patient sort of sigh, "I hope the answer will come in time for me to see it;" then, turning away his face, laid the flowers against his lips, as if to hide some quiver of emotion at the thought of such a sudden sundering of all the dear home ties.

These things had happened two days before; now John was dying, and the letter had not come. I had been summoned to many death beds in my life, but to none that made my heart ache as it did then, since my mother called me to watch the departure of a spirit akin to this in its gentleness and patient strength. As I went in, John stretched out both hands:

"I knew you'd come! I guess I'm moving on, ma'am."

He was; and so rapidly that, even while he spoke, over his face I saw the grey veil falling that no human hand can lift. I sat down by him, wiped the drops from his forehead, stirred the air about him with the slow wave of a fan, and waited to help him die. He stood in sore need of help—and I could do so little; for, as the doctor had foretold, the strong body rebelled against death, and fought every inch of the way, forcing him to draw each breath with a spasm, and clench his hands with an imploring look, as if he asked, "How long must I endure this, and be still!" For hours he suffered dumbly, without a moment's respite, or a moment's murmuring; his limbs grew cold, his face damp, his lips white, and, again and again, he tore the covering off his breast, as if the lightest weight added to his agony; yet through it all, his eyes never lost their perfect serenity, and the man's soul seemed to sit therein, undaunted by the ills that vexed his flesh.

One by one, the men woke, and round the room appeared a circle of pale faces and watchful eyes, full of awe and pity; for, though a stranger, John was beloved by all. Each man there had wondered at his patience, respected his piety, admired his fortitude, and now lamented his hard death; for the influence of an upright nature had made itself deeply felt, even in one little week. Presently, the Jonathan who so loved this comely David, came creeping from his bed for a last look and word. The kind soul was full of trouble, as the choke in his voice, the grasp of his hand, betrayed; but there were no tears, and the farewell of the friends was the more touching for its brevity.

"Old boy, how are you?" faltered the one.

"Most through, thank heaven!" whispered the other.

"Can I say or do anything for you anywheres?"

"Take my things home, and tell them that I did **my best.**"

"I will! I will!"

"Good bye, Ned."

"Good bye, John, good bye!"

They kissed each other, tenderly as women, and so parted, for poor Ned could not stay to see his comrade die. For a little while, there was no sound in the room but the drip of water, from a stump or two, and John's distressful gasps, as he slowly breathed his life away. I thought him nearly gone, and had just laid down the fan, believing its help to be no longer needed, when suddenly he rose up in his bed, and cried out with a bitter cry that broke the silence, sharply startling every one with its agonized appeal:

"For God's sake, give me air!"

It was the only cry pain or death had wrung from him, the only boon he had asked; and none of us could grant it, for all the airs that blew were useless now. Dan flung up the window. The first red streak of dawn was warming the grey east, a herald of the coming sun; John saw it, and with the love of light which lingers in us to the end, seemed to read in it a sign of hope of help, for, over his whole face there broke that mysterious expression, brighter than any smile, which often comes to eyes that look their last. He laid himself gently down; and, stretching out his strong right arm, as if to grasp and bring the blessed air to his lips in a fuller flow, lapsed into a merciful unconsciousness, which assured us that for him suffering was forever past. He died then; for, though the heavy breaths still tore their way up for a little longer, they were but the waves of an ebbing tide that beat unfelt against the wreck, which an immortal voyager had deserted with a smile. He never spoke again, but to the end held my hand close, so close that when he was asleep at last, I could not draw it away. Dan helped me, warning me as he did so that it was unsafe for dead and living flesh to lie so long together; but though my hand was strangely cold and stiff, and four white marks remained across its back, even when warmth and color had returned elsewhere, I could not but be glad that, through its touch, the presence of human sympathy, perhaps, had lightened that hard hour.

When they had made him ready for the grave, John lay in state for half an hour, a thing which seldom happened in that busy place; but a universal sentiment of reverence and affection seemed to fill the hearts of all who had known or heard of him; and when the rumor of his death went through the house, always astir, many came to see him, and I felt a tender sort of pride in my lost patient; for he looked a most heroic figure, lying there stately and still as the statue of some young knight asleep upon his tomb. The lovely expression which so often beautifies dead faces, soon replaced the marks of pain, and I longed for those who loved him best to see him when half an hour's acquaintance with Death had made them friends. As we stood looking at him, the ward master handed me a letter, saying it had been forgotten the night before. It was John's letter, come just an hour too late to gladden the eyes that had longed and looked for it so eagerly! but he had it; for, after I had cut some brown locks for his mother, and taken off the ring to send her, telling how well the talisman had done its work, I kissed this good son for her sake, and laid the letter in his hand, still folded as when I drew my own away, feeling that its place was there, and making myself happy with the thought, that, even in his solitary grave in the "Government Lot," he would not be without some token of the love which makes life beautiful and outlives death. Then I left him, glad to have known so genuine a man, and carrying with me an enduring memory of the brave Virginia blacksmith, as he lay serenely waiting for the dawn of that long day which knows no night.

CHAPTER V.

OFF DUTY.

"My dear girl, we shall have you sick in your bed, unless you keep yourself warm and quiet for a few days. Widow Wadman can take care of the ward alone, now the men are so comfortable, and have her vacation when you are about again. Now do be prudent in time, and don't let me have to add a Periwinkle to my bouquet of patients."

This advice was delivered, in a paternal manner, by the youngest surgeon in the hospital, a kind-hearted little gentleman, who seemed to consider me a frail young blossom, that needed much cherishing, instead of a stout spinster, who had been knocking about the world for thirty years. At the time I write of, he discovered me sitting on the stairs, with a fine cloud of unwholesome steam rising from the washroom; a party of January breezes disporting themselves in the halls; and perfumes, by no means from "Araby the blest," keeping them company; while I enjoyed a fit of coughing, which caused my head to spin in a way that made the application of a cool banister both necessary and agreeable, as I waited for the frolicsome wind to restore the breath I'd lost; cheering myself, meantime, with a secret conviction that pneumonia was waiting for me round the corner. This piece of advice had been offered by several persons for a week, and refused by me with the obstinacy with which my sex is so richly gifted. But the last few hours had developed several surprising internal and external phenomena, which impressed upon me the fact that if I didn't make a masterly retreat very soon, I should tumble down somewhere, and have to be borne ignominiously from the field. My head felt like a cannon ball; my feet had a tendency to cleave to the floor; the walls at times undulated in a most disagreeable manner; people looked unnaturally big; and the very bottles on the mantle piece appeared to dance derisively before my eyes. Taking these things into consideration, while blinking stupidly at Dr. Z., I resolved to retire gracefully, if I must; so, with a valedictory to my boys, a private lecture to Mrs. Wadman, and a fervent wish that I could take off my body and work in my soul, I mournfully ascended to my apartment, and Nurse P. was reported off duty.

For the benefit of any ardent damsel whose patriotic fancy may have surrounded hospital life with a halo of charms, I will briefly describe the bower to which I retired, in a somewhat ruinous condition. It was well ventilated, for five panes of glass had suffered compound fractures, which all the surgeons and nurses had failed to heal; the two windows were draped with sheets, the church hospital opposite being a brick and mortar Argus, and the female mind cherishing a prejudice in favor of retiracy during the night-capped periods of existence. A bare floor supported two narrow iron beds, spread with thin mattrasses like plasters, furnished with pillows in the last stages of consumption. In a fire place, guiltless of shovel, tongs, andirons, or grate, burned a log, inch by inch, being too long to go on all at once; so, while the fire blazed away at one end, I did the same at the other, as I tripped over it a dozen times a day, and flew up to poke it a dozen times at night. A mirror (let us be elegant!) of the dimensions of a muffin, and about as reflective, hung over a tin basin, blue pitcher, and a brace of yellow mugs. Two invalid tables, ditto chairs, wandered here and there, and the closet contained a varied collection of bonnets, bottles, bags, boots, bread and butter, boxes and bugs. The closet was a regular Blue Beard cupboard to me; I always opened it with fear and trembling, owing to rats, and shut it in anguish of spirit; for time and space were not to be had, and chaos reigned along with the rats. Our chimney-piece was decorated with a flat-iron, a Bible, a candle minus stick, a lavender bottle, a new tin pan, so brilliant that it served nicely for a pier-glass, and such of the portly black bugs as preferred a warmer climate than the rubbish hole afforded. Two arks, commonly called trunks, lurked behind the door, containing the worldly goods of the twain who laughed and cried, slept and scrambled, in this refuge; while from the white-washed walls above either bed, looked down the pictured faces of those whose memory could make for us —

"One little room an everywhere."

For a day or two I managed to appear at meals; for the human grub must eat till the butterfly is ready to break loose, and no one had time to come up two flights while it was possible for me to come down. Far be it from me to add another affliction or reproach to that enduring man, the steward; for, compared with his predecessor, he was a horn of plenty; but — I put it to any candid mind — is not the following bill of fare susceptible of improvement, without plunging the nation madly into debt? The three meals were "pretty much of a muchness," and consisted of beef, evidently put down for the men of '76; pork, just in from the street; army bread, composed of saw-dust and saleratus; butter, salt as if churned by Lot's wife; stewed blackberries, so much like preserved cockroaches, that only those devoid of imagination could partake thereof with relish; coffee, mild and muddy; tea, three dried huckleberry leaves to a quart of water — flavored with lime — also animated and unconscious of any approach to clearness. Variety being the spice of life, a small pinch of the article would have been appreciated by the hungry, hard-working sisterhood, one of whom, though accustomed to plain fare, soon found herself reduced to bread and water; having an inborn repugnance to the fat of the land, and the salt of the earth.

Another peculiarity of these hospital meals was the rapidity with which the edibles vanished, and the impossibility of getting a drop or crumb after the usual time. At the first ring of the bell, a general stampede took place; some twenty hungry souls rushed to the dining-room, swept over the table like a swarm of locusts, and left no fragment for any tardy creature who arrived fifteen minutes late. Thinking it of more importance that the patients should be well and comfortably fed, I took my time about my own meals for the first day or two after I came, but was speedily enlightened by Isaac, the black waiter, who bore with me a few times, and then informed me, looking as stern as fate:

"I say, mam, ef you comes so late you can't have no vittles, — 'cause I'm 'bleeged fer ter git things ready fer de doctors 'mazin' spry arter you nusses and folks is done. De gen'lemen don't kere fer ter wait, no more does I; so you jes' please ter come at de time, and dere won't be no frettin' nowheres."

It was a new sensation to stand looking at a full table, painfully conscious of one of the vacuums which Nature abhors, and receive orders to right about face, without partaking of the nourishment which your inner woman clamorously demanded. The doctors always fared better than we; and for a moment a desperate impulse prompted me to give them a hint, by walking off with the mutton, or confiscating the pie. But Ike's eye was on me, and, to my shame be it spoken, I walked meekly away; went dinnerless that day, and that evening went to market, laying in a small stock of crackers, cheese and apples, that my boys might not be neglected, nor myself obliged to bolt solid and liquid dyspepsias, or starve. This plan would have succeeded admirably had not the evil star under which I was born, been in the ascendant during that month, and cast its malign influences even into my " 'umble " larder; for the rats had their dessert off my cheese, the bugs set up housekeeping in my cracker-bag, and the apples like all worldly riches, took to themselves wings and flew away; whither no man could tell, though certain black imps might have thrown light upon the matter, had not the plaintiff in the case been loth to add another to the many trials of long-suffering Africa. After this failure I resigned myself to fate, and, remembering that bread was called the staff of life, leaned pretty exclusively upon it; but it proved a broken reed, and I came to the ground after a few weeks of prison fare, varied by an occasional potato or surreptitious sip of milk.

Very soon after leaving the care of my ward, I discovered that I had no appetite, and cut the bread and butter interests almost entirely, trying the exercise and sun cure instead.

Flattering myself that I had plenty of time, and could see all that was to be seen, so far as a lone lorn female could venture in a city, one-half of whose male population seemed to be taking the other half to the guard-house, — every morning I took a brisk run in one direction or another; for the January days were as mild as Spring. A rollicking north wind and occasional snow storm would have been more to my taste, for the one would have braced and refreshed tired body and soul, the other have purified the air, and spread a clean coverlid over the bed, wherein the capital of these United States appeared to be dozing pretty soundly just then.

One of these trips was to the Armory Hospital, the neatness, comfort, and convenience of which makes it an honor to its presiding genius, and arouses all the covetous propensities of such nurses as came from other hospitals to visit it.

The long, clean, warm, and airy wards, built barrack-fashion, with the nurse's room at the end, were fully appreciated by Nurse Periwinkle, whose ward and private bower were cold, dirty, inconvenient, up stairs and down stairs, and in everybody's chamber. At the Armory, in ward K, I found a cheery, bright-eyed, white-aproned little lady, reading at her post near the stove; matting under her feet; a draft of fresh air flowing in above her head; a table full of trays, glasses, and such matters, on one side, a large, well-stocked medicine chest on the other; and all her duty seemed to be going about now and then to give doses, issue orders, which well-trained attendants executed, and pet, advise, or comfort Tom, Dick, or Harry, as she found best. As I watched the proceedings, I recalled my own tribulations, and contrasted the two hospitals in a way that would have caused my summary dismissal, could it have been reported at headquarters. Here, order, method, common sense and liberality seemed to rule in a style that did one's heart good to see; at the Hurly burly Hotel, disorder, discomfort, bad management, and no visible head, reduced things to a condition which I despair of describing. The circumlocution fashion prevailed, forms and fusses tormented our souls, and unnecessary strictness in one place was counterbalanced by unpardonable laxity in another. Here is a sample: I am dressing Sam Dammer's shoulder; and, having cleansed the wound, look about for some strips of adhesive plaster to hold on the little square of wet linen which is to cover the gunshot wound; the case is not in the tray; Frank, the sleepy, half-sick attendant, knows nothing of it; we rummage high and low; Sam is tired, and fumes; Frank dawdles and yawns; the men advise and laugh at the flurry; I feel like a boiling tea-kettle, with the lid ready to fly off and damage somebody.

"Go and borrow some from the next ward, and spend the rest of the day in finding ours," I finally command. A pause; then Frank scuffles back with the message: "Miss Peppercorn ain't got none, and says you ain't no business to lose your own duds and go borrowin' other folkses." I say nothing, for fear of saying too much, but fly to the surgery. Mr. Toddypestle informs me that I can't have anything without an order from the surgeon of my ward. Great heavens! where is he? and away I rush, up and down, here and there, till at last I find him, in a state of bliss over a complicated amputation, in the fourth story. I make my demand; he answers: "In five minutes," and works away, with his head upside down, as he ties an artery, saws a bone, or does a little needle-work, with a visible relish and very sanguinary pair of hands. The five minutes grow to fifteen, and Frank appears, with the remark that, "Dammer wants to know what in thunder you are keeping him there with his finger on a wet rag for?" Dr. P.

tears himself away long enough to scribble the order, with which I plunge downward to the surgery again, find the door locked, and, while hammering away on it, am told that two friends are waiting to see me in the hall. The matron being away, her parlor is locked, and there is no where to see my guests but in my own room, and no time to enjoy them till the plaster is found. I settle this matter, and circulate through the house to find Toddypestle, who has no right to leave the surgery till night. He is discovered in the dead house, smoking a cigar, and very much the worse for his researches among the spirituous preparations that fill the surgery shelves. He is inclined to be gallant, and puts the finishing blow to the fire of my wrath; for the tea-kettle lid flies off, and driving him before me to his post, I fling down the order, take what I choose; and, leaving the absurd incapable kissing his hand to me, depart, feeling as Grandma Riglesty is reported to have done, when she vainly sought for chips, in Bimleck Jackwood's " shif less paster."

I find Dammer a well acted charade of his own name, and, just as I get him done, struggling the while with a burning desire to clap an adhesive strip across his mouth, full of heaven-defying oaths, Frank takes up his boot to put it on, and exclaims :

" I'm blest ef here ain't that case now ! I recollect seeing it fall in this mornin', but forgot all about it, till my heel went smash inter it. Here, ma'am, ketch hold on it, and give the boys a sheet on't all round, 'gainst it tumbles inter t'other boot next time yer want it."

. If a look could annihilate, Francis Saucebox would have ceased to exist; but it couldn't; therefore, he yet lives, to aggravate some unhappy woman's soul, and wax fat in some equally congenial situation.

Now, while I'm freeing my mind, I should like to enter my protest against employing convalescents as attendants, instead of strong, properly trained, and cheerful men. How it may be in other places I cannot say; but here it was a source of constant trouble and confusion, these feeble, ignorant men trying to sweep, scrub, lift, and wait upon their sicker comrades. One, with a diseased heart, was expected to run up and down stairs, carry heavy trays, and move helpless men; he tried it, and grew rapidly worse than when he first came: and, when he was ordered out to march away to the convalescent hospital, fell, in a sort of fit, before he turned the corner, and was brought back to die. Another, hurt by a fall from his horse, endeavored to do his duty, but failed entirely, and the wrath of the ward master fell upon the nurse, who must either scrub the rooms herself, or take the lecture; for the boy looked stout and well, and the master never happened to see him turn white with pain, or hear him groan in his sleep when an involuntary motion strained his poor back. Constant complaints were being made of incompetent attendants, and some dozen women did double duty, and then were blamed for breaking down. If any hospital director fancies this a good and economical arrangement, allow one used up nurse to tell him it isn't, and beg him to spare the sisterhood, who sometimes, in their sympathy, forget that they are mortal, and run the risk of being made immortal, sooner than is agreeable to their partial friends.

Another of my few rambles took me to the Senate Chamber, hoping to hear and see if this large machine was run any better than some small ones I knew of. I was too late, and found the Speaker's chair occupied by a colored gentleman of ten; while two others were on their legs, having a hot debate on the cornball question, as they gathered the waste paper strewn about the floor into bags; and several white members played leap-frog over the desks, a much wholesomer relaxation than some of the older Senators indulge in, I fancy. Finding the coast clear, I likewise gambolled up and down, from gallery to gallery; sat in Sumner's chair, and cudgelled an imaginary Brooks within an inch of his life; examined Wilson's books in the coolest possible manner; warmed my feet at one of the national registers; read people's names on scattered envelopes, and pocketed a castaway autograph or two; watched the somewhat unparliamentary proceedings going on about me, and wondered who in the world all the sedate gentlemen were, who kept popping out of odd doors here and there, like respectable Jacks-in-the-box. Then I wandered over the palatial residence of Mrs. Columbia, and examined its many beauties, though I can't say I thought her a tidy housekeeper, and didn't admire her taste in pictures, for the eye of this humble individual soon wearied of expiring patriots, who all appeared to be quitting their earthly tabernacles in convulsions, ruffled shirts, and a whirl of torn banners, bomb shells, and buff and blue arms and legs.

The statuary also was massive and concrete. but rather wearying to examine; for the colossal ladies and gentlemen carried no cards of introduction in face or figure; so whether the meditative party in a kilt, with well-developed legs, shoes like army slippers, and a ponderous nose, was Columbus, Cato, or Cockelorum Tibby the tragedian, was more than I could tell. Several robust ladies attracted me; but which was America and which Pocahontas was a mystery; for all affected much looseness of costume, dishevelment of hair, swords, arrows, lances scales, and other ornaments quite *passé* with damsels of our day, whose effigies should go down to posterity armed with fans, crochet needles, riding whips, and parasols, with here and there one holding pen or pencil, rolling-pin or broom. The statue of Liberty I recognized at once, for it had no pedestal as yet, but stood flat in the mud, with Young America most symbolically making dirt pies, and chip forts, in its shadow. But high above the squabbling little throng and their petty plans, the sun shone full on Liberty's broad forehead, and, in her hand, some summer bird had built its nest. I accepted the good omen then, and, on the first of January, the Emancipation Act gave the statue a nobler and more enduring pedestal than any marble or granite ever carved and quarried by human hands.

One trip to Georgetown Heights, where cedars sighed overhead, dead leaves rustled underfoot, pleasant paths led up and down, and a brook wound like a silver snake by the blackened ruins of some French Minister's house, through the poor gardens of the black washerwomen who congregated there, and, passing the cemetery with a murmurous lullaby, rolled away to pay its little tribute to the river. This breezy run was the last I took ; for, on the morrow, came rain and wind : and confinement soon proved a powerful reinforcement to the enemy, who was quietly preparing to spring a mine, and blow me five hundred miles from the position I had taken in what I called my Chickahominy Swamp.

Shut up in my room, with no voice, spirits, or books, that week was not a holiday, by any means. Finding meals a humbug, I stopped away altogether, trusting that if this sparrow was of any worth, the Lord would not let it fall to the ground. Like a flock of friendly ravens, my sister nurses fed me, not only with food for the body, but kind words for the mind ; and soon, from being half starved, I found myself so beteaed and betoasted, petted and served, that I was nearly killed with kindness, in spite of cough, headache, a painful consciousness of my pleura, and a realizing sense of bones in the human frame. From the pleasant house on the hill, the home in the heart of Washington, and the Willard caravansary, came friends new and old, with bottles, baskets, carriages and invitations for the invalid; and daily our Florence Nightingale climbed the steep stairs, stealing a moment from her busy life, to watch over the stranger, of whom she was as thoughtfully tender as any mother. Long may she wave! Whatever others may think or say, Nurse Periwinkle is forever grateful; and among her relics of that Washington defeat, none is more valued than the little book which appeared on her pillow, one dreary day; for the D D. written in it means to her far more than Doctor of Divinity.

Being forbidden to meddle with fleshly arms and legs, I solaced myself by mending cotton ones, and, as I sat sewing at my window, watched the moving panorama that passed below; amusing myself with taking notes of the most striking figures in it. Long trains of army wagons kept up a perpetual rumble from morning till night; ambulances rattled to and fro with busy surgeons, nurses taking an airing, or convalescents going in parties to be fitted to artificial limbs. Strings of sorry looking horses passed, saying as plainly as dumb creatures could, "Why, in a city full of them, is there no *horse*pital for us?" Often a cart came by, with several rough coffins in it, and no mourners following; barouches, with invalid officers, rolled round the corner, and carriage loads of pretty children, with black coachmen, footmen, and maids. The women who took their walks abroad, were so extinguished in three story bonnets, with overhanging balconies of flowers, that their charms were obscured; and all I can say of them is, that they dressed in the worst possible taste, and walked like ducks.

The men did the picturesque, and did it so well that Washington looked like a mammoth masquerade. Spanish hats, scarlet lined riding cloaks, swords and sashes, high boots and bright spurs, beards and mustaches, which made plain faces comely, and comely faces heroic; these vanities of the flesh transformed our butchers, bakers, and candlestick makers into gallant riders of gaily caparisoned horses, much handsomer than themselves; and dozens of such figures were constantly prancing by, with private prickings of spurs, for the benefit of the perambulating flower-bed. Some of these gentlemen affected painfully tight uniforms, and little caps, kept on by some new law of gravitation, as they covered only the bridge of the nose, yet never fell off; the men looked like stuffed fowls, and rode as if the safety of the nation depended on their speed alone. The fattest, greyest officers dressed most, and ambled statelily along, with orderlies behind, trying to look as if they didn't know the stout party in front, and doing much caracoling on their own account.

The mules were my especial delight; and an hour's study of a constant succession of them introduced me to many of their characteristics; for six of these odd little beasts drew each army wagon, and went hopping like frogs through the stream of mud that gently rolled along the street. The coquettish mule had small feet, a nicely trimmed tassel of a tail, perked up ears, and seemed much given to little tosses of the head, affected skips and prances; and, if he wore the bells, or were bedizzened with a bit of finery, put on as many airs as any belle. The moral mule was a stout, hard-working creature, always tugging with all his might; often pulling away after the rest had stopped, laboring under the conscientious delusion that food for the entire army depended upon his private exertions. I respected this style of mule; and, had

I possessed a juicy cabbage, would have pressed it upon him, with thanks for his excellent example. The historical mule was a melo-dramatic quadruped, prone to startling humanity by erratic leaps, and wild plunges, much shaking of his stubborn head, and lashing out of his vicious heels; now and then falling flat, and apparently dying *a la* Forrest: a gasp — a squirm — a flop, and so on, till the street was well blocked up, the drivers all swearing like demons in bad hats, and the chief actor's circulation decidedly quickened by every variety of kick, cuff, jerk and haul. When the last breath seemed to have left his body, and "Doctors were in vain," a sudden resurrection took place; and if ever a mule laughed with scornful triumph, that was the beast, as he leisurely rose, gave a comfortable shake; and, calmly regarding the excited crowd seeemed to say — "A hit! a decided hit! for the stupidest of animals has bamboozled a dozen men. Now, then! what are *you* stopping the way for?" The pathetic mule was, perhaps, the most interesting of all; for, though he always seemed to be the smallest, thinnest, weakest of the six, the postillion, with big boots, long-tailed coat, and heavy whip, was sure to bestride this one, who struggled feebly along, head down, coat muddy and rough, eye spiritless and sad, his very tail a mortified stump, and the whole beast a picture of meek misery, fit to touch a heart of stone. The jovial mule was a roly poly, happy-go-lucky little piece of horse-flesh, taking everything easily, from cudgeling to caressing; strolling along with a roguish twinkle of the eye, and, if the thing were possible, would have had his hands in his pockets, and whistled as he went. If there ever chanced to be an apple core, a stray turnip, or wisp of hay, in the gutter, this Mark Tapley was sure to find it, and none of his mates seemed to begrudge him his bite. I suspected this fellow was the peacemaker, confidant and friend of all the others, for he had a sort of "Cheer-up,-old-boy,-I'll-pull-you-through" look, which was exceedingly engaging.

Pigs also possessed attractions for me, never having had an opportunity of observing their graces of mind and manner, till I came to Washington, whose porcine citizens appeared to enjoy a larger liberty than many of its human ones. Stout, sedate looking pigs, hurried by each morning to their places of business, with a preoccupied air, and sonorous greeting to their friends. Genteel pigs, with an extra curl to their tails, promenaded in pairs, lunching here and there, like gentlemen of leisure. Rowdy pigs pushed the passers by off the side walk; tipsy pigs hiccoughed their version of "We wont go home till morning," from the gutter; and delicate young pigs tripped daintily through the mud, as if they plumed themselves upon their ankles, and kept themselves particularly neat in point of stockings. Maternal pigs, with their interesting families, strolled by in the sun; and often the pink, baby-like squealers lay down for a nap, with a trust in Providence worthy of human imitation.

But more interesting than officers, ladies, mules, or pigs, were my colored brothers and sisters, because so unlike the respectable members of society I'd known in moral Boston.

Here was the genuine article — no, not the genuine article at all, we must go to Africa for that — but the sort of creatures generations of slavery have made them: obsequious, trickish, lazy and ignorant, yet kind-hearted, merry-tempered, quick to feel and accept the least token of the brotherly love which is slowly teaching the white hand to grasp the black, in this great struggle for the liberty of both the races.

Having been warned not to be too rampant on the subject of slavery, as secesh principles flourished even under the shadow of Father Abraham, I had endeavored to walk discreetly, and curb my unruly member; looking about me with all my eyes the while, and saving up the result of my observations for future use. I had not been there a week before the neglected, devil-may care expression in many of the faces about me, seemed an urgent appeal to leave nursing white bodies, and take some care for these black souls. Much as the lazy boys and saucy girls tormented me, I liked them, and found that any show of interest or friendliness brought out the better traits which live in the most degraded and forsaken of us all. I liked their cheerfulness, for the dreariest old hag, who scrubbed all day in that pestilential steam, gossipped and grinned all the way out, when night set her free from drudgery. The girls romped with their dusky sweethearts, or tossed their babies, with the tender pride that makes mother-love a beautifier to the homeliest face. The men and boys sang and whistled all day long; and often, as I held my watch, the silence of the night was sweetly broken by some chorus from the street, full of real melody, whether the song was of heaven, or of hoe-cakes; and, as I listened, I felt that we never should doubt nor despair concerning a race which, through such griefs and wrongs, still clings to this good gift, and seems to solace with it the patient hearts that wait and watch and hope until the end.

I expected to have to defend myself from accusations of a prejudice against color; but was surprised to find things just the other way, and daily shocked some neighbor by treating the blacks as I did the whites. The men *would* swear at the "darkies," would put two *gs* into negro, and scoff at the idea of any good coming from such trash. The nurses were willing to be served by the colored people, but seldom thanked them, never praised, and scarcely recognized them in the street;

whereat the blood of two generations of abolitionists waxed hot in my veins, and, at the first opportunity, proclaimed itself, and asserted the right of free speech as doggedly as the irrepressible Folsom herself.

Happening to catch up a funny little black baby, who was toddling about the nurses' kitchen, one day, when I went down to make a mess for some of my men, a Virginia woman standing by elevated her most prominent feature, with a sniff of disapprobation, exclaiming:

"Gracious, Miss P.! how can you? I've been here six months, and never so much as touched the little toad with a poker."

"More shame for you, ma'am," responded Miss P.; and, with the natural perversity of a Yankee, followed up the blow by kissing "the toad," with ardor. His face was providentially as clean and shiny as if his mamma had just polished it up with a corner of her apron and a drop from the tea-kettle spout, like old Aunt Chloe. This rash act, and the anti-slavery lecture that followed, while one hand stirred gruel for sick America, and the other hugged baby Africa, did not produce the cheering result which I fondly expected; for my comrade henceforth regarded me as a dangerous fanatic, and my protegé nearly came to his death by insisting on swarming up stairs to my room, on all occasions, and being walked on like a little black spider.

I waited for New Year's day with more eagerness than I had ever known before; and, though it brought me no gift, I felt rich in the act of justice so tardily performed toward some of those about me. As the bells rung midnight, I electrified my room-mate by dancing out of bed, throwing up the window, and flapping my handkerchief, with a feeble cheer, in answer to the shout of a group of colored men in the street

"One hand stirred gruel for sick America, and the other hugged baby Africa." — PAGE 76.

below. All night they tooted and tramped, fired crackers, sung "Glory, Hallelujah," and took comfort, poor souls! in their own way. The sky was clear, the moon shone benignly, a mild wind blew across the river, and all good omens seemed to usher in the dawn of the day whose noontide cannot now be long in coming. If the colored people had taken hands and danced around the White House, with a few cheers for the much abused gentleman who has immortalized himself by one just act, no President could have had a finer levee, or one to be prouder of.

While these sights and sounds were going on without, curious scenes were passing within, and I was learning that one of the best methods of fitting oneself to be a nurse in a hospital, is to be a patient there. For then only can one wholly realize what the men suffer and sigh for; how acts of kindness touch and win; how much or little we are to those about us; and for the first time really see that in coming there we have taken our lives in our hands, and may have to pay dearly for a brief experience. Every one was very kind; the attendants of my ward often came up to report progress, to fill my wood-box, or bring messages and presents from my boys. The nurses took many steps with those tired feet of theirs, and several came each evening, to chat over my fire and make things cosy for the night. The doctors paid daily visits, tapped at my lungs to see if pneumonia was within, left doses without names, and went away, leaving me as ignorant, and much more uncomfortable than when they came. Hours began to get confused; people looked odd; queer faces haunted the room, and the nights were one long fight with weariness and pain. Letters from home grew anxious; the doctors lifted their eyebrows, and nodded ominously; friends said "Don't stay," and an internal rebellion seconded the advice;

but the three months were not out, and the idea of giving up so soon was proclaiming a defeat before I was fairly routed; so to all "Don't stays" I opposed "I wills," till, one fine morning, a gray-headed gentleman rose like a welcome ghost on my hearth; and, at the sight of him, my resolution melted away, my heart turned traitor to my boys, and, when he said, "Come home," I answered, "Yes, father;" and so ended my career as an army nurse.

I never shall regret the going, though a sharp tussle with typhoid, ten dollars, and a wig, are all the visible results of the experiment; for one may live and learn much in a month. A good fit of illness proves the value of health; real danger tries one's mettle; and self-sacrifice sweetens character. . Let no one who sincerely desires to help the work on in this way, delay going through any fear; for the worth of life lies in the experiences that fill it, and this is one which cannot be forgotten. All that is best and bravest in the hearts of men and women, comes out in scenes like these; and, though a hospital is a rough school, its lessons are both stern and salutary; and the humblest of pupils there, in proportion to his faithfulness, learns a deeper faith in God and in himself. I, for one, would return tomorrow, on the "up-again,-and-take-another" principle, if I could; for the amount of pleasure and profit I got out of that month compensates for all after pangs; and, though a sadly womanish feeling, I take some satisfaction in the thought that, if I could not lay my head on the altar of my country, I have my hair; and that is more than handsome Helen did for her dead husband, when she sacrificed only the ends of her ringlets on his urn. Therefore, I close this little chapter of hospital experiences, with the regret that they were no better worth recording; and add the poetical gem with which I console myself for the untimely demise of "Nurse Periwinkle:"

> Oh, lay her in a little pit,
> With a marble stone to cover it;
> And carve thereon a gruel spoon,
> To show a "nuss" has died too soon.

CHAPTER VI.

A POSTSCRIPT.

My Dear S.:— As inquiries like your own have come to me from various friendly readers of the Sketches, I will answer them *en masse*, and in printed form, as a sort of postscript to what has gone before. One of these questions was, " Are there no services by hospital death-beds, or on Sundays ?"

In most Hospitals I hope there are ; in ours, the men died, and were carried away, with as little ceremony as on a battle-field. The first event of this kind which I witnessed was so very brief, and bare of anything like reverence, sorrow, or pious consolation, that I heartily agreed with the bluntly expressed opinion of a Maine man lying next his comrade, who died with no visible help near him, but a compassionate woman and a tender-hearted Irishman, who dropped upon his knees, and told his beads, with Catholic fervor, for the good of his Protestant brother's parting soul :

"If, after gettin' all the hard knocks, we are left to die

this way, with nothing but a Paddy's prayers to help us, I guess Christians are rather scarce round Washington."

I thought so too; but though Miss Blank, one of my mates, anxious that souls should be ministered to, as well as bodies, spoke more than once to the Chaplain, nothing ever came of it. Unlike another Shepherd, whose earnest piety weekly purified the Senate Chamber, this man did not feed as well as fold his flock, nor make himself a human symbol of the Divine Samaritan, who never passes by on the other side.

I have since learned that our non-commital Chaplain had been a Professor in some Southern College; and, though he maintained that he had no secesh proclivities, I can testify that he seceded from his ministerial duties, I may say, skedaddled; for, being one of his own words, it is as appropriate as inelegant. He read Emerson, quoted Carlyle, and tried to be a Chaplain; but, judging from his success, I am afraid he still hankered after the hominy pots of Rebeldom.

Occasionally, on a Sunday afternoon, such of the nurses, officers, attendants, and patients as could avail themselves of it, were gathered in the Ball Room, for an hour's service, of which the singing was the better part. To me it seemed that if ever strong, wise, and loving words were needed; it was then; if ever mortal man had living texts before his eyes to illustrate and illuminate his thought, it was there; and if ever hearts were prompted to devoutest self-abnegation, it was in the work which brought us to anything but a Chapel of Ease. But some spiritual paralysis seemed to have befallen our pastor; for, though many faces turned toward him, full of the dumb hunger that often comes to men when suffering or danger brings them nearer to the heart of things, they were offered the chaff of divinity, and its wheat was left for less needy gleaners, who knew where to look. Even the fine old Bible stories, which may be made as lifelike as any history of our day by a vivid fancy and pictorial diction, were robbed of all their charms by dry explanations and literal applications, instead of being useful and pleasant lessons to those men, whom weakness had rendered as docile as children in a father's hands.

I watched the listless countenances all about me, while we listened to a dull sermon, delivered with a monotonous tone, a business-like manner, and a very visible desire to get the uninteresting job done as expeditiously as possible; which demonstrations were most successful in making the Sunday services a duty, not a pleasure. Listless they were at the beginning, and listless at the end; but the instant some stirring old hymn was given out, sleepy eyes brightened, lounging figures sat erect, and many a poor lad rose up in his bed, or stretched an eager hand for the book, while all broke out with a heartiness that proved that somewhere at the core of even the most abandoned, there still glowed some remnant of the native piety that flows in music from the heart of every little child. Even the big rebel joined, and boomed away in a thunderous bass, singing—

"Salvation! let the echoes fly,"

as energetically as if he felt the need of a speedy execution of the command.

That was the pleasantest moment of the hour, for then it seemed a homelike and happy spot; the groups of men looking over one another's shoulders as they sang; the few silent figures in the beds; here and there a woman noiselessly performing some necessary duty, and singing as she worked;

while in the arm chair standing in the midst, I placed, for my own satisfaction, the imaginary likeness of a certain faithful pastor, who took all outcasts by the hand, smote the devil in whatever guise he came, and comforted the indigent in spirit with the best wisdom of a great and tender heart, which still speaks to us from its Italian grave. With that addition, my picture was complete; and I often longed to take a veritable sketch of a Hospital Sunday, for, despite its drawbacks, consisting of continued labor, the want of proper books, the barren preaching that bore no fruit, this day was never like the other six.

True to their home training, our New England boys did their best to make it what it should be. With many, there was much reading of Testaments, humming over of favorite hymns, and looking at such books as I could cull from a miscellaneous library. Some lay idle, slept, or gossiped; yet, when I came to them for a quiet evening chat or reading, they often talked freely and well of themselves; would blunder out some timid hope that their troubles might "do 'em good, and keep 'em stiddy;" would choke a little, as they said good night, and turned their faces to the wall to think of mother, wife, or home, these human ties seeming to be the most vital religion which they yet knew. I observed that some of them did not wear their caps on this day, though at other times they clung to them like Quakers; wearing them in bed, putting them on to read the paper, eat an apple, or write a letter, as if, like a new sort of Samson, their strength lay, not in their hair, but in their hats. Many read no novels, swore less, were more silent, orderly, and cheerful, as if the Lord were an invisible Ward-master, who went his rounds but once a week, and must find all things at their best. I liked all this in the poor, rough boys, and could have found it in my heart to put down sponge and tea-pot, and preach a little sermon then and there, while homesickness and pain had made these natures soft, that some good seed might be cast therein, to blossom and bear fruit here or hereafter.

Regarding the admission of friends to nurse their sick, I can only say, it was not allowed at Hurlyburly House; though one indomitable parent took my ward by storm, and held her position, in spite of doctors, matron, and Nurse Periwinkle. Though it was against the rules, though the culprit was an acid, frost-bitten female, though the young man would have done quite as well without her anxious fussiness, and the whole room-full been much more comfortable, there was something so irresistible in this persistent devotion, that no one had the heart to oust her from her post. She slept on the floor, without uttering a complaint; bore jokes somewhat of the rudest; fared scantily, though her basket was daily filled with luxuries for her boy; and tended that petulant personage with a never-failing patience beautiful to see.

I feel a glow of moral rectitude in saying this of her; for, though a perfect pelican to her young, she pecked and cackled (I don't know that pelicans usually express their emotions in that manner,) most obstreperously. when others invaded her premises; and led me a weary life, with "George's tea-rusks," "George's foot-bath," "George's measles," and "George's mother;" till, after a sharp passage of arms and tongues with the matron, she wrathfully packed up her rusks, her son, and herself, and departed, in an ambulance, scolding to the very last.

This is the comic side of the matter. The serious one is harder to describe; for the presence, however brief, of relations and friends by the bedsides of the dead or dying, is always a trial to the bystanders. They are not near enough to know how best to comfort, yet too near to turn their backs upon the sorrow that finds its only solace in listening to recitals of last words, breathed into nurse's ears, or receiving the tender legacies of love and longing bequeathed through them.

To me, the saddest sight I saw in that sad place, was the spectacle of a grey-haired father, sitting hour after hour by his son, dying from the poison of his wound. The old father, hale and hearty; the young son, past all help, though one could scarcely believe it; for the subtle fever, burning his strength away, flushed his cheeks with color, filled his eyes with lustre, and lent a mournful mockery of health to face and figure, making the poor lad comelier in death than in life. His bed was not in my ward; but I was often in and out, and, for a day or two, the pair were much together, saying little, but looking much. The old man tried to busy himself with book or pen, that his presence might not be a burden; and once, when he sat writing, to the anxious mother at home, doubtless, I saw the son's eyes fixed upon his face, with a look of mingled resignation and regret, as if endeavoring to teach himself to say cheerfully the long good bye. And again, when the son slept, the father watched him, as he had himself been watched; and though no feature of his grave countenance changed, the rough hand, smoothing the lock of hair upon the pillow, the bowed attitude of the grey head, were more pathetic than the loudest lamentations. The son died; and the father took home the pale relic of the life he gave, offering a little money to the nurse, as the only visible return it was in his power to make her; for, though very grateful, he was poor. Of course, she did not take it, but found a richer compensation in the old man's earnest declaration:

"My boy couldn't have been better cared for if he'd been at home; and God will reward you for it, though I can't."

My own experiences of this sort began when my first man died. He had scarcely been removed, when his wife came in. Her eye went straight to the well-known bed; it was empty; and feeling, yet not believing the hard truth, she cried out, with a look I never shall forget:

"Why, where's Emanuel?"

I had never seen her before, did not know her relationship to the man whom I had only nursed for a day, and was about to tell her he was gone, when McGee, the tender-hearted Irishman before mentioned, brushed by me with a cheerful — "It's shifted to a better bed he is, Mrs. Connel. Come out, dear, till I show ye;" and, taking her gently by the arm, he led her to the matron, who broke the heavy tidings to the wife, and comforted the widow.

Another day, running up to my room for a breath of fresh air and a five minutes' rest after a disagreeable task, I found a stout young woman sitting on my bed, wearing the miserable look which I had learned to know by that time. Seeing her, reminded me that I had heard of some one's dying in the night, and his sister's arriving in the morning. This must be she, I thought. I pitied her with all my heart. What could I say or do? Words always seem impertinent at such times; I did not know the man; the woman was neither interesting in herself nor graceful in her grief; yet, having known a sister's sorrow myself, I could not leave her alone with her trouble in that strange place, without a word. So, feeling heart-sick, home-sick, and not knowing what else to do, I just put my arms about her, and began to cry in a very helpless but hearty way; for, as I seldom indulge in this moist luxury, I like to enjoy it with all my might, when I do.

It so happened I could not have done a better thing; for, though not a word was spoken, each felt the other's sympathy; and, in the silence, our handkerchiefs were more eloquent than words. She soon sobbed herself quiet; and, leaving her on my bed, I went back to work, feeling much refreshed by the shower, though I'd forgotten to rest, and had washed my face instead of my hands. I mention this successful experiment as a receipt proved and approved, for the use of any nurse who may find herself called upon to minister to these wounds of the heart. They will find it more efficacious than cups of tea, smelling-bottles, psalms, or sermons; for a friendly touch and a companionable cry, unite the consolations of all the rest for womankind; and, if genuine, will be found a sovereign cure for the first sharp pang so many suffer in these heavy times.

I am gratified to find that my little Sergeant has found favor in several quarters, and gladly respond to sundry calls for news of him, though my personal knowledge ended five months ago. Next to my good John — I hope the grass is green above him, far away there in Virginia! — I placed the Sergeant on my list of worthy boys; and many a jovial chat have I enjoyed with the merry-hearted lad, who had a fancy for fun, when his poor arm was dressed. While Dr. P. poked and strapped, I brushed the remains of the Sergeant's brown mane — shorn sorely against his will — and gossiped with all my might, the boy making odd faces, exclamations, and appeals, when nerves got the better of nonsense, as they sometimes did:

"I'd rather laugh than cry, when I must sing out anyhow, so just say that bit from Dickens again, please, and I'll stand it like a man." He did; for "Mrs. Cluppins," "Chadband," and "Sam Weller," always helped him through;

thereby causing me to lay another offering of love and admiration on the shrine of the god of my idolatry, though he does wear too much jewelry and talk slang.

The Sergeant also originated, I believe, the fashion of calling his neighbors by their afflictions instead of their names; and I was rather taken aback by hearing them bandy remarks of this sort, with perfect good humor and much enjoyment of the new game.

"Hallo, old Fits is off again!" "How are you, Rheumatiz?" "Will you trade apples, Ribs?" "I say, Miss P., may I give Typus a drink of this?" "Look here, No Toes, lend us a stamp, there's a good feller," etc. He himself was christened "Baby B.," because he tended his arm on a little pillow, and called it his infant.

Very fussy about his food was Sergeant B., and much trotting of attendants was necessary when he partook of nourishment. Anything more irresistibly wheedlesome I never saw, and constantly found myself indulging him, like the most weak-minded parent, merely for the pleasure of seeing his blue eyes twinkle, his merry mouth break into a smile, and his one hand execute a jaunty little salute that was entirely captivating. I am afraid that Nurse P. damaged her dignity, frolicking with this persuasive young gentleman, though done for his well-being. But "boys will be boys," is perfectly applicable to the case; for, in spite of years, sex, and the "prunes-and-prisms" doctrine laid down for our use, I have a fellow feeling for lads, and always owed Fate a grudge because I wasn't a lord of creation instead of a lady.

Since I left, I have heard, from a reliable source, that my Sergeant has gone home; therefore, the small romance that budded the first day I saw him, has blossomed into its second chapter, and I now imagine "dearest Jane" filling my place, tending the wounds I tended, brushing the curly jungle I brushed, loving the excellent little youth I loved, and eventually walking altarward, with the Sergeant stumping gallantly at her side. If she doesn't do all this, and no end more, I'll never forgive her; and sincerely pray to the guardian saint of lovers, that "Baby B" may prosper in his wooing, and his name be long in the land.

One of the lively episodes of hospital life, is the frequent marching away of such as are well enough to rejoin their regiments, or betake themselves to some convalescent camp. The ward master comes to the door of each room that is to be thinned, reads off a list of names, bids their owners look sharp and be ready when called for; and, as he vanishes, the rooms fall into an indescribable state of topsy-turvyness, as the boys begin to black their boots, brighten spurs, brush clothes, overhaul knapsacks, make presents; are fitted out with needfuls, and — well, why not? — kissed sometimes, as they say, good by; for in all human probability we shall never meet again, and a woman's heart yearns over anything that has clung to her for help and comfort. I never liked these breakings-up of my little household: though my short stay showed me but three. I was immensely gratified by the hand shakes I got, for their somewhat painful cordiality assured me that I had not tried in vain. The big Prussian rumbled out his unintelligible *adieux*, with a grateful face and a premonitory smooth of his yellow moustache, but got no farther, for some one else stepped up, with a large brown hand extended, and this recommendation of our very faulty establishment:

"We're off, ma'am, and I'm powerful sorry, for I'd no idea a 'orspittle was such a jolly place. Hope I'll git another ball somewheres easy, so I'll come back, and be took care on again. Mean, ain't it?"

I didn't think so, but the doctrine of inglorious ease was not the the right one to preach up. so I tried to look shocked, failed signally, and consoled myself by giving him the fat pincushion he had admired as the "cutest little machine agoin." Then they fell into line in front of the house, looking rather wan and feeble, some of them, but trying to step out smartly and march in good order, though half the knapsacks were carried by the guard, and several leaned on sticks instead of shouldering guns. All looked up and smiled, or waved heir hands and touched their caps, as they passed under our windows down the long street, and so away, some to their homes in this world, and some to that in the next; and, for the rest of the day, I felt like Rachel mourning for her children, when I saw the empty beds and missed the familiar faces.

You ask if nurses are obliged to witness amputations and such matters, as a part of their duty? I think not, unless they wish; for the patient is under the effects of ether, and needs no care but such as the surgeons can best give. Our work begins afterward, when the poor soul comes to himself, sick, faint, and wandering; full of strange pains and confused visions, of disagreeable sensations and sights. Then we must sooth and sustain, tend and watch; preaching and practicing patience, till sleep and time have restored courage and self-control.

I witnessed several operations; for the height of my ambition was to go to the front after a battle, and feeling that the sooner I inured myself to trying sights, the more useful I should be. Several of my mates shrunk from such things; for though the spirit was wholly willing, the flesh was inconveniently weak. One funereal lady came to try her powers as a nurse; but, a brief conversation eliciting the facts that she fainted at the sight of blood, was afraid to watch alone, couldn't possibly take care of delirious persons, was nervous about infections, and unable to bear much fatigue, she was mildly dismissed. I hope she found her sphere, but fancy a comfortable bandbox on a high shelf would best meet the requirements of her case.

Dr. Z. suggested that I should witness a dissection; but I never accepted his invitations, thinking that my nerves belonged to the living, not to the dead, and I had better finish my education as a nurse before I began that of a surgeon. But I never met the little man skipping through the hall, with oddly shaped cases in his hand, and an absorbed expression of countenance, without being sure that a select party of surgeons were at work in the dead house, which idea was a rather trying one, when I knew the subject was some person whom I had nursed and cared for.

But this must not lead any one to suppose that the surgeons were willfully hard or cruel, though one of them remorsefully confided to me that he feared his profession blunted his sensibilities, and, perhaps, rendered him indifferent to the sight of pain.

I am inclined to think that in some cases it does; for, though a capital surgeon and a kindly man, Dr. P., through long acquaintance with many of the ills flesh is heir to, had acquired a somewhat trying habit of regarding a man and his wound as separate institutions, and seemed rather annoyed that the former should express any opinion upon the latter, or claim any right in it, while under his care. He had a way of twitching off a bandage, and giving a limb a comprehensive sort of clutch, which, though no doubt entirely scientific, was rather startling than soothing, and highly objectionable as a means of preparing nerves for any fresh trial. He also expected the patient to assist in small operations, as he considered them, and to restrain all demonstrations during the process.

"Here, my man, just hold it this way, while I look into it a bit," he said one day to Fitz G., putting a wounded arm into the keeping of a sound one, and proceeding to poke about among bits of bone and visible muscles, in a red and black chasm made by some infernal machine of the shot or shell description. Poor Fitz held on like grim Death, ashamed to show fear before a woman, till it grew more than he could bear in silence; and, after a few smothered groans, he looked at me imploringly, as if he said, "I wouldn't, ma'am, if I could help it," and fainted quietly away.

Dr. P. looked up, gave a compassionate sort of cluck, and poked away more busily than ever, with a nod at me and a brief — "Never mind; be so good as to hold this till I finish."

I obeyed, cherishing the while a strong desire to insinuate a few of his own disagreeable knives and scissors into him, and see how he liked it. A very disrespectful and ridiculous fancy, of course; for he was doing all that could be done, and the arm prospered finely in his hands. But the human mind is prone to prejudice; and, though a personable man, speaking French like a born "Parley voo," and whipping off legs like an animated guillotine, I must confess to a sense of relief when he was ordered elsewhere; and suspect that several of the men would have faced a rebel battery with less trepidation than they did Dr. P., when he came briskly in on his morning round.

As if to give us the pleasures of contrast, Dr. Z. succeeded him, who, I think, suffered more in giving pain than did his patients in enduring it; for he often paused to ask: "Do I hurt you?" and, seeing his solicitude, the boys invariably answered: "Not much; go ahead, Doctor," though the lips that uttered this amiable fib might be white with pain as they spoke. Over the dressing of some of the wounds, we used to carry on conversations upon subjects foreign to the work in hand, that the patient might forget himself in the charms of our discourse. Christmas eve was spent in this way; the Doctor strapping the little Sergeant's arm, I holding the lamp, while all three laughed and talked, as if anywhere but in a hospital ward; except when the chat was broken by a long-drawn "Oh!" from "Baby B.," an abrupt request from the Doctor to "Hold the lamp a little higher, please," or an encouraging, "Most through, Sergeant," from Nurse P.

The chief Surgeon, Dr. O., I was told, refused the higher salary, greater honor, and less labor, of an appointment to the Officer's Hospital, round the corner, that he might serve the poor fellows at Hurlyburly House, or go to the front, working there day and night, among the horrors that succeed the glories of a battle. I liked that so much, that the quiet, brown-eyed Doctor was my especial admiration; and when my own turn came, had more faith in him than in all the rest put together, although he did advise me to go home, and authorize the consumption of blue pills.

Speaking of the surgeons reminds me that, having found all manner of fault, it becomes me to celebrate the redeeming feature of Hurlyburly House. I had been prepared by the accounts of others, to expect much humiliation of spirit from the surgeons, and to be treated by them like a door-mat, a worm, or any other meek and lowly article, whose mission it is to be put down and walked upon; nurses being considered as mere servants, receiving the lowest pay, and, it's my private opinion, doing the hardest work of any part of the army, except the mules. Great, therefore, was my surprise, when I found myself treated with the utmost courtesy and kindness. Very soon my carefully prepared meekness was laid upon the shelf; and, going from one extreme to the other, I more than once expressed a difference of opinion regarding sundry messes it was my painful duty to administer.

As eight of us nurses chanced to be off duty at once, we had an excellent opportunity of trying the virtues of these gentlemen; and I am bound to say they stood the test admirably, as far as my personal observation went. Dr. O.'s stethescope was unremitting in its attentions; Dr. S. brought his buttons into my room twice a day, with the regularity of a medical clock; while Dr. Z. filled my table with neat little bottles, which I never emptied, prescribed Browning, bedewed me with Cologne, and kept my fire going, as if, like the candles in St. Peter's, it must never be permitted to die out. Waking one cold night, with the certainty that my last spark had expired, and consequently hours of coughing were in store for me, I was much amazed to see a ruddy light dancing on the wall, a jolly blaze roaring up the chimney, and, down upon his knees before it, Dr. Z., whittling shavings. I ought to have risen up and thanked him on the spot; but, knowing that he was one of those who like to do good by stealth, I only peeped at him as if he were a friendly ghost; till, having made things as cozy as the most motherly of nurses could have done, he crept away, leaving me to feel, as somebody says, "as if angels were a watching of me in my sleep;" though that species of wild fowl do not usually descend in broadcloth and glasses. I afterwards discovered that he split the wood himself on that cool January midnight, and went about making or mending fires for the poor old ladies in their dismal dens; thus causing himself to be regarded as a bright and shining light in more ways than one. I never thanked him as I ought; therefore, I publicly make a note of it, and further aggravate that modest M. D. by saying that if this was not being the best of doctors and the gentlest of gentlemen, I shall be happy to see any improvement upon it.

To such as wish to know where these scenes took place, I must respectfully decline to answer; for Hurly-burly House has ceased to exist as a hospital; so let it rest, with all its sins upon its head,— perhaps I should say chimney top. When the nurses felt ill, the doctors departed, and the patients got well, I believe the concern gently faded from existence, or was merged into some other and better establishment, where I hope the washing of three hundred sick people is done out of the house, the food is eatable, and mortal women are not expected to possess an angelic exemption from all wants, and the endurance of truck horses.

Since the appearance of these hasty Sketches, I have heard from several of my comrades at the Hospital; and their approval assures me that I have not let sympathy and fancy run away with me, as that lively team is apt to do when harnessed to a pen. As no two persons see the same thing with the same eyes, my view of hospital life must be taken through my glass, and held for what it is worth. Certainly, nothing was set down in malice, and to the serious-minded party who objected to a tone of levity in some portions of the Sketches, I can only say that it is a part of my religion to look well after the cheerfulnesses of life, and let the dismals shift for themselves; believing, with good Sir Thomas More, that it is wise to "be merrie in God."

The next hospital I enter will, I hope, be one for the colored regiments, as they seem to be proving their right to the admiration and kind offices of their white relations, who owe them so large a debt, a little part of which I shall be proud to pay.

   Yours,
    With a firm faith
     In the good time coming,
      TRIBULATION PERIWINKLE.

CONCORD April, 1863.

CAMP AND FIRESIDE STORIES.

THE KING OF CLUBS

AND

THE QUEEN OF HEARTS.

A STORY FOR YOUNG AMERICA.

FIVE-and-twenty ladies, all in a row, sat on one side of the hall, looking very much as if they felt like the little old woman who fell asleep on the king's highway and awoke with abbreviated drapery, for they were all arrayed in gray tunics and Turkish continuations, profusely adorned with many-colored trimmings. Five-and-twenty gentlemen, all in a row, sat on the opposite side of the hall, looking somewhat subdued, as men are apt to do when they fancy they are in danger of making fools of themselves. They, also, were *en* costume, for all the dark ones had grown piratical in red shirts, the light ones nautical in blue; and a few boldly appeared in white, making up in starch and studs what they lost in color, while all were more or less Byronic as to collar.

On the platform appeared a pile of dumb-bells, a regiment of clubs, and a pyramid of bean-bags, and stirring nervously among them a foreign-looking gentleman, the new leader of a class lately formed by Dr. Thor Turner, whose mission it was to strengthen the world's spine, and convert it to a belief in air and exercise, by setting it to balancing its poles and spinning merrily, while enjoying the "Sun-cure" on a large scale. His advent formed an epoch in the history of the town; for it was a quiet old village, guiltless of bustle, fashion, or parade, where each man stood for what he was; and, being a sagacious set, every one's true value was pretty accurately known. It was a neighborly town, with gossip enough to stir the social atmosphere with small gusts of interest or wonder, yet do no harm. A sensible, free-and-easy town, for the wisest man in it wore the worst boots, and no one thought the less of his understanding; the belle of the village went shopping with a big sun-bonnet and tin pail, and no one found her beauty lessened; oddities of all sorts ambled peacefully about on their various hobbies, and no one suggested the expediency of a trip on the wooden horse upon which the chivalrous South is always eager to mount an irrepressible abolitionist. Restless people were soothed by the lullaby the river sang in its slow journey to the sea, old people found here a pleasant place to make ready to die in, young people to survey the world from, before taking their first flight, and strangers looked back upon it, as a quiet nook full of ancient legends and modern lights, which would keep its memory green when many a gayer spot was quite forgotten. Anything based upon common sense found favor with the inhabitants, and Dr. Turner's theories, being eminently so, were accepted at once, and energetically carried out. A sort of heathen revival took place, for even the ministers and deacons turned Musselmen; old ladies tossed beanbags till their caps were awry, and winter-roses blossomed on their cheeks; school-children proved the worth of the old proverb, "An ounce of prevention is worth a pound of cure," by getting their backs ready before the burdens came; pale girls grew blithe and strong swinging their dumb namesakes; and jolly lads marched to and fro embracing clubs as if longevity were corked up in those wooden bottles, and they all took "modest quenchers" by the way.

August Bopp, the new leader of the class, was a German possessing but a small stock of English, though a fine gymnast; and being also a bashful man, the appointed moment had no sooner arrived than he found his carefully prepared sentences slipping away from his memory as the ice appears to do from under unhappy souls first mounted upon skates. An awful silence reigned: Mr. Bopp glanced nervously over his shoulder at the staring rows, more appalling in their stillness than if they had risen up and hooted at him; then piling up the bags for the seventh time, he gave himself a mental shake, and, with a crimson visage, was about to launch his first "Ladees und gentlemen," when the door opened, and a small, merry-faced figure appeared, looking quite at ease in the novel dress, as, with a comprehensive nod, it marched straight across the hall to its place among the weaker vessels.

A general glance of approbation followed from the gentlemen's side, a welcoming murmur ran along the ladies', and the fifty pairs of eyes changed their focus for a moment. Taking advantage of which, Mr. Bopp righted himself, and burst out with a decided, —

"Ladees und gentlemen: the time have arrived that we shall begin. Will the gentlemen serve the ladees to a wand, each one, then spread theirselves about the hall, and follow the motions I will make as I shall count."

Five minutes of chaos, then all fell into order, and nothing was heard but the leader's voice and the stir of many bodies movings imultaneously. An uninitiated observer would have thought himself in Bedlam; for, as the evening wore on, the laws of society seemed given to the winds, and humanity gone mad. Bags flew in all directions, clubs hurtled through the air, and dumb-bells played a castinet accompaniment to peals of laughter that made better music than any band. Old and young gave themselves up to the universal merriment, and, setting dignity aside, played like happy-hearted children for an hour. Stout Dr. Quackenboss gasped twice round the hall on one toe; stately Mrs. Primmins ran like a girl of fifteen to get her pins home before her competitor; Tommy Inches, four feet three, trotted away with Deacon Stone on his shoulder, while Mr. Steepleton and Miss Maypole hopped together like a pair of lively young ostriches, and Ned Amandine, the village beau, blew arrows through a pop-gun, like a modern Cupid in pegtops instead of pinions.

The sprightly young lady whose entrance had been so opportune seemed a universal favorite, and was overwhelmed with invitations to "bag," "hop," and "blow" from the gentlemen who hovered about her, cheerfully distorting themselves to the verge of dislocation in order to win a glance of approbation from the merry black eyes which were the tapers where all these muscular moths singed their wings. Mr. Bopp had never seen such a little piece of earnestness before, and began to think the young lady must be training for a boat-race or the ring. Her dumb-bells flew about till a pair of white arms looked like the sails of a windmill; she hit out from the shoulder with a vigor that would have done execution had there been anything but empty air to "punish"; and the "one, two, three!" of the Zouave movement went off with a snap; while the color deepened from pink to scarlet in her cheeks, the black braids tumbled down upon her shoulders, and the clasp of her belt flew asunder; but her eye seldom left the leader's face, and she followed every motion with an agility and precision quite inspiring. Mr. Bopp's courage rose as he watched her, and a burning desire to excel took possession of him, till he felt as if his muscles were made of india-rubber, and his nerves of iron. He went into his work heart and soul, shaking a brown mane out of his eyes, issuing commands like a general at the head of his troops, and keeping both interest and fun in full blast till people laughed who had not laughed heartily for years; lungs got their fill for once, unsuspected muscles were suddenly developed, and when the clock struck ten, all were bubbling over with that innocent jollity which makes youth worth possessing, and its memory the sunshine of old age.

The last exercise was drawing to a close, and a large ring of respectable members of society were violently sitting down and rising up in a manner which would have scandalized Miss Wilhelmina Carolina Amelia Skeggs to the last degree, when Mr. Bopp was seen to grow very pale, and drop in a manner which it was evident his pupils were not expected to follow.

At this unexpected performance, the gentlemen took advantage of their newly-acquired agility to fly over all obstacles and swarm on to the platform, while the ladies successfully lessened their unusual bloom by staring wildly at one another and suggesting awful impossibilities. The bustle subsided as suddenly as it arose; and Mr. Bopp, rather damp about the head and dizzy about the eye, but quite composed, appeared, saying, with the broken English and appealing manner which caused all the ladies to pronounce him "a dear" on the spot, —

"I hope you will excoose me for making this lesson to be more short than it should; but I have exercise nine hours this day, and being just got well from a illness, I have not recover the strength I have lost. Next week I shall be able to take time by the hair, so that I will not have so much engagements in one day. I thank you for your kindness, and say good-efening."

After a round of applause, as a last vent for their spirits, the class dispersed, and Mr. Bopp was wrestling with a vicious pin as he put on his collar ("a sure sign he has no ma to see to his buttons, poor lamb!" thought Mrs. Fairbairn, watching him from afar); when the sprightly young lady, accompanied by a lad the masculine image of herself, appeared upon the platform, saying, with an aspect as cordial as her words, —

"Good-evening, sir. Allow me to introduce my brother and myself, Dick and Dolly Ward, and ask you, in my mother's name, to come home with us; for the tavern is not a cosy place, and after all this exertion you should be made comfortable. Please come, for Dr. Turner always stayed with us, and we promised to do the honors of the town to any gentleman he might send to supply his place."

"Of course we did; and mother is probably freezing

her blessed nose off watching for us; so don't disappoint her, Bopp. It's all settled; the sleigh's at the door, and here's your coat; so, come on!"

Dick was a fine sample of young America in its best aspect, and would have said "How are you?" to Louis Napoleon if he had been at hand, and have done it so heartily that the great Frenchman would have found it hard to resist giving as frank an answer. Therefore, no wonder that Mr. Bopp surrendered at once; for the young gentleman took possession of him bodily, and shook him into his coat with an amiable impetuosity which developed a sudden rent in the well-worn sleeve thereof, and caused an expression of dismay to dawn upon the owner's countenance.

"Beg pardon; never mind; mother'll sew you up in two seconds, and your overcoat will hide the damage. Where is it? I'll get it, and then we'll be off."

Mr. Bopp colored distressfully, looked up, looked down, and then straight into the lad's face, saying simply, —

"Thank you; I haf no coat but one."

Dick opened his eyes, and was about opening his mouth also, for the exit of some blunderingly good-natured reply, when a warning poke from his sister restrained him; while Dolly, with the innocent hypocrisy which is as natural to some women as the art of tying bows, said, as she led the way out, —

"You see the worth of gymnastics, Dick, in this delightful indifference to cold. I sincerely hope we may reach a like enviable state of health, and look upon great-coats as effeminate, and mufflers a weakness of the flesh. Do you think we shall, Mr. Bopp?"

He shook his head with a perceptible shiver as the keen

north wind smote him in the face, but answered, with a look half merry, half sad, —

"It is not choice, but what you call necessitee, with me; and I truly hope you may never haf to exercise to keep life in you when you haf sold your coat to pay your doctor's bill, or teach the art of laughing while your heart is heavy as one stone. You would not like that, I think, yet it is good, too; for small things make much happiness for me, and a kind word is often better than a rix-dollar."

There was something in the young man's tone and manner which touched and won his hearers at once. Dolly secretly resolved to put an extra blanket on his bed, and shower kind words upon him, while Dick tucked him up in buffalo robes, where he sat helplessly beaming down upon the red hood at his side.

A roaring fire shone out hospitably as they came, and glorified the pleasant room, dancing on ancient furniture and pictured walls till the jolly old portraits seemed to wink a visible welcome. A cheery-faced little woman, like an elder Dolly, in a widow's cap, stood on the threshold, with a friendly greeting for the stranger, which warmed him as no fire could have done.

If August Bopp had been an Englishman, he would have felt much, but said less on that account; if he had been an American, he would have tried to conceal his poverty, and impress the family with his past grandeur, present importance, or future prospects; being a German, he showed exactly what he was, with the childlike frankness of his race. Having had no dinner, he ate heartily of what was offered him; being cold, he basked in the generous warmth; being homesick and solitary, he enjoyed the genial influences that surrounded him, and told his story, sure of sympathy; for even in prosaic Yankeedom he had found it, as travellers find Alpine flowers among the snow.

It was a simple story of a laborious boyhood, being early left an orphan, with a little sister dependent on him, till an opening in America tempted him to leave her, and come to try and earn a home for her and for himself. Sickness, misfortune, and disappointment had been his companions for a year; but he still worked, still hoped, and waited for the happy hour when little Ulla should come to him across the sea. This was all; yet as he told it, with the magical accompaniments of gesture, look, and tone, it seemed full of pathos and romance to his listeners, whose faces proved their interest more flatteringly than their words.

Mrs. Ward mended the torn coat with motherly zeal, and gave it many of those timely stitches which thrifty women love to sew. The young folks devoted themselves to their guest, each in a characteristic manner. Dick, as host, offered every article of refreshment the house afforded, goaded the fire to a perpetual roar, and discussed gymnastics, with bursts of boyish admiration for the grace and skill of his new leader, whom he christened King of Clubs on the spot. Dolly made the stranger one of them at once by talking bad German, as an offset to his bad English, and unconsciously symbolized his future bondage by giving him a tangled skein to hold for the furtherance of her mother's somewhat lengthened job.

The Cupid of the present day was undoubtedly "raised" in Connecticut; for the ingenuity and shrewdness of that small personage could have sprung from no other soil. In former times his stratagems were of the romantic order. Colin bleated forth his passion in rhyme, and cast sheep's eyes from among his flock, while Phyllis coquetted with her crook and stuck posies in his hat; royal Ferdinand and Miranda played at chess; Ivanhoe upset his fellow-men like nine-pins for love of lackadaisical Rowena; and "sweet Moll" turned the pages while her lover, Milton, sang. But in our day, the jolly little god, though still a heathen in the severe simplicity of his attire, has become modernized in his arts, and invented huskings, apple-bees, sleigh-rides, "dropins," gymnastics, and, among his finer snares, the putting on of skates, drawing of patterns, and holding skeins, — the last-named having superior advantages over the others, as all will testify who have enjoyed one of those hand-to-hand skirmishes.

August Bopp was three-and-twenty, imaginative, grateful and heart-whole; therefore, when he found himself sitting opposite a blooming little damsel, with a head bound by a pretty red snood bent down before him, and very close to his own a pair of distracting hands, every finger of which had a hit to make, and made it, it is not to be denied that he felt himself entering upon a new and very agreeable experience. Where could he look but in the face opposite, sometimes so girlishly merry and sometimes so beautifully shy? It was a winning face, full of smooth curves, fresh colors, and sunshiny twinkles, — a face every one liked, for it was as changeful as an April day, and always pleasant, whether mischievous, mournful or demure.

Like one watching a new picture, Mr. Bopp inspected every feature of the countenance so near his own; and as his admiration "grew by what it fed on," he fell into

Like one watching a new picture, Mr. Bopp inspected every feature of the countenance so near his own. — PAGE 108

a chronic state of stammer and blush; for the frank eyes were very kind, the smooth cheeks reflected a pretty shade of his own crimson, and the smiling lips seemed constantly suggesting, with mute eloquence, that they were made for kissing, while the expressive hands picked at the knots till August felt like a very resigned fly in the web of a most enticing young spider.

If the King of Clubs saw a comely face, the Queen of Hearts saw what observing girls call a "good face"; and with a womanly respect for strength, the manliest attribute of man, she admired the broad shoulders and six feet one of her new master. This face was not handsome, for, true to his fatherland, Bopp had an eminent nose, a blonde beard, and a crop of "bonnie brown hair" long enough to have been gathered into a ribbon, as in the days of Schiller and Jean Paul; but Dolly liked it, for its strength was tempered with gentleness; patience and courage gave it dignity, and the glance that met her own was both keen and kind.

The silk was wound at last, — the coat repaired. Dick with difficulty concealed the growing stiffness of his shoulders, while Dolly turned up the lamp, which bluntly hinted bedtime, and Mrs. Ward successfully devoured six gapes behind her hand, but was detected in the seventh by Mr. Bopp, who glanced at the clock, stopped in the middle of a sentence, and, with a hurried "gootnight," made for the door without the least idea whither he was going. Piloted by Dick, he was installed in the "best chamber," where his waking dreams were enlivened by a great fire, and his sleeping ones by an endless succession of skeins, each rapturously concluded in the style of Sam Weller when folding carpets with the pretty maid

"I TELL you, Dolly, it won't do, and I'm not going to have it."

"Oh, indeed; and how will you help it, you absurd boy?"

"Why, if you don't stop it, I'll just say to Bopp, — 'Look here, my dear fellow; this sister of mine is a capital girl, but she will flirt, and ' — "

"Add it's a family failing, Dick," cut in Dolly.

"Not a bit of it. I shall say, 'Take care of your heart, Bopp, for she has a bad habit of playing battledore and shuttlecock with these articles; and, though it may be very good fun for a time, it makes them ache when they get a last knock and are left to lie in a corner.' "

"What eloquence! But you'd never dare to try it on Mr. Bopp; and I shouldn't like to predict what would happen to you if you did."

"If you say 'dare,' I'll do it the first minute I see him. As for consequences, I don't care that for 'em;" and Dick snapped his fingers with an aspect of much disdain. But something in his sister's face suggested the wisdom of moderation, and moved him to say, less like a lord of creation, and more like a brother who privately adored his sister, but of course was not going to acknowledge such a weakness, —

"Well, but soberly, now, I wish you wouldn't plague Bopp; for it's evident to me that he is hit; and from the way you've gone on these two months, what else was to be expected? Now, as the head of the family, — you needn't laugh, for I am, — I think I ought to interfere; and so I put it to you, — do you like him, and will you have him? or are you merely amusing yourself, as you have done ever since you were out of pinafores? If you like him, all serene. I'd rather have him for a brother than any one I know, for he's a regular trump, though he *is* poor; but if you don't, I won't have the dear old fellow floored just because you like to see it done."

It may here be remarked that Dolly quite glowed to hear her brother praise Mr. Bopp, and that she endorsed every word with mental additions of double warmth; but Dick had begun all wrong, and, manlike, demanded her confidence before she had made up her mind to own she had any to bestow; therefore nothing came of it but vexation of spirit; for it is a well-known fact that, on some subjects, if boys *will* tease, girls *will* fib, and both maintain that it is right. So Dolly whetted her feminine weapon, and assumed a lofty superiority.

"Dear me! what a sudden spasm of virtue; and why, if it is such a sin, has not the 'head of the house' taken his sister to task before, instead of indulging in a like degeneracy, and causing several interesting persons to tear their hair, and bewail his forgetfulness, when they ought to have blessed their stars he was out of the way?"

Dick snow-balled a dozing crow and looked nettled; for he had attained that age when "Tom Brown at Oxford" was the book of books, the twelfth chapter being the favorite, and five young ladies having already been endowed with the significant heliotrope flower, — all of which facts Dolly had skilfully brought to mind, as a return-shot for his somewhat personal remarks.

"Bah! they were only girls, and it don't amount to anything among us young folks; but Bopp is a grown man, and you ought to respect him too much to play such pranks with him. Besides, he's a German, and more tender-hearted than we rough Yankees, as any one can see by the way he acts when you snub him. He is proud, too, for all his meekness, and waits till he's sure you like him before he says anything; and he'll need the patience of a family of Jobs at the rate you're going on, — a honey-pot one day and a pickle-jar the next. Do make up your mind, and say yes or no, right off, Dolly."

"Would you have me meet him at the door with a meek courtesy, and say, 'Oh, if you please, I'm ready to say, Yes, thank you, if you'll be good enough to say, Will you'?"

"Don't be a goose, child; you know I mean nothing of the kind; only you girls never will do anything straight ahead if you can dodge and fuss and make a mess of it. Just tell me one thing: Do you, or don't you, like old Bopp?"

"What an elegant way to put it! Of course I like him well enough as a leader; he is clever, and sort of cunning, and I enjoy his funny ways; but what in the world should I do with a great yellow-haired laddie who could put me in his pocket, and yet is so meek that I should never find the heart to hen-peck him? You are welcome to him; and since you love him so much, there's no need of my troubling myself on his account; for with you for a friend, he can have no earthly wish ungratified."

"Don't try to be cutting, Dolly, because you look homely when you do, and it's a woman's business to be pretty always. All I've got to say is, you will be in a nice state of mind if you damage Bopp; for every one likes him, and will be down upon you for a heartless little wretch; and I shan't blame them, I promise you."

"I wish the town wouldn't put its fingers in other

people's pies, and you may tell it so, with my compliments; and all *I* have to say is, that you men have more liberty than you know what to do with, and we women haven't enough; so it's perfectly fair that we should show you the worth of the thing by taking it away now and then. I shall do exactly as I please: dance, walk, ride and flirt, whenever and with whomever I see fit; and the whole town, with Mr. Dick Ward at their head, can't stop me if I choose to go on. Now then, what next?" After which declaration of independence Dolly folded her arms and wheeled about and faced her brother, a spirited statuette of Self-Will, in a red hood and mittens.

Dick sternly asked, —

"Is that your firm decision, ma'am?"

"Yes."

"And you will not give up your nonsense?"

"No."

"You are quite sure you don't care for Bopp?"

"I could slap him with all my heart."

"Very good. I shall see that you don't get a chance."

"I wouldn't try a skirmish, for you'll get beaten, Dick."

"We'll prove that, ma'am."

"We will, sir."

And the belligerents loftily paced up the lawn, with their purpose so well expressed by outward signs that Mrs. Ward knew, by the cock of Dick's hat and the decided tap of Dolly's heels, that a storm was brewing, before they entered the door.

This fraternal conversation took place some two months from the evening of Mr. Bopp's advent, as the young folks were strolling home from school, which school must be briefly alluded to in order to explain the foregoing remarks. It was an excellent institution in all respects; for its presiding genius stood high in the townfolks' esteem, and might have served as an example to Dr. Watts' "busy bee," in the zeal with which he improved his "shining hours," and laid up honey against the winter, which many hoped would be long in coming. All manner of aids were provided for sprouting souls and bodies, diversions innumerable, and the best society. But, sad to relate, in spite of all these blessings, the students who resorted to this academy possessed an Adam-and-Eve-like proclivity for exactly what they hadn't got and didn't need; and, not contented with the pleasures provided, must needs play truant with that young scamp Eros, and turn the ancient town topsy-turvy with modern innovations, till scandalized spinsters predicted that the very babies would catch the fever, refuse their panada in jealous gloom, send billets-doux in their rattles, elope in wicker-carriages, and set up housekeeping in dolls' houses, after the latest fashion.

Certain inflammable Southerners introduced the new game, and left such romantic legends of their loves behind them that their successors were fired with an ambition to do the like, and excel in all things, from cricket to captivation.

This state of things is not to be wondered at; for America, being renowned as a "fast" nation, has become a sort of hot-bed, and seems to force humanity into early bloom. Therefore, past generations must not groan over the sprightly present, but sit in the chimney-corner and see boys and girls play the game which is too apt to end in a checkmate for one of the players. To many of the lookers-on, the new order of things was as good as a puppet-show; for, with the enthusiasm of youth, the actors performed their parts heartily, forgetting the audience in their own earnestness. Bless us! what revolutions went on under the round jackets, and what love-tokens lay in the pockets thereof. What plots and counterplots occupied the heads that wore the innocent-looking snoods, and what captives were taken in the many-colored nets that would come off and have to be taken care of. What romances blossomed like dandelions along the road to school, and what tales the river might have told if any one could have learned its musical speech. How certain gates were glorified by daily lingerings thereat, and what tender memories hung about dingy desks, old pens, and books illustrated with all manner of symbolical designs.

Let those laugh who will: older and wiser men and women might have taken lessons of these budding heroes and heroines; for here all was honest, sincere, and fresh; the old world had not taught them falsehood, self-interest, or mean ambitions. When they lost or won, they frankly grieved or rejoiced, and wore no masks except in play, and then got them off as soon as possible. If blue-eyed Lizzie frowned, or went home with Joe, Ned, with a wisdom older lovers would do well to imitate, went in for another game of foot-ball, gave the rejected apple to little Sally, and whistled "Glory Hallelujah" instead of "Annie Laurie," which was better than blowing a rival's brains out, or glowering at womankind forever after. Or, when Tom put on Clara's skates three successive days, and danced with her three successive evenings, leaving Kitty to freeze her feet in the one instance and fold her hands in the other, she just had a " good cry," gave her mother an extra kiss, and waited till the recreant Tom returned to his allegiance, finding his little friend a sweetheart in nature as in name.

Dick and Dolly were foremost in the ranks, and expert in all the new amusements. Dick worshipped at many shrines, but most faithfully at that of a meek divinity, who returned charming answers to the ardent epistles which he left in her father's garden wall, where, Pyramus and Thisbe-like, they often chatted through a chink; and Dolly was seldom seen without a staff of aids who would have " fought, bled, and died " for her as cheerfully as the Little Corporal's Old Guard, though she paid them only in words; for her Waterloo had not yet come.

WITH the charming perversity of her sex in such matters, no sooner had Dolly declared that she didn't like Mr. Bopp, than she began to discover that she did; and so far from desiring " to slap him," a tendency to regard him with peculiar good-will and tenderness developed itself, much to her own surprise; for with all her coquetry and seeming coldness, Dolly had a right womanly heart of her own, though she had never acknowledged the fact till August Bopp looked at her with so much love and longing in his honest eyes. Then she found a little fear mingling with her regard, felt a strong desire to be respected by him, discovered a certain something which she called conscience, restraining a reckless use of her power, and, soon after her lofty denial to Dick, was forced to own that Mr. Bopp had become her master in the finer species of gymnastics that came in with Adam and Eve, and have kept all creation turning somersets ever since. Of course these discoveries were unconfessed, even to that best bosom friend which any of us can have; yet her mother suspected them, and, with much anxiety, saw all, yet held her peace, knowing that her little daughter would, sooner or later, give her a fuller confidence than could be demanded; and remembering the happiest moments of her own happy past, when an older Dick wooed another Dolly, she left that flower, which never can be forced, to open at its own sweet will.

Meanwhile, Mr. Bopp, though carrying his heart upon his sleeve, believed his secret buried in the deepest gloom, and enjoyed all the delightful miseries lovers insist upon making for themselves. When Dolly was quiet or absent, he became pensive, the lesson dragged, and people fancied they were getting tired of the humbug; when Dolly was blithe and bland, he grew radiant, exercised within an inch of his life as a vent for his emotions, and people went home declaring gymnastics to be the crowning triumph of the age; and when Dolly was capricious, Mr. Bopp became a bewildered weathercock, changing as the wind changed, and dire was the confusion occasioned thereby.

Like the sage fowl in the story, Dick said nothing, but "kept up a terrible thinking," and, not having had experience enough to know that when a woman says No she is very apt to mean Yes, he took Dolly at her word. Believing it to be his duty to warn "Old Bopp," he resolved to do it like a Roman brother, regardless of his own feelings or his sister's wrath, quite unconscious that the motive power in the affair was a boyish love of ruling the young person who ruled every one else.

Matters stood thus, when the town was electrified by a general invitation to the annual jubilee at Jollyboys Hall, which this spring flowered into a masquerade, and filled the souls of old and young with visions of splendor, frolic and fun. Being an amiable old town, it gave itself up, like a kind grandma, to the wishes of its children, let them put its knitting away, disturb its naps, keep its hands busy with vanities of the flesh, and its mind in a state of chaos for three mortal weeks. Young ladies were obscured by tarlatan fogs, behind which they concocted angels' wings, newspaper gowns, Minnehaha's wampum, and Cinderella's slippers. Inspired but incapable boys undertook designs that would have daunted a costumer of the first water, fell into sloughs of despond, and, emerging, settled down from peers and paladins into jovial tars, friar waterproofs, and officers in miscellaneous uniforms. Fathers laughed or grumbled at the whole thing, and advanced pecuniary loans with good or ill grace, as the case might be; but the mothers, whose interest in their children's pleasure is a sort of evergreen that no snows of time can kill, sewed spangles by the bushel, made wildernesses of tissue-paper blossom as the rose, kept tempers sweet, stomachs full, and domestic machinery working smoothly through it all, by that maternal magic which makes them the human providences of this naughty world.

"What shall I go as?" was the universal cry. Garrets were taken by storm, cherished relics were teased out of old ladies' lavendered chests (happy she who saw them again!), hats were made into boots, gowns into doublets, cloaks into hose, Sunday bonnets despoiled of their plumage, silken cauliflowers sown broadcast over the land, and cocked-up caps erected in every style of architecture, while "Tag, Rag, and Bobtail" drove a smashing business, and everybody knew what everybody else was going to be, and solemnly vowed they didn't, — which transparent falsehood was the best joke of the whole.

Dolly allowed her mates to believe she was to be the Queen of Hearts, but privately laid hold of certain brocades worn by a trim grandmother half a century ago, and one evening burst upon her brother in a charming "Little Bo-Peep" costume, which, for the benefit of future distressed damsels, may be described as a white silk skirt, scarlet overdress, "neatly bundled up behind," as ancient ladies expressed it, blue hose with red clocks, high-heeled shoes with silver buckles, a nosegay in the tucker, and a fly-way hat perched on the top of black curls, which gave additional archness to Dolly's face as she entered, singing that famous ditty.

Dick surveyed her with approval, turning her about like a lay figure, and expressing his fraternal opinion that she was "the sauciest little turnout he ever saw," and then wet-blanketed the remark by adding, "Of course you don't call it a disguise, do you? and don't flatter yourself that you won't be known; for Dolly Ward is as plainly written in every curl, bow, and gimcrack, as if you wore a label on your back."

"Then I shan't wear it"; and off went the hat at one fell blow, as Dolly threw her crook in one corner, her posy in another, and sat down an image of despair.

"Now don't be a goose, and rip everything to bits,

just wear a domino over all, as Fan is going to, and then, when you've had fun enough, take it off and do the pretty. It will make two rigs, you see, and bother the boys to your heart's content."

"Dick, I insist upon kissing you for that brilliant suggestion; and then you may run and get me eight yards of cambric, just the color of Fan's; but if you tell any one, I'll keep her from dancing with you the whole evening;" with which bribe and threat Dolly embraced her brother, and shut the door in his face, while he, putting himself in good humor by imagining she was somebody else, departed on his muddy mission.

If the ghosts of the first settlers had taken their walks abroad on the eventful Friday night, they would have held up their shadowy hands at the scenes going on under their venerable noses; for strange figures flitted through the quiet streets, and, instead of decorous slumber, there was decidedly —

"A sound of revelry by night."

Spurs clanked and swords rattled over the frosty ground, as if the British were about to make another flying call; hooded monks and nuns paced along, on carnal thoughts intent; ancient ladies and bewigged gentlemen seemed hurrying to enjoy a social cup of tea, and groan over the tax; barrels staggered and stuck through narrow ways, as if temperance were still among the lost arts, while bears, apes, imps and elves pattered or sparkled by, as if a second Walpurgis Night had come, and all were bound for Blocksberg.

"Hooray for the rooster!" shouted Young Ireland, encamped on the sidewalk to see the show, as Mephistopheles' red cock's feather skimmed up the stairs, and he left a pink domino at the ladies' dressing-room door, with the brief warning, "Now cut your own capers and leave me to mine," adding, as he paused a moment at the great door, —

"By Jove! isn't it a jolly sight, though?"

And so it was; for a mammoth boot stood sentinel at the entrance; a Bedouin Arab leaned on his spear in one corner, looking as if ready to say, —

"Fly to the desert, fly with me,"

to the pretty Jewess on his arm; a stately Hamlet, with irreproachable legs, settled his plumage in another, still undecided to which Ophelia he would first address —

"The honey of his music vows."

Bluff King Hal's representative was waltzing in a way that would have filled that stout potentate with respectful admiration, while Queen Katherine flirted with a Fire Zouave. Alcibiades whisked Mother Goose about the room till the old lady's conical hat tottered on her head, and the Union held fast to a very little Mac. Flocks of friars, black, white and gray, pervaded the hall, with flocks of ballet-girls, intended to represent peasants, but failing for lack of drapery; morning and evening stars rose or set, as partners willed; lively red demons harassed meek nuns, and knights of the Leopard, the Lion, or Griffin, flashed by, looking heroically uncomfortable in their gilded cages; court ladies promenaded with Jack-tars, and dukes danced with dairy-maids, while **Brother Jonathan** whittled, **Aunt Dinah** jabbered, **Ingo-**

mar flourished his club, and every one felt warmly enthusiastic and vigorously jolly.

"Ach himmel! Das ist wunder schön!" murmured a tall, gray monk, looking in, and quite unconscious that he spoke aloud.

"Hullo, Bopp! I thought you weren't coming," cried Mephistopheles in an emphatic whisper.

"Ah, I guess you! yes, you are well done. I should like to be a Faust for you, but I haf no time, no purse for a dress, so I throw this on, and run up for a hour or two. Where is, — who is all these people? Do you know them?"

"The one with the Pope, Fra Diavolo, the telegraph, and two knights asking her to dance, is Dolly, if that's what you want to know. Go in and keep it up, Bopp, while you can; I am off for Fan;" and Mephistopheles departed over the banisters with a weird agility that delighted the beholders; while the gray friar stole into a corner and watched the pink domino for half an hour, at the end of which time his regards were somewhat confused by discovering that there were two pink damsels so like that he could not tell which was the one pointed out by Dick, and which the new-comer.

"She thinks I will not know her, but I shall go now and find out for myself;" and, starting into sudden activity, the gray brother strode up to the nearest pink lady, bowed, and offered his arm. With a haughty little gesture of denial to several others, she accepted it, and they joined the circle of many-colored promenaders that eddied round the hall. As they went, Mr. Bopp scrutinized his companion, but saw only a slender figure shrouded from head to foot, and the tip of a white glove resting on his arm.

"I will speak; then her voice will betray her," he thought, forgetting that his own was undisguisable.

"Madame, permit me that I fan you, it is so greatly warm."

A fan was surrendered with a bow, and the masked face turned fully towards his own, while the hood trembled as if its wearer laughed silently.

"Ah, it is you, — I know the eyes, the step, the laugh. Miss Dolly, did you think you could hide from me?"

"I did not wish to," was the whispered answer.

"Did you think I would come?"

"I hoped so."

"Then you are not displease with me?"

"No; I am very glad; I wanted you."

The pink head drooped a little nearer, and another white glove went to meet its mate upon his arm with a pretty, confiding gesture. Mr. Bopp instantly fell into a state of bliss, — the lights, music, gay surroundings, and, more than all, this unwonted demonstration, put the crowning glory to the moment; and, fired with the hopeful omen, he allowed his love to silence his prudence, and lead him to do, then and there, the very thing he had often resolved never to do at all.

"Ah, Miss Dolly, if you knew how much, how very much you haf enlarged my happiness, and made this efening shine for me, you would more often be a little friendly, for this winter has been all summer to me, since I knew you and your kind home, and now I haf no sorrow but that after the next lesson I come no more unless you gif me leaf. See now I must say this even here, when so much people are about us, because I cannot stop it; and you will forgif me that I cannot wait any longer."

"Mr. Bopp, please don't, please stop!" began the pink domino in a hurried whisper. But Mr. Bopp was not to be stopped. He had dammed up the stream so long, that now it rushed on fast, full and uncontrollable; for, leading her into one of the curtained recesses near by, he sat down beside her, and, still plying the fan, went on impetuously, —

"I feel to say that I lofe you, and tho' I try to kill it, my lofe will not die, because it is more strong than my will, more dear than my pride, for I haf much, and I do not ask you to be meine Frau till I can gif you more than my heart and my poor name. But hear now: I will work, and save, and wait a many years if at the end you will take all I haf and say, 'August, I lofe you.' Do not laugh at me because I say this in such poor words; you are my heart's dearest, and I must tell it or never come again. Speak to me one kind yes, and I will thank Gott for so much joy."

The pink domino had listened to this rapid speech with averted head, and, when it ended, started up, saying eagerly, "You are mistaken, sir, I am not Dolly;" but as she spoke her words were belied, for the hasty movement partially displaced her mask, and Mr. Bopp saw Dolly's eyes, a lock of dark hair, and a pair of burning cheeks, before the screen was readjusted. With redoubled earnestness he held her back, whispering, —

"Do not go mitout the little word, Yes, or No; it is not much to say."

"Well then, No!"

"You mean it? Dolly! truly mean it?"

"Yes, let me go at once, sir."

Mr. Bopp stood up, saying, slowly,—"Yes, go now; they told me you had no heart; I beliefe it, and thank you for that No;" then bowed, and walked straight out of the hall, while the pink domino broke into a fit of laughter, saying to herself,—

"I've done it! I've done it! but what a piece of work there'll be to-morrow."

"Dick, who was that tall creature Fan was parading with last night? No one knew, and he vanished before the masks were taken off," asked Dolly, as she and her brother lounged in opposite corners of the sofa the morning after the masquerade, "talking it over."

"That was old Bopp, Mrs. Peep."

"Gracious me! why, he said he wasn't coming."

"People sometimes say what they don't mean, as you may have discovered."

"But why didn't he come and speak to a body, Dick?"

"Better employed, I suppose."

"Now don't be cross, dear, but tell me all about it, for I don't understand how you allowed him to monopolize Fan so."

"Oh, don't bother, I'm sleepy."

"No you're not; you look wicked; I know you've been in mischief, and I insist upon hearing all about it, so come and tell this instant."

Dolly proceeded to enforce her command by pulling away his pillow and dragging her brother into a sitting posture, in spite of his laughing resistance and evident desire to exhaust her patience; for Dick excelled in teasing, and kept his sister in a fidget from morning till night, with occasional fits of penitence and petting which lasted till next time. Therefore, though dying to tell, he was undecided as to the best method of executing that task in the manner most aggravating to his listener and most agreeable to himself, and sat regarding her with twinkling eyes, and his curly pate in a high state of rumple, trying to appear innocently meek, but failing signally.

"Now, then, begin," commanded Dolly.

"Well, if you won't take my head off till I'm done, I'll tell you the best joke of the season. Are you sure the pink domino with Bopp wasn't yourself, — for she looked and acted very like you?"

"Of course I am. I didn't even know he was there, and think it very rude and ungentlemanly in him not to come and speak to me. You know it was Fan, so do go on."

"But it wasn't, for she changed her mind and wore a black domino; I saw her put it on myself. Her Cousin Jack came unexpectedly, and she thought if she altered her dress and went with him, you wouldn't know her."

"Who could it have been, Dick?"

"That's the mystery, for, do you know, Bopp proposed to her."

"He didn't!" and Dolly flew up with a startled look, at, to adopt a phrase from his own vocabulary, was "nuts" to her brother.

"Yes he did; I heard him."

"When, where, and how?"

"In one of those flirtation boxes; they dropped the curtain, but I heard him do it, on my honor I did."

"Persons of honor don't listen at curtains and key-holes. What did they say?"

"Oh, if it wasn't honorable to listen, it isn't to hear; so I won't tell, though I could not help knowing it."

"Mercy! don't stop now, or I shall die with curiosity. I dare say I should have done the same; no one minds at such a place, you know. But I don't see the joke yet," said Dolly dismally.

"I do," and Dick went off into a shout.

"You idiotic boy, take that pillow out of your mouth, and tell me the whole thing, — what he said, what she said, and what they both did. It was all fun, of course, but I'd like to hear about it."

"It may have been fun on her part, but it was solemn earnest on his, for he went it strong I assure you. I'd no idea the old fellow was so sly, for he appeared smashed with you, you know, and there he was finishing up with this unknown lady. I wish you could have heard him go on, with tears in his eyes ——"

"How do you know, if you didn't see him?"

"Oh, well, that's only a figure of speech; I thought so from his voice. He was ever so tender, and took to Dutch when English was too cool for him. It was really touching, for I never heard a fellow do it before; and, upon my word, I should think it was rather a tough job to say that sort of thing to a pretty woman, mask or no mask."

"What did she say?" asked Dolly, with her hands

pressed tight together, and a curious little quiver of the lips.

"She said No, as short as pie-crust; and when he rushed out with his heart broken all to bits, apparently, she just burst out laughing, and went and polked at a two-forty pace for half an hour."

Dora unclasped her hands, took a long breath, and cried out, —

"She was a wicked, heartless hussy! and if I know her, I'll never speak to her again; for if he was really in earnest, she ought to be killed for laughing at him."

"So ought you, then, for making fun of poor Fisher when he went down on his knees behind the berry bushes last summer. He was earnest enough, for he looked as blue as his berries when he got home. Your theory is all right, ma'am, but your practice is all bosh."

"Hold your tongue about that silly thing. Boys in college think they know everything, can do everything, have everything, and only need beckon, and all womankind will come and adore. It made a man of him, and he'll thank me for taking the sentimental nonsense and conceit out of him. You will need just such a lesson at the rate you go on, and I hope Fan will give it to you."

"When the lecture is over, I'll go on with the joke, if you want to know it."

"Isn't this all?"

"Oh, bless you, no! the cream of it is to come. What would you give to know who the lady was?"

"Five dollars, down, this minute."

"Very good, hand 'em over, and I'll tell you."

"Truly, Dick?"

"Yes, and prove it."

Dolly produced her purse, and, bill in hand, sat waiting for the disclosure. Dick rose with a melo-dramatic bow, —

"Lo, it was I."

"That's a great fib, for I saw you flying about the whole evening."

"You saw my dress, but I was not in it."

"Oh! oh! who *did* I keep going to, then? and what *did* I do to make a fool of myself, I wonder?"

Purse and bill dropped out of Dolly's hand, and she looked at her brother with a distracted expression of countenance. Dick rubbed his hands and chuckled.

"Here's a jolly state of things! Now I'll tell you the whole story. I never thought of doing it till I saw Bopp and told him who you were; but on my way for Fan I wondered if he'd get puzzled between you two; and then a grand idea popped into my head to puzzle him myself, for I can take you off to the life. Fan didn't want me to, but I made her, so she lent me hoops, and gown, and the pink domino, and if ever I thanked my stars I wasn't tall, I did then, for the things fitted capitally as to length, though I kept splitting something down the back, and scattering hooks and eyes in all directions. I wish you could have heard Jack roar while they rigged me. He had no dress, so I lent him mine, till just before the masks were taken off, when we cut home and changed. He told me how you kept running to him to tie up your slippers, find your fan, and tell him funny things, thinking it was me. I never enjoyed anything so much in my life."

"Go on," said Dolly, in a breathless sort of voice, and the deluded boy obeyed.

"I knew Bopp, and hovered near till he came to find out who I was. I took you off in style, and it deceived him, for I'm only an inch or two taller than you, and kept my head down in the lackadaisical way you girls do; I whispered, so my voice didn't betray me; and was very clinging, and sweet, and fluttery, and that blessed old goose was sure it was you. I thought it was all over once, for when he came the heavy in the recess I got a bit flustered, he was so serious about it, my mask slipped, but I caught it, so he only saw my eyes and forehead, which are just like yours, and that finished him, for I've no doubt I looked as red and silly as you would have done in a like fix."

"Why did you say No?" and Dolly looked as stern as fate.

"What else should I say? You told me you wouldn't have him, and I thought it would save you the bother of saying it, and him the pain of asking twice. I told him some time ago that you were a born flirt; he said he knew it; so I was surprised to hear him go on at such a rate, but supposed that I was too amiable, and that misled him. Poor old Bopp, I kept thinking of him all night, as he looked when he said, 'They told me you had no heart, now I believe it, and I thank you for that No.' It was rather a hard joke for him, but it's over now, and he won't have to do it again. You said I wouldn't *dare* tell him about you; didn't I? and haven't I won the ———"

The rest of the sentence went spinning dizzily through Dick's head, as a sudden tingling sensation pervaded his left ear, followed by a similar smart in the right; and, for a moment, chaos seemed to have come again. Whatever Dolly did was thoroughly done: when she danced, the soles of her shoes attested the fact; when she flirted, it was warm work while it lasted; and when she was angry, it thundered, lightened, and blew great guns till the shower came, and the whole affair ended in a rainbow. Therefore, being outwitted, disappointed, mortified and hurt, her first impulse was to find a vent for these conflicting emotions; and possessing skilful hands, she left them to avenge the wrong done her heart, which they did so faithfully, that if ever a young gentleman's ears were vigorously and completely boxed, Dick was that young individual. As the thunder-clap ceased, the gale began, and blew steadily for several minutes.

"You think it a joke, do you? I tell you it's a wicked, cruel thing; you've told a lie; you've broken August's heart, and made me so angry that I'll never forgive you as long as I live. What do you know about my feelings? and how dare you take it upon yourself to answer for me? You think because we are nearly the same age that I am no older than you, but you're mistaken, for a boy of eighteen *is* a boy, a girl of seventeen is often a woman, with a woman's hopes and plans; you don't understand this any more than you do August's love for me, which you listened to and laughed at. I said I didn't like him, and I didn't find out till afterward that I did; then I was afraid to tell you, lest you'd twit me with it. But now I care for no one, and I say I *do* like him, — yes, I love him with all my heart, and soul, and might, and I'd die this minute if I could undo the harm you've done, and see him happy! I know I've been selfish, vain, and thoughtless, but I am not now; I hoped he'd love me, hoped he'd see I cared for him, that I'd done trifling, and didn't mind if he *was* poor, for I'd enough for both; that I longed to make his life pleasant after all his troubles; that I'd send for the little sister he loves so well, and never let him suffer any more; for he is so good, so patient, so generous, and dear to me, I cannot do enough for him. Now it's all spoilt; now I can never tell him this, never comfort him in any way, never be happy again all my life, and *you* have done it!"

As Dolly stood before her brother, pouring out her words with glittering eyes, impetuous voice, and face pale with passionate emotion, he was scared; for, as his scattered wits returned to him, he felt that he had been playing with edge-tools, and had cut and slashed in rather a promiscuous manner. Dazed and dizzy, he sat staring at the excited figure before him, forgetting the indignity he had received, the mistake he had made, the damage he had done, in simple wonder at the revolutions going on under his astonished eyes. When Dolly stopped for breath, he muttered with a contrite look, —

"I'm very sorry, — it was only fun; and I thought it would help you both, for how the deuce should I know you liked the man when you said you hated him?"

"I never said that, and if I'd wanted advice I should have gone to mother. You men go blundering off with half an idea in your heads, and never see your stupidity till you have made a mess that can't be mended; we women don't work so, but save people's feelings, and are called hypocrites for our pains. I never meant to tell you, but I will now, to show you how I've been serving you, while you've been harming me: every one of those notes from Fan which you admire so much, answer so carefully, and wear out in your pocket, though copied by her, were written by me."

"The dickins they were!" Up flew Dick, and clapping his hand on the left-breast pocket, out came a dozen pink notes tied up with a blue ribbon, and much the worse for wear. He hastily turned them over as Dolly went on.

"Yes, I did it, for she didn't know how to answer your notes, and came to me. I didn't laugh at them, or make fun of her, but helped her silly little wits, and made you a happy boy for three months, though you teased me day and night, for I loved you, and hadn't the heart to spoil your pleasure."

"You've done it now with a vengeance, and you're a pair of deceitful minxes. I've paid *you* off. I'll give Fan one more note that will keep her eyes red for a month; and I'll never love or trust a girl again as long as I live, — never! never!"

Red with wrath, Dick threw the treasured packet into the fire, punched it well down among the coals, flung away the poker, and turned about with a look and gesture which would have been very comical if they had not been decidedly pathetic, for, in spite of his years, a very tender heart beat under the blue jacket, and it was grievously wounded at the perfidy of the gentle little divinity whom he worshipped with daily increasing ardor. His eyes filled, but he winked resolutely; his lips trembled, but he bit them hard; his hands doubled themselves up, but he remembered his adversary was a woman; and, as a last effort to preserve his masculine dignity, he began to whistle.

As if the inconsistencies of womankind were to be shown him as rapidly as possible, at this moment the shower came on; for, taking him tenderly about the neck,

Dolly fell to weeping so infectiously, that, after standing rigidly erect till a great tear dropped off the end of his nose, Dick gave in, and laying his head on Dolly's shoulder, the brother and sister quenched their anger, washed away their malice, and soothed their sorrow by one of those natural processes so kindly provided for poor humanity, and so often despised as a weakness when it might prove a better strength than any pride.

DICK cleared up first, with no sign of the tempest but a slight mist through which his native sunshine glimmered pensively.

"Don't, dear, don't cry so; it will make you sick, and won't do any good, for things will come right, or I'll make 'em, and we'll be comfortable all round."

"No, we never can be as we were, and it's all my fault. I've betrayed Fan's confidence, I've spoiled your little romance, I've been a thoughtless, wicked girl, I've lost August; and, oh, dear me, I wish I was dead!" with which funereal climax Dolly cried despairingly.

"Oh, come now, don't be dismal, and blame yourself for every trouble under the sun. Sit down and talk it over, and see what can be done. Poor old girl, I forgive you the notes, and say I *was* wrong to meddle with Bopp. I got you into the scrape, and I'll get you out if the sky don't fall, or Bopp blow his brains out, like a second Werther, before to-morrow."

Dick drew the animated fountain to the wide chair, where they had sat together since they were born, wiped her eyes, and patted her back, with an idea that it was soothing to babies, and why not to girls?

"I wish mother was at home," sighed Dolly, longing for that port which was always a haven of refuge in domestic squalls like this.

"Write, and tell her not to stay till Saturday."

"No; it would spoil her visit, and you know she deferred it to help us through this dreadful masquerade. But I don't know what to do."

"Why, bless your heart, it's simple enough. I'll tell Bopp, beg his pardon, say 'Dolly's willing,' and there you are all taut and ship-shape again."

"I wouldn't for the world, Dick. It would be very hard for you, very awkward for me, and do no good in the end; for August is so proud he'd never forgive you for such a trick, would never believe that I 'had a heart' after all you've said and I've done; and I should only hear with my own ears that he thanked me for that No. Oh, why can't people know when they are in love, and not go heels over head before they are ready!"

"Well, if that don't suit, I'll let it alone, for that is all I can suggest; and if you like your woman's way better, try it, only you'll have to fly round, because to-morrow is the last night, you know."

"I shan't go, Dick."

"Why not? we are going to give him the rosewood set of things, have speeches, cheers for the King of Clubs, and no end of fun."

"I can't help it; there would be no fun for me, and I couldn't look him in the face after all this."

"Oh, pooh! yes you could, or it will be the first time you dared not do damage with those wicked eyes of yours."

"It is the first time I ever loved any one." Dolly's

voice was so low, and her head drooped so much, that this brief confession was apparently put away in Dick's pocket; and, being an exceedingly novel one, filled that ardent youth with a desire to deposit a similar one in the other pocket, which, being emptied of its accustomed contents, left a somewhat aching void in itself and the heart underneath. After a moment's silence, he said, —

"Well, if you won't go, you can settle it when he comes here, though I think we should all do better to confess coming home in the dark."

"He won't come here again, Dick."

"Won't he! that shows you don't know Bopp as well as I. He'll come to say good-by, to thank mother for her kindness, and you and me for the little things we've done for him (I wish I'd left the last undone!), and go away like a gentleman, as he is, — see if he don't."

"Do you think so? Then I must see him."

"I'm sure he will, for we men don't bear malice and sulk and bawl when we come to grief this way, but stand up and take it without winking, like the young Spartan brick when the fox was digging into him, you know."

"Then of course you'll forgive Fan."

"I'll be hanged if I do," growled Dick.

"Ah ha! your theory is very good, sir, but your practice is bosh," quoted Dolly, with a gleam of the old mischief in her face.

Dick took a sudden turn through the room, burst out laughing, and came back, saying heartily, —

"I'll own up; it is mean to feel so, and I'll think about forgiving you both; but she may stop up the hole in the wall, for she won't get any more letters just yet; and you may devote your epistolary powers to A. Bopp in future. Well, what is it? free your mind, and have done with it; but don't make your nose red, or take the starch out of my collar with any more salt water, if you please."

"No, I won't; and I only want to say that, as you owe the explanation to us both, perhaps it would be best for you to tell August your part of the thing as you come home to-morrow, and then leave the rest to fate. I can't let him go away thinking me such a heartless creature, and once gone it will be too late to mend the matter. Can you do this without getting me into another scrape, do you think?"

"I haven't a doubt of it, and I call that sensible. I'll fix it capitally, — go down on my knees in the mud, if it is necessary; treat you like eggs for fear of another smash-up; and bring him home in such a tip-top state, you'll only have to nod and find yourself Mrs. B. any day you like. Now let's kiss and be friends, and then go pitch into that pie for luncheon."

So they did; and an hour afterward were rioting in the garret under pretence of putting grandma's things away; for at eighteen, in spite of love and mischief, boys and girls have a spell to exorcise blue devils, and a happy faculty of forgetting that "the world is hollow, and their dolls stuffed with sawdust."

Dick was right, for on the following evening, after the lesson, Mr. Bopp did go home with him, "to say good-by, like a gentleman as he was." Dolly got over the first greeting in the dusky hall, and as her guest passed on to the parlor, she popped her head out to ask anxiously, —

"Did you say anything, Dick?"

"I couldn't; something has happened to him; he'll

tell you about it. I'm going to see to the horse, so take your time, and do what you like;" with which vague information Dick vanished, and Dolly wished herself anywhere but where she was.

Mr. Bopp sat before the fire, looking so haggard and worn-out that the girl's conscience pricked her sorely for her part in the change; but plucking up her courage, she stirred briskly among the tea-cups, asking, —

"What shall I give you, sir?"

"Thank you, I haf no care to eat."

Something in his spiritless mien and sorrowful voice made Dolly's eyes fill; but knowing she must depend upon herself now, and make the best of her position, she said kindly, yet nervously, —

"You look tired: let me do something for you if I can; shall I sing for you a little? you once said music rested you."

"You are kind; I could like that I think. Excoose me if I am dull, I haf, — yes, a little air if you please."

More and more disturbed by his absent, troubled manner, Dolly began a German song he had taught her, but before the first line was sung he stopped her with an imploring, —

"For Gott sake not that! I cannot hear it this night; it was the last I sung her in the Vaterland."

"Mr. Bopp, what is it? Dick says you have a trouble; tell me, and let us help you if we can. Are you ill, in want, or has any one injured you in any way? Oh, let me help you!"

Tears had been streaming down Mr. Bopp's cheeks, but as she spoke he checked them, and tried to answer steadily, —

"No, I am not ill; I haf no wants now, and no one has hurt me but in kindness; yet I haf so great a grief, I could not bear it all alone, and so I came to ask a little sympathy from your good Mutter, who has been kind to me as if I was a son. She is not here, and I thought I would stop back my grief; but that moosic was too much; you pity me, and so I tell you. See, now! when I find things go bright with me, and haf a hope of much work, I take the little store I saved, I send it to my friend Carl Hoffman, who is coming from my home, and say, 'Bring Ulla to me now, for I can make life go well to her, and I am hungry till I haf her in my arms again.' I tell no one, for I am bold to think that one day I come here with her in my hand, to let her thank you in her so sweet way for all you haf done for me. Well, I watch the wind, I count the days, I haf no rest for joy; and when Carl comes, I fly to him. He gifs me back my store, he falls upon my neck and does not speak, then I know my little girl will never come, for she has gone to Himmel before I could make a home for her on earth. Oh, my Ulla! it is hard to bear;" and poor Mr. Bopp covered his face, and laid it down on his empty plate, as if he never cared to lift it up again.

Then Dolly forgot herself in her great sympathy, and, going to him, she touched the bent head with a soothing hand; let her tears flow to comfort his; and whispered in her tenderest voice, —

"Dear Mr. Bopp, I wish I could cure this sorrow, but as I cannot, let me bear it with you; let me tell you how we loved the little child, and longed to see her; how we should have rejoiced to know you had so dear a friend to make your life happy in this strange land; how we shall grieve for your great loss, and long to prove our respect and love for you. I cannot say this as I ought, but, oh, be comforted, for you will see the child again, and, remembering that she waits for you, you will be glad to go when God calls you to meet your Ulla in that other Fatherland."

"Ah, I will go now! I haf no wish to stay, for all my life is black to me. If I had found that other little friend to fill her place, I should not grieve so much, because she is weller there above than I could make her here; but no: I wait for that other one; I save all my heart for her; I send it, but it comes back to me; then I know my hope is dead, and I am all alone in the strange land."

There was neither bitterness nor reproach in these broken words, only a patient sorrow, a regretful pain, as if he saw the two lost loves before him, and uttered over them an irrepressible lament. It was too much for Dolly, and with sudden resolution she spoke out fast and low, —

"Mr. Bopp, that was a mistake. It was not me you saw at the masque; it was Dick. He played a cruel trick; he insulted you and wronged me by that deceit, and I find it very hard to pardon him."

"What! what is that?" and Mr. Bopp looked up with tears still shining in his beard, and intense surprise in every feature of his face.

Dolly turned scarlet, and her heart beat fast as she repeated with an unsteady voice, —

"It was Dick, not me."

A cloud swept over Mr. Bopp's face, and he knit his brows a moment as if Dolly had not been far from right when she said "he never would forgive the joke." Presently, he spoke in a tone she had never heard before,—cold and quiet,—and in his eye she thought she read contempt for her brother and herself:

"I see now, and I say no more but this; it was not kind when I so trusted you. Yet it is well, for you and Richart are so one, I haf no doubt he spoke your wish."

Here was a desperate state of things. Dolly had done her best, yet he did not, or would not, understand, and before she could restrain them, the words slipped over her tongue,—

"No! Dick and I never agree."

Mr. Bopp started, swept three spoons and a tea-cup off the table as he turned, for something in the hasty whisper reassured him. The color sprang up to his cheek, the old warmth to his eye, the old erectness to his figure, and the eager accent to his voice. He rose, drew Dolly nearer, took her face between his hands, and bending, fixed on her a look tender, yet commanding, as he said, with an earnestness that stirred her as words had never done before,—

"Dollee, *he* said No! do *you* say Yes?"

She could not speak, but her heart stood up in her eyes, and answered him so eloquently that he was satisfied.

"Thank the Lord, it's all right!" thought Dick, as, peeping in at the window ten minutes later, he saw Dolly enthroned upon Mr. Bopp's knee, both her hands in his, and an expression in her April countenance which proved that she found it natural and pleasant to be sitting there, with her head on the kind heart that loved her; to hear herself called "*meine leibchen*"; to know that she alone could comfort him for little Ulla's loss, and fill her empty place.

"They make a very pretty landscape, but too much honey isn't good for 'em, so I'll go in, and we'll eat, drink, and be merry, in honor of the night."

He rattled the latch and tramped on the mat, to warn them of his approach, and appeared just as Dolly was skimming into a chair, and Mr. Bopp picking up the spoons, which he dropped again to meet Dick, and kissing him on both cheeks, after the fashion of his country, as he said, pointing to Dolly, —

"See, it is all fine again. I forgif you, and leave all blame to that bad spirit, Mephistopheles, who has much pranks like that, but never pays one for their pain, as you haf me. Heart's dearest, come and say a friendly word to Richart, then we will haf a little health: Long life and happiness to the King of Clubs and the Queen of Hearts."

"Yes, August, and as he's to be a farmer, we'll add another: 'Wiser wits and better manners to the Knave of Spades.'"

MRS. PODGERS' TEAPOT.

"AH, dear me, dear me, I'm a deal too comfortable!"
Judging from appearances, Mrs. Podgers certainly had some cause for that unusual exclamation. To begin with, the room was comfortable. It was tidy, bright, and warm; full of cosy corners and capital contrivances for quiet enjoyment. The chairs seemed to extend their plump arms invitingly; the old-fashioned sofa was so hospitable, that whoever sat down upon it was slow to get up; the pictures, though portraits, did not stare one out of countenance, but surveyed the scene with an air of tranquil enjoyment; and the unshuttered windows allowed the cheery light to shine out into the snowy street through blooming screens of Christmas roses and white chrysanthemums.

The fire was comfortable; for it was neither hidden in a stove nor imprisoned behind bars, but went rollicking up the wide chimney with a jovial roar. It flickered over the supper-table as if curious to discover what savory viands were concealed under the shining covers. It touched up the old portraits till they seemed to wink; it covered the walls with comical shadows, as if the portly chairs had set their arms akimbo and were dancing a jig; it flashed out into the street with a voiceless greeting to every passer-by; it kindled mimic fires in the brass andirons and the teapot simmering on the hob, and, best of all, it shone its brightest on Mrs. Podgers, as if conscious that it couldn't do a better thing.

Mrs. Podgers was comfortable as she sat there, buxom, blooming, and brisk, in spite of her forty years and her widow's cap. Her black gown was illuminated to such an extent that it couldn't look sombre; her cap had given up trying to be prim long ago, and cherry ribbons wouldn't have made it more becoming as it set off her crisp black hair, and met in a coquettish bow under her plump chin; her white apron encircled her trim waist, as if conscious of its advantages; and the mourning-pin upon her bosom actually seemed to twinkle with satisfaction at the enviable post it occupied.

The sleek cat, purring on the hearth, was comfortable, so was the agreeable fragrance of muffins that pervaded the air, so was the drowsy tick of the clock in the corner; and if anything was needed to give a finishing touch to the general comfort of the scene, the figure pausing in the doorway supplied the want most successfully.

Heroes are always expected to be young and comely, also fierce, melancholy, or at least what novel-readers call "interesting"; but I am forced to own that my present hero was none of these. Half the real beauty, virtue, and romance of the world gets put into humble souls, hidden in plain bodies. Mr. Jerusalem Turner was an example of this; and, at the risk of shocking my sentimental readers, I must frankly state that he was fifty, stout, and bald, also that he used bad grammar, had a double chin, and was only the Co. in a prosperous grocery store. A hale and hearty old gentleman, with cheerful brown eyes, a ruddy countenance, and curly gray hair sticking up all round his head, with an air of energy and independence that was pleasant to behold. There he stood, beaming upon the unconscious Mrs. Podgers, softly rubbing his hands, and smiling to himself with the air of a man enjoying the chief satisfaction of his life, as he was.

"Ah, dear me, dear me, I'm a deal too comfortable!" sighed Mrs. Podgers, addressing the teapot.

"Not a bit, mum, not a bit."

In walked the gentleman, and up rose the lady, saying, with a start and an aspect of relief, —

"Bless me, I didn't hear you! I began to think you were never coming to your tea, Mr. 'Rusalem."

Everybody called him Mr. 'Rusalem, and many people were ignorant that he had any other name. He liked it, for it began with the children, and the little voices had endeared it to him, not to mention the sound of it from Mrs Podgers' lips for ten years.

"I know I'm late, mum, but I really couldn't help it. To-night's a busy time, and the lads are just good for nothing with their jokes and spirits, so I stayed to steady 'em, and do a little job that turned up unexpected."

"Sit right down and have your tea while you can, then. I've kept it warm for you, and the muffins are done lovely."

Mrs. Podgers bustled about with an alacrity that seemed to give an added relish to the supper; and when her companion was served, she sat smiling at him with her hand on the teapot, ready to replenish his cup before he could ask for it.

"Have things been fretting of you, mum? You looked down-hearted as I came in, and that ain't an cordin' to the time of year, which is merry," said Mr. 'Rusalem, stirring his tea with a sense of solid satisfaction that would have sweetened a far less palatable draught.

"It's the teapot; I don't know what's got into it to-night; but, as I was waiting for you, it set me thinking of one thing and another, till I declare I felt as if it had up and spoke to me, showing me how I wasn't grateful enough for my blessings, but a deal more comfortable than I deserved."

While speaking, Mrs. Podgers' eyes rested on an inscription which encircled the corpulent little silver teapot: "*To our Benefactor.—They who give to the poor lend to the Lord.*" Now one wouldn't think there was anything in the speech or the inscription to disturb Mr 'Rusalem; but there seemed to be, for he fidgeted in his chair, dropped his fork, and glanced at the teapot with a very odd expression. It was a capital little teapot, solid, bright as hands could make it, and ornamented with a robust young cherub perched upon the lid, regardless of the warmth of his seat. With her eyes still fixed upon it, Mrs. Podgers continued meditatively, —

"You know how fond I am of the teapot for poor Podgers' sake. I really feel quite superstitious about it; and when thoughts come to me, as I sit watching it, I have faith in them, because they always remind me of the past."

Here, after vain efforts to restrain himself, Mr. 'Rusalem broke into a sudden laugh, so hearty and infectious that Mrs. Podgers couldn't help smiling, even while she shook her head at him.

"I beg pardon, mum, it's hysterical; I'll rever do it

again," panted Mr. 'Rusalem, as he got his breath, and went soberly on with his supper.

It was a singular fact that whenever the teapot was particularly alluded to he always behaved in this incomprehensible manner, — laughed, begged pardon, said it was hysterical, and promised never to do it again. It used to trouble Mrs. Podgers very much, but she had grown used to it; and having been obliged to overlook many oddities in the departed Podgers, she easily forgave 'Rusalem his only one. After the laugh there was a pause, during which Mrs. Podgers sat absently polishing up the silver cherub, with the memory of the little son who died two Christmases ago lying heavy at her heart, and Mr. 'Rusalem seemed to be turning something over in his mind as he watched a bit of butter sink luxuriously into the warm bosom of a muffin. Once or twice he paused as if listening, several times he stole a look at Mrs. Podgers, and presently said, in a somewhat anxious tone, —

"You was saying just now that you was a deal too comfortable, mum; would you wish to be made uncomfortable in order to realize your blessings?"

"Yes, I should. I'm getting lazy, selfish, and forgetful of other folks. You leave me nothing to do, and make everything so easy for me that I'm growing young and giddy again. Now that isn't as it should be, 'Rusalem."

"It meets my views exactly, mum. You've had your hard times, your worryments and cares, and now it's right to take your rest."

"Then why don't you take yours? I'm sure you've

earned it drudging thirty years in the store, with more extra work than holidays for your share."

"Oh well, mum, it's different with me, you know. Business is amusing; and I'm so used to it I shouldn't know myself if I was out of the store for good."

"Well, I hope you are saving up something against the time when business won't be amusing. You are so generous, I'm afraid you forget you can't work for other people all your days."

"Yes, mum, I've put by a little sum in a safe bank that pays good interest, and when I'm past work I'll fall back and enjoy it."

To judge from the cheerful content of the old gentleman's face he was enjoying it already, as he looked about him with the air of a man who had made a capital investment, and was in the receipt of generous dividends. Seeing Mrs. Podgers' bright eye fixed upon him, as if she suspected something, and would have the truth out of him in two minutes, he recalled the conversation to the point from which it had wandered.

"If you would like to try how a little misery suits you, mum, I can accommodate you if you'll step upstairs."

"Good gracious, what do you mean? Who's up there? Why didn't you tell me before?" cried Mrs. Podgers, in a flutter of interest, curiosity, and surprise, as he knew she would be.

"You see, mum, I was doubtful how you'd like it. I did it without stopping to think, and then I was afraid you'd consider it a liberty."

Mr. 'Rusalem spoke with some hesitation; but Mrs. Podgers didn't wait to hear him, for she was already at the door, lamp in hand, and would have been off had she known where to go, "up-stairs" being a somewhat vague expression. The old gentleman led the way to the room he had occupied for thirty years, in spite of Mrs. Podgers' frequent offers of a better and brighter one. He was attached to it, small and dark as it was, for the joys and sorrows of more than half his life had come to him in that little room, and somehow when he was there it brightened up amazingly. Mrs. Podgers looked well about her, but saw nothing new, and her conductor said, as he paused beside the bed, —

"Let me tell you how I found it before I show it. You see, mum, I had to step down the street just at dark, and passing the windows I give a glance in, as I've a bad habit of doing when the lamps is lighted and you a setting there alone. Well, mum, what did I see outside but a ragged little chap a flattening his nose against the glass, and staring in with all his eyes. I didn't blame him much for it, and on I goes without a word. When I came back I see him a lying close to the wall, and mistrusting that he was up to some game that might give you a scare, I speaks to him: he don't answer; I touches him: he don't stir; then I picks him up, and seeing that he's gone in a fit or a faint, I makes for the store with a will. He come to rapid; and finding that he was most froze and starved, I fed and warmed and fixed him a trifle, and then tucked him away here, for he's got no folks to worry for him, and was too used up to go out again to-night. That's the story, mum; and now I'll produce the little chap if I can find him."

With that Mr. 'Rusalem began to grope about the bed, chuckling, yet somewhat anxious, for not a vestige of an occupant appeared, till a dive downward produced a sudden agitation of the clothes, a squeak, and the unexpected appearance out at the foot of the bed of a singular figure, that dodged into a corner, with one arm up, as if to ward off a blow, while a sleepy little voice exclaimed beseechingly, "I'm up, I'm up, don't hit me!"

"Lord love the child, who'd think of doing that! Wake up, Joe, and see your friends," said Mr. 'Rusalem, advancing cautiously.

At the sound of his voice down went the arm, and Mrs. Podgers saw a boy of nine or ten, arrayed in a flannel garment that evidently belonged to Mr. 'Rusalem, for though none too long it was immensely broad, and the voluminous sleeves were pinned up, showing a pair of wasted arms, chapped with cold and mottled with bruises. A large blue sock still covered one foot, the other was bound up as if hurt. A tall cotton nightcap, garnished with a red tassel, looked like a big extinguisher on a small candle; and from under it a pair of dark, hollow eyes glanced sharply with a shrewd, suspicious look, that made the little face more pathetic than the marks of suffering, neglect, and abuse, which told the child's story without words. As if quite reassured by 'Rusalem's presence, the boy shuffled out of his corner, saying coolly, as he prepared to climb into his nest again, —

"I thought it was the old one when you grabbed me. Ain't this bed a first-rater, though?"

Mr. 'Rusalem lifted the composed young personage into the middle of the big bed, where he sat bolt upright, surveying the prospect from under the extinguisher with an equanimity that quite took the good lady's breath away. But Mr. 'Rusalem fell back and pointed to him, saying, "There he is, mum," with as much pride and satisfaction as if he had found some rare and valuable treasure; for the little child was very precious in his sight. Mrs. Podgers really didn't know whether to laugh or cry, and settled the matter by plumping down beside the boy, saying cordially, as she took the grimy little hands into her own, —

"He's heartily welcome, 'Rusalem. Now tell me all about it, my poor dear, and don't be afraid."

"Ho, I ain't afraid a you nor he. I ain't got nothin' to tell, only my name's Joe and I'm sleepy."

"Who is your mother, and where do you live, deary?" asked Mrs. Podgers, haunted with the idea that some woman must be anxious for the child.

"Ain't got any, we don't have 'em where I lives. The old one takes care a me."

"Who is the old one?"

"Granny. I works for her, and she lets me stay alonger her."

"Bless the dear! what work can such a mite do?"

"Heaps a things. I sifs ashes, picks rags, goes beggin', runs arrants, and sometimes the big fellers lets me call papers. That's fun, only I gets knocked round, and it hurts, you'd better believe."

"Did you come here begging, and, being afraid to ring, stand outside looking in at me enjoying myself, like a selfish creeter as I am?"

"I forgot to ask for the cold vittles a lookin' at warm ones, and thinkin' if they was mine what I'd give the little fellers when I has my tree."

"Your what, child?"

"My Christmas-tree. Look a here, I've got it, and all these to put on it to-morrer."

From under his pillow the boy produced a small branch of hemlock, dropped from some tree on its passage to a gayer festival than little Joe's; also an old handkerchief which contained his treasures, — only a few odds and ends picked up in the streets: a gnarly apple, half-a-dozen nuts, two or three dingy bonbons, gleaned from the sweepings of some store, and a bit of cheese, which last possession he evidently prized highly.

"That's for the old one; she likes it, and I kep it for her, — cause she don't hit so hard when I fetch her goodies. You don't mind, do you?" he said, looking inquiringly at Mr. 'Rusalem, who blew his nose like a trumpet, and patted the big nightcap with a fatherly gesture more satisfactory than words.

"What have you kept for yourself, dear?" asked Mrs. Podgers, with an irrepressible sniff, as she looked at the poor little presents, and remembered that they "didn't have mothers" where the child lived.

"Oh, I had my treat alonger him," said the boy, nodding toward 'Rusalem, and adding enthusiastically, "Wasn't that prime! It was real Christmasy a settin' by the fire, eating lots and not bein' hit."

Here Mrs. Podgers broke down; and, taking the boy in her arms, sobbed over him as if she had found her lost Neddy in this sad shape. The little lad regarded her demonstration with some uneasiness at first, but there is a magic about a genuine woman that wins its way everywhere, and soon the outcast nestled to her feeling that this wonderful night was getting more "Christmasy" every minute.

Mrs. Podgers was herself again directly; and seeing that the child's eyelids were heavy with weakness and weariness, she made him comfortable among the pillows, and began to sing the lullaby that used to hush her little son to sleep. Mr. 'Rusalem took something from his drawer, and was stealing away, when the child opened his eyes and started up, calling out as he nodded, till the tassel danced on this preposterous cap, —

"I say! good night, good night!"

Looking much gratified, Mr. 'Rusalem returned, shook the little hand extended to him, kissed the grateful face, and went away to sit on the stairs with tear after tear dropping off the end of his nose, as he listened to the voice that, after two years of silence, sung the air this simple soul thought the loveliest in the world. At first, it was more sob than song, but soon the soothing music flowed on unbroken, and the wondering child, for the first time within his memory, fell asleep in the sweet shelter of a woman's arms.

When Mrs. Podgers came out, she found Mr. 'Rusalem intent on stuffing another parcel into a long gray stocking already full to overflowing.

"For the little chap, mum. He let fall that he'd never done this sort of thing in his life, and as he hadn't any stockings of his own, poor dear, I took the liberty of lending him one of mine," explained Mr. 'Rusalem, surveying the knobby article with evident regret that it wasn't bigger.

Mrs. Podgers said nothing, but looked from the stocking to the fatherly old gentleman who held it; and it is my private belief, that if Mrs. Podgers had obeyed the impulse of her heart, she would have forgotten decorum, and kissed him on the spot. She didn't, however, but went briskly into her own room, whence she presently returned with red eyes, and a pile of small garments in her hands. Having nearly exhausted his pincushion in trying to suspend the heavy stocking, Mr. 'Rusalem had just succeeded as she appeared. He saw what she carried, watched her arrange the little shirt, jacket and trousers, the half-worn shoes and tidy socks, beside the bed, with motherly care, and stand looking at the unconscious child, with an expression which caused Mr. 'Rusalem to dart down stairs, and compose himself by rubbing his hair erect, and shaking his fist in the painted face of the late Podgers.

An hour or two later the store was closed, the room cleared, Mrs. Podgers in her arm-chair on one side of the hearth, with her knitting in her hand, Mr. 'Rusalem in his arm-chair on the other side, with his newspaper on his knee, both looking so cosy and comfortable that any one would have pronounced them a Darby and Joan on the spot. Ah, but they weren't, you see, and that spoilt the illusion, to one party at least. Both were rather silent, both looked thoughtfully at the fire, and the fire gave them both excellent counsel, as it seldom fails to do when it finds any kindred warmth and brightness in the hearts and souls of those who study it. Mrs. Podgers kindled first, and broke out suddenly with a nod of great determination.

"'Rusalem, I'm going to keep that boy if it's possible!"

"You shall, mum, whether it's possible or not," he answered, nodding back at her with equal decision.

"I don't know why I never thought of such a thing

before. There's a many children suffering for mothers, and heaven knows I'm wearying for some little child to fill my Neddy's place. I wonder if you didn't think of this when you took that boy in; it would be just like you!"

Mr. 'Rusalem shook his head, but looked so guilty, that Mrs. Podgers was satisfied, called him "a thoughtful dear," within herself, and kindled still more.

"Between you, and Joe, and the teapot, I've got another idea into my stupid head, and I know you won't laugh at it. That loving little soul has tried to get a tree for some poor babies who have no one to think of them but him, and even remembered the old one, who must be a wretch to hit that child, and hit hard, too, I know by the looks of his arms. Well, I've a great longing to go and give him a tree,—a right good one, like those Neddy used to have; to get in the 'little fellers' he tells of, give them a good dinner, and then a regular Christmas frolic. Can't it be done?"

"Nothing could be easier, mum;" and Mr. 'Rusalem, who had been taking counsel with the fire till he quite glowed with warmth and emotion, nodded, smiled, and rubbed his hands, as if Mrs. Podgers had invited him to a Lord Mayor's feast, or some equally gorgeous jollification.

"I suppose it's the day, and thinking of how it came to be, that makes me feel as if I wanted to help everybody, and makes this Christmas so bright and happy that I never can forget it," continued the good woman, with a heartiness that made her honest face quite beautiful to behold.

If Mrs. Podgers had only known what was going on under the capacious waistcoat opposite, she would have held her tongue; for the more charitable, earnest, and tender-hearted she grew, the harder it became for Mr. 'Rusalem to restrain the declaration which had been hovering on his lips ever since old Podgers died. As the comely relict sat there talking in that genial way, and glowing with good-will to all mankind, it was too much for Mr. 'Rusalem; and finding it impossible to resist the desire to know his fate, he yielded to it, gave a portentous hem, and said abruptly, —

"Well, mum, have I done it?"

"Done what?" asked Mrs. P., going on with her work.

"Made you uncomfortable, according to promise."

"Oh dear, no, you've made me very happy, and will have to try again," she answered, laughing.

"I will, mum."

As he spoke Mr. 'Rusalem drew his chair nearer, leaned forward, and looking straight at her, said deliberately, though his voice shook a little, —

"Mrs. Podgers, I love you hearty; would you have any objections to marrying of me?"

Not a word said Mrs. Podgers; but her knitting dropped out of her hand, and she looked as uncomfortable as she could desire.

"I thought that would do it," muttered Mr. 'Rusalem, but went on steadily, though his ruddy face got paler and paler, his voice huskier and huskier, and his heart fuller and fuller every word he attempted.

"You see, mum, I have took the liberty of loving you ever since you came, more than ten years ago. I was eager to make it known long before this, but Podgers spoke first and then it was no use. It come hard for a time, but I learned to give you up, though I couldn't learn not to love you, being as it was impossible. Since Podgers died I've turned it over in my mind frequent, but felt as if I was too old, and rough, and poor every way to ask so much. Lately, the wish has growed too strong for me, and to-night it won't be put down. If you want a trial, mum, I should be that I'll warrant, for do my best, I could never be all I'm wishful of being for your sake. Would you give it name, and if not agreeable, we'll let it drop, mum, we'll let it drop."

If it hadn't been for the teapot, Mrs. Podgers would have said Yes at once. The word was on her lips, but as she looked up the fire flashed brightly on the teapot (which always occupied the place of honor on the sideboard, for Mrs. P. was intensely proud of it), and she stopped to think, for it reminded her of something. In order to explain this, we must keep Mr. 'Rusalem waiting for his answer a minute.

Rather more than ten years ago, old Podgers happening to want a housekeeper, invited a poor relation to fill that post in his bachelor establishment. He never would have thought of marrying her, though the young woman was both notable and handsome, if he hadn't discovered that his partner loved her. Whereupon the perverse old fellow immediately proposed, lest he should lose his housekeeper, and was accepted from motives of gratitude. Mrs. Podgers was a dutiful wife, but not a very happy one, for the world said that Mr. P. was a hard, miserly man, and his wife was forced to believe the world in the right, till the teapot changed her opinion. There happened to be much suffering among the poor one year, owing to the burning of the mills, and contributions were solicited for their relief. Old Podgers, though a rich man, refused to give a penny, but it was afterwards discovered that his private charities exceeded many more ostentatious ones, and the word "miserly" was changed to "peculiar." When times grew prosperous again, the workmen, whose families had been so quietly served, clubbed together, got the teapot, and left it at Mr. Podgers' door one Christmas Eve. But the old gentleman never saw it; his dinner had been too much for him, and apoplexy took him off that very afternoon.

In the midst of her grief Mrs. Podgers was surprised, touched and troubled by this revelation, for she had known nothing of the affair till the teapot came. Woman-like, she felt great remorse for what now seemed like blindness and ingratitude; she fancied she owed him some atonement, and remembering how often he had expressed a hope that she wouldn't marry again after he was gone, she resolved to gratify him. The buxom widow had had many opportunities of putting off her weeds, but she had refused all offers without regret till now. The teapot reminded her of Podgers and her vow; and though her heart rebelled, she thought it her duty to check the answer that sprung to her lips, and slowly, but decidedly, replied, —

"I'm truly grateful to you, 'Rusalem, but I couldn't do it. Don't think you'd ever be a trial, for you're the last man to be that to any woman. It's a feeling I have that it wouldn't be kind to Podgers. I can't forget how much I owe him, how much I wronged him, and how much I can please him by staying as I am, for his frequent words were, 'Keep the property together, and don't marry, Jane.'"

"Very well, mum, then we'll let it drop, and fall back into the old ways. Don't fret yourself about it, I shall bear up, and —" there Mr. 'Rusalem's voice gave out, and he sat frowning at the fire, bent on bearing up manfully, though it was very hard to find that Podgers dead as well as Podgers living was to keep from him the happiness he had waited for so long. His altered face and broken voice were almost too much for Mrs. P., and she found it necessary to confirm her resolution by telling it. Laying one hand on his shoulder, she pointed to the teapot with the other, saying gently, —

"The day that came and I found out how good he was, too late to beg his pardon and love him for it, I said to myself, 'I'll be true to Podgers till I die, because that's all I can do now to show my repentance and respect.' But for that feeling and that promise I couldn't say No to you, 'Rusalem, for you've been my best friend all these years, and I'll be yours all my life, though I can't be anything else, my dear."

For the first time since its arrival, the mention of the teapot did not produce the accustomed demonstration from Mr. 'Rusalem. On the contrary, he looked at it with a momentary expression of indignation and disgust, strongly suggestive of an insane desire to cast the precious relic on the floor and trample on it. If any such temptation did assail him, he promptly curbed it, and looked about the room with a forlorn air, that made Mrs. Podgers hate herself, as he meekly answered, —

"I'm obliged to you, mum; the feeling does you

honor. Don't mind me, it's rather a blow, but I'll be up again directly."

He retired behind his paper as he spoke. and Mrs. Podgers spoilt her knitting in respectful silence, till Mr. 'Rusalem began to read aloud as usual, to assure her that in spite of the blow he *was* up again.

In the gray dawn the worthy gentleman was roused from his slumbers, by a strange voice whispering shrilly in his ear, —

"I say, there's two of em. Ain't it jolly?"

Starting up, he beheld a comical little goblin standing at his bedside, with a rapturous expression of countenance, and a pair of long gray stockings in its hands. Both were heaping full, but one was evidently meant for Mr. 'Rusalem, for every wish, whim and fancy of his had been guessed, and gratified in a way that touched him to the heart. If it were not indecorous to invade the privacy of a gentleman's apartment, I could describe how there were two boys in the big bed that morning; how the old boy revelled in the treasures of his stocking as heartily as the young one; how they laughed and exclaimed, pulled each others nightcaps off, and had a regular pillow fight; how little Joe was got into his new clothes, and strutted like a small peacock in them; how Mr. 'Rusalem made himself splendid in his Sunday best, and spent ten good minutes in tying the fine cravat somebody had hemmed for him. But lest it should be thought improper, I will merely say, that nowhere in the city did the sun shine on happier faces than these two showed Mrs. Podgers, as Mr. 'Rusalem came in with Joe on his shoulder, both wishing her a merry Christmas, as heartily as if this were the first the world had ever seen.

Mrs. Podgers was as brisk and blithe as they, though she must have sat up one-half the night making presents for them, and laid awake the other half making plans for the day. As soon as she had hugged Joe, toasted him red, and heaped his plate with everything on the table, she told them the order of performances.

"As soon as ever you can't eat any more you must order home the tree, 'Rusalem, and then go with Joe to invite the party, while I see to dinner, and dress up the pine as well as I can in such a hurry."

"Yes, mum," answered Mr. 'Rusalem with alacrity; though how she was going to do her part was not clear to him. But he believed her capable of working any miracle within the power of mortal woman; and having plans of his own, he soon trudged away with Joe prancing at his side, so like the lost Neddy, in the little cap and coat, that Mrs. Podgers forgot her party to stand watching them down the crowded street, with eyes that saw very dimly when they looked away again.

Never mind how she did it, the miracle was wrought, for Mrs. Podgers and her maid Betsey fell to work with a will, and when women set their hearts on anything it is a known fact that they seldom fail to accomplish it. By noon everything was ready, the tree waiting in the best parlor, the dinner smoking on the table, and Mrs. Podgers at the window to catch the first glimpse of her coming guests. A last thought struck her as she stood waiting. There was but one high chair in the house, and the big ones would be doubtless too low for the little people. Bent on making them as comfortable as her motherly heart could desire, she set about mending the matter by bringing out from Podgers' bookcase several fat old ledgers, and arranging them in the chairs. While busily dusting one of these it slipped from her hands, and as it fell a paper fluttered from among the leaves. She picked it up, looked at it, dropped her duster, and became absorbed. It was a small sheet filled with figures, and here and there short memoranda, — not an interesting looking document in the least; but Mrs. Podgers stood like a statue till she had read it several times; then she caught her breath, clapped her hands, laughed and cried together, and put the climax to her extraordinary behavior by running across the room and embracing the astonished little teapot.

How long she would have gone on in this wild manner it is impossible to say, had not the the jingle of bells, and a shrill, small cheer announced that the party had arrived. Whisking the mysterious paper into her pocket, and dressing her agitated countenance in smiles, she hastened to open the door before chilly fingers could find the bell.

Such a merry load as that was! Such happy faces looking out from under the faded hoods and caps! Such a hearty "Hurrah for Mrs. Podgers!" greeted her straight from the grateful hearts that loved her the instant she appeared! And what a perfect Santa Claus Mr. 'Rusalem made, with his sleigh full of bundles as well as children, his face full of sunshine, his arms full of babies, whom he held up that they too might clap their little hands, while he hurrahed with all his might. I really don't think reindeers, or the immemorial white beard and fur cap, could have improved the picture; and the neighbors were of my opinion, I suspect.

It was good to see Mrs. Podgers welcome them all in a way that gave the shyest courage, made the poorest forget patched jackets or ragged gowns, and caused them all to feel that this indeed was merry Christmas. It was better still to see Mrs. Podgers preside over the table, dealing out turkey and pudding with such a bounteous hand, that the small feasters often paused, in sheer astonishment, at the abundance before them, and then fell to again with renewed energy, as if they feared to wake up presently and find the whole a dr...
It was best of all to see Mrs. Podgers gather t... about her afterwards, hearing their little stories, learning their many wants, and winning their young hearts by such gentle wiles that they soon regarded her as some beautiful, benignant fairy, who had led them from a cold, dark world into the land of innocent delights they had imagined, longed for, yet never hoped to find.

Then came the tree, hung thick with bonbons, fruit and toys, gay mittens and tippets, comfortable socks and hoods, and, lower down, more substantial but less showy gifts; for Mrs Podgers had nearly exhausted the Dorcas basket that fortunately chanced to be with her just then. There was no time for candles, but, as if he understood the matter and was bent on supplying all deficiencies, the sun shone gloriously on the little tree, and made it doubly splendid in the children's eyes.

It would have touched the hardest heart to watch the poor little creatures, as they trooped in and stood about the wonderful tree. Some seemed ready to go wild with delight, some folded their hands and sighed with solemn satisfaction, others looked as if bewildered by such unwonted and unexpected good fortune; and when Mr.

'Rusalem told them how this fruitful tree had sprung up from their loving playmate's broken bough, little Joe hid his face in Mrs. Podgers' gown, and could find no vent for his great happiness but tears. It was not a large tree, but it took a long while to strip it; and even when the last gilded nut was gone the children still lingered about it, as if they regarded it with affection as a generous benefactor, and were loath to leave it.

Next they had a splendid round of games. I don't know what will be thought of the worthy souls, but Mr. 'Rusalem and Mrs. Podgers played with all their might. Perhaps the reason why he gave himself up so freely to the spirit of the hour was, that his disappointment was very heavy; and, according to his simple philosophy, it was wiser to soothe his wounded heart and cheer his sad spirit with the sweet society of little children, than to curse fate and reproach a woman. What was Mrs. Podgers' reason it is impossible to tell, but she behaved as if some secret satisfaction filled her heart so full that she was glad to let it bubble over in this harmless fashion. Both tried to be children again, and both succeeded capitally, though now and then their hearts got the better of them. When Mr. 'Rusalem was blinded he tossed all the little lads up to the ceiling when he caught them, kissed all the little girls, and, that no one might feel slighted, kissed Mrs. Podgers also. When they played "Open the gates," and the two grown people stood hand in hand while the mirthful troops marched under the tall arch, Mrs. Podgers never once looked Mr. 'Rusalem in the face, but blushed and kept her eyes on the ground, as if she was a bashful girl playing games with some boyish sweetheart. The children saw nothing of all this, and, bless their innocent little hearts! they wouldn't have understood it if they had; but it was perfectly evident that the gray-headed gentleman and the mature matron had forgotten all about their years, and were in their teens again; for true love is gifted with immortal youth.

When weary with romping, they gathered round the fire, and Mr. 'Rusalem told fairy tales, as if his dull ledgers had preserved these childish romances like flowers between their leaves, and kept them fresh in spite of time. Mrs. Podgers sung to them, and made them sing with her, till passers-by smiled and lingered as the childish voices reached them, and, looking through the screen of roses, they caught glimpses of the happy little group singing in the ruddy circle of that Christmas fire.

It was a very humble festival, but with these poor guests came also Love and Charity, Innocence and Joy, — the strong, sweet spirits who bless and beautify the world; and though eclipsed by many more splendid celebrations, I think the day was the better and the blither for Mrs. Podgers' little party.

When it was all over, — the grateful farewells and riotous cheers as the children were carried home, the twilight raptures of Joe, and the long lullaby before he could extinguish himself enough to go to sleep, the congratulations and clearing up, — then Mr. 'Rusalem and Mrs. Podgers sat down to tea. But no sooner were they alone together than Mrs. P. fell into a curious flutter, and did the oddest things. She gave Mr. 'Rusalem warm water instead of tea, passed the slop-bowl when he asked for the sugar-basin, burnt her fingers, laid her handkerchief on the tray, and tried to put her fork in her pocket, and went on in such a way that Mr. 'Rusalem began to fear the day had been too much for her.

"You're tired, mum," he said presently, hearing her sigh.

"Not a bit," she answered briskly, opening the teapot to add more water, but seemed to forget her purpose, and sat looking into its steamy depths as if in search of something. If it was courage, she certainly found it, for all of a sudden she handed the mysterious paper to Mr. 'Rusalem, saying solemnly, —

"Read that, and tell me if it's true."

He took it readily, put on his glasses, and bent to examine it, but gave a start that caused the spectacles to fly off his nose, as he exclaimed, —

"Lord bless me, he said he'd burnt it!"

"Then it *is* true? Don't deny it, 'Rusalem; it's no use, for I've caught you at last!" and in her excitement Mrs. Podgers slapped down the teapot-lid as if she had got him inside.

"I assure you, mum, he promised to burn it. He made me write down the sums, and so on, to satisfy him that I hadn't took more'n my share of the profits. It was my own; and though he called me a fool he let me do as I liked, but I never thought it would come up again like this, mum."

"Of course you didn't, for it was left in one of the old ledgers we had down for the dears to sit on. I found it, I read it, and I understood it in a minute. It was you who helped the mill-people, and then hid behind Podgers because you didn't want to be thanked. When he died, and the teapot came, you saw how proud I was of it, — how I took comfort in thinking he did the kind things;

and for my sake you never told the truth, not even last night, when a word would have done so much. Oh, 'Rusalem, how could you deceive me all these years?"

If Mr. 'Rusalem had desired to answer he would have had no chance; for Mrs. Podgers was too much in earnest to let any one speak but herself, and hurried on, fearing that her emotion would get the better of her before she had had her say.

"It was like you, but it wasn't right, for you've robbed yourself of the love and honor that was your due; you've let people praise Podgers when he didn't deserve it; you've seen me take pride in this because I thought he'd earned it; and you've only laughed at it all as if it was a fine joke to do generous things and never take the credit of 'em. Now I know what bank you've laid up your hard earnings in, and what a blessed interest you'll get by and by. Truly they who give to the poor lend to the Lord, — and you don't need to have the good words written on silver, for you keep 'em always in your heart."

Mrs. Podgers stopped a minute for breath, and felt that she was going very fast; for 'Rusalem sat looking at her with so much humility, love, and longing in his honest face, that she knew it would be all up with her directly.

"You saw how I grieved for Neddy, and gave me this motherless boy to fill his place; you knew I wanted some one to make the house seem like home again, and you offered me the lovingest heart that ever was. You found I wasn't satisfied to lead such a selfish life, and you showed me how beautiful Charity could make it; you taught me to find my duty waiting for me at my own door; and, putting by your own trouble, you've helped to make this day the happiest Christmas of my life."

If it hadn't been for the teapot Mrs. Podgers would have given out here; but her hand was still on it, and something in the touch gave her steadiness for one more burst.

"I loved the little teapot for Podgers' sake; now I love it a hundred times more for yours, because you've brought its lesson home to me in a way I never can forget, and have been my benefactor as well as theirs, who shall soon know you as well as I do. 'Rusalem, there's only one way in which I can thank you for all this, and I do it with my whole heart. Last night you asked me for something, and I thought I couldn't give it to you. Now I'm sure I can, and if you still want it why ——"

Mrs. Podgers never finished that sentence; for, with an impetuosity surprising in one of his age and figure, Mr. 'Rusalem sprang out of his chair and took her in his arms, saying tenderly, in a voice almost inaudible, between a conflicting choke and chuckle, —

"**My dear! my dear! God bless you!**"

MY CONTRABAND.

DOCTOR FRANCK came in as I sat sewing up the rents in an old shirt, that Tom might go tidily to his grave. New shirts were needed for the living, and there was no wife or mother to "dress him handsome when he went to meet the Lord," as one woman said, describing the fine funeral she had pinched herself to give her son.

"Miss Dane, I'm in a quandary," began the Doctor, with that expression of countenance which says as plainly as words, "I want to ask a favor, but I wish you'd save me the trouble."

"Can I help you out of it?"

"Faith! I don't like to propose it, but you certainly can, if you please."

"Then name it, I beg."

"You see a Reb has just been brought in crazy with typhoid; a bad case every way; a drunken, rascally little captain somebody took the trouble to capture, but whom nobody wants to take the trouble to cure. The wards are full, the ladies worked to death, and willing to be for our own boys, but rather slow to risk their lives for a Reb. Now, you've had the fever, you like queer patients, your mate will see to your ward for a while, and

I will find you a good attendant. The fellow won't last long, I fancy; but he can't die without some sort of care, you know. I've put him in the fourth story of the west wing, away from the rest. It is airy, quiet, and comfortable there. I'm on that ward, and will do my best for you in every way. Now, then, will you go?"

"Of course I will, out of perversity, if not common charity; for some of these people think that because I'm an abolitionist I am also a heathen, and I should rather like to show them that, though I cannot quite love my enemies, I am willing to take care of them."

"Very good; I thought you'd go; and speaking of abolition reminds me that you can have a contraband for servant, if you like. It is that fine mulatto fellow who was found burying his rebel master after the fight, and, being badly cut over the head, our boys brought him along. Will you have him?"

"By all means, — for I'll stand to my guns on that point, as on the other; these black boys are far more faithful and handy than some of the white scamps given me to serve, instead of being served by. But is this man well enough?"

"Yes, for that sort of work, and I think you'll like him. He must have been a handsome fellow before he got his face slashed; not much darker than myself; his master's son, I dare say, and the white blood makes him rather high and haughty about some things. He was in a bad way when he came in, but vowed he'd die in the street rather than turn in with the black fellows below; so I put him up in the west wing, to be out of the way, and he's seen to the captain all the morning. When can you go up?"

"As soon as Tom is laid out, Skinner moved, Haywood washed, Marble dressed, Charley rubbed, Downs taken up, Upham laid down, and the whole forty fed."

We both laughed, though the Doctor was on his way to the dead-house and I held a shroud on my lap. But in a hospital one learns that cheerfulness is one's salvation; for, in an atmosphere of suffering and death, heaviness of heart would soon paralyze usefulness of hand, if the blessed gift of smiles had been denied us.

In an hour I took possession of my new charge, finding a dissipated-looking boy of nineteen or twenty raving in the solitary little room, with no one near him but the contraband in the room adjoining. Feeling decidedly more interest in the black man than in the white, yet remembering the Doctor's hint of his being "high and mighty," I glanced furtively at him as I scattered chloride of lime about the room to purify the air, and settled matters to suit myself. I had seen many contrabands, but never one so attractive as this. All colored men are called "boys," even if their heads are white; this boy was five-and-twenty at least, strong-limbed and manly, and had the look of one who never had been cowed by abuse or worn with oppressive labor. He sat on his bed doing nothing; no book, no pipe, no pen or paper anywhere appeared, yet anything less indolent or restless than his attitude and expression I never saw. Erect he sat, with a hand on either knee, and eyes fixed on the bare wall opposite, so rapt in some absorbing thought as to be unconscious of my presence, though the door stood wide open and my movements were by no means noiseless. His face was half averted, but I instantly approved the Doctor's taste, for the profile which I saw possessed all the attributes of comeliness belonging to his mixed race. He was more quadroon than mulatto, with Saxon features, Spanish complexion darkened by exposure, color in lips and cheek, waving hair, and an eye full of the passionate melancholy which in such men always seems to utter a mute protest against the broken law that doomed them at their birth. What could he be thinking of? The sick boy cursed and raved, I rustled to and fro, steps passed the door, bells rang, and the steady rumble of army-wagons came up from the street, still he never stirred. I had seen colored people in what they call "the black sulks," when, for days, they neither smiled nor spoke, and scarcely ate. But this was something more than that; for the man was not dully brooding over some small grievance; he seemed to see an all-absorbing fact or fancy recorded on the wall, which was a blank to me. I wondered if it were some deep wrong or sorrow, kept alive by memory and impotent regret; if he mourned for the dead master to whom he had been faithful to the end; or if the liberty now his were robbed of half its sweetness by the knowledge that some one near and dear to him still languished in the cell from which he had escaped. My heart quite warmed to him at that idea; I wanted to know and comfort him; and, following the impulse of the moment, I went in and touched him on the shoulder.

In an instant the man vanished and the slave appeared. Freedom was too new a boon to have wrought its blessed changes yet; and as he started up, with his hand at his temple, and an obsequious "Yes, Missis," any romance that had gathered round him fled away, leaving the saddest of all sad facts in living guise before me. Not only did the manhood seem to die out of him, but the comeliness that first attracted me; for, as he turned, I saw the ghastly wound that had laid open cheek and forehead. Being partly healed, it was no longer bandaged, but held together with strips of that transparent plaster which I never see without a shiver, and swift recollections of the scenes with which it is associated in my mind. Part of his black hair had been shorn away, and one eye was nearly closed; pain so distorted, and the cruel sabre-cut so marred that portion of his face, that, when I saw it, I felt as if a fine medal had been suddenly reversed, showing me a far more striking type of human suffering and wrong than Michael Angelo's bronze prisoner. By one of those inexplicable processes that often teach us how little we understand ourselves, my purpose was suddenly changed; and, though I went in to offer comfort as a friend, I merely gave an order as a mistress.

"Will you open these windows? this man needs more air."

He obeyed at once, and, as he slowly urged up the unruly sash, the handsome profile was again turned toward me, and again I was possessed by my first impression so strongly that I involuntarily said, —

"Thank you."

Perhaps it was fancy, but I thought that in the look of mingled surprise and something like reproach which he gave me, there was also a trace of grateful pleasure. But he said, in that tone of spiritless humility these poor souls learn so soon, —

"I isn't a white man, Missis, I'se a contraband."

"Yes, I know it; but a contraband is a free man, and I heartily congratulate you."

He liked that; his face shone, he squared his shoulders, lifted his head, and looked me full in the eye with a brisk, —

"Thank ye, Missis; anything more to do fer yer?"

"Doctor Franck thought you would help me with this man, as there are many patients and few nurses or attendants. Have you had the fever?"

"No, Missis."

"They should have thought of that when they put him here; wounds and fevers should not be together. I'll try to get you moved."

He laughed a sudden laugh: if he had been a white man, I should have called it scornful; as he was a few shades darker than myself, I suppose it must be considered an insolent, or at least an unmannerly one.

"It don't matter, Missis. I'd rather be up here with the fever than down with those niggers; and there isn't no other place fer me."

Poor fellow! that was true. No ward in all the hospital would take him in to lie side by side with the most miserable white wreck there. Like the bat in Æsop's fable, he belonged to neither race; and the pride of one and the helplessness of the other, kept him hovering alone in the twilight a great sin has brought to overshadow the whole land.

"You shall stay, then; for I would far rather have you than my lazy Jack. But are you well and strong enough?"

"I guess I'll do, Missis."

He spoke with a passive sort of acquiescence, — as if

did not much matter if he were not able, and no one would particularly rejoice if he were.

"Yes, I think you will. By what name shall I call you?"

"Bob, Missis."

Every woman has her pet whim; one of mine was to teach the men self-respect by treating them respectfully. Tom, Dick, and Harry would pass, when lads rejoiced in those familiar abbreviations; but to address men often old enough to be my father in that style did not suit my old-fashioned ideas of propriety. This "Bob" would never do; I should have found it as easy to call the chaplain "Gus" as my tragical-looking contraband by a title so strongly associated with the tail of a kite.

"What is your other name?" I asked. "I like to call my attendants by their last names rather than by their first."

"I'se got no other, Missis; we has our master's names, or do without. Mine's dead, and I won't have anything of his 'bout me."

"Well, I'll call you Robert, then, and you may fill this pitcher for me, if you will be so kind."

He went; but, through all the tame obedience years of servitude had taught him, I could see that the proud spirit his father gave him was not yet subdued, for the look and gesture with which he repudiated his master's name were a more effective declaration of independence than any Fourth-of-July orator could have prepared.

We spent a curious week together. Robert seldom left his room, except upon my errands; and I was a prisoner all day, often all night, by the bedside of the rebel. The fever burned itself rapidly away, for there seemed little vitality to feed it in the feeble frame of this old young man, whose life had been none of the most righteous, judging from the revelations made by his unconscious lips; since more than once Robert authoritatively silenced him, when my gentler hushings were of no avail, and blasphemous wanderings or ribald camp-songs made my cheeks burn and Robert's face assume an aspect of disgust. The captain was a gentleman in the world's eye, but the contraband was the gentleman in mine;—I was a fanatic, and that accounts for such depravity of taste, I hope. I never asked Robert of himself, feeling that somewhere there was a spot still too sore to bear the lightest touch; but, from his language, manner, and intelligence, I inferred that his color had procured for him the few advantages within the reach of a quick-witted, kindly-treated slave. Silent, grave, and thoughtful, but most serviceable, was my contraband; glad of the books I brought him, faithful in the performance of the duties I assigned to him, grateful for the friendliness I could not but feel and show toward him. Often I longed to ask what purpose was so visibly altering his aspect with such daily deepening gloom. But I never dared, and no one else had either time or desire to pry into the past of this specimen of one branch of the chivalrous " F. F. Vs."

On the seventh night, Dr. Franck suggested that it would be well for some one, besides the general watchman of the ward, to be with the captain, as it might be his last. Although the greater part of the two preceding nights had been spent there, of course I offered to remain,—for there is a strange fascination in these scenes, which renders one careless of fatigue and unconscious of fear until the crisis is past.

"Give him water as long as he can drink, and if he drops into a natural sleep, it may save him. I'll look in at midnight, when some change will probably take place. Nothing but sleep or a miracle will keep him now. Good-night."

Away went the Doctor; and, devouring a whole mouthful of gapes, I lowered the lamp, wet the captain's head, and sat down on a hard stool to begin my watch. The captain lay with his hot, haggard face turned toward me, filling the air with his poisonous breath, and feebly muttering, with lips and tongue so parched that the sanest speech would have been difficult to understand. Robert was stretched on his bed in the inner room, the door of which stood ajar, that a fresh draught from his open window might carry the fever-fumes away through mine. I could just see a long, dark figure, with the lighter outline of a face, and, having little else to do just then, I fell to thinking of this curious contraband, who evidently prized his freedom highly, yet seemed in no haste to enjoy it. Dr. Franck had offered to send him on to safer quarters, but he had said, "No, thank yer, sir, not yet," and then had gone away to fall into one of those black moods of his, which began to disturb me, because I had no power to lighten them. As I sat listening to the clocks from the steeples all about us, I amused myself with planning Robert's future, as I often did my own, and had dealt out to him a generous hand of trumps wherewith to play this game of life which hitherto had gone so cruelly against him, when a harsh choked voice called,—

"Lucy!"

It was the captain, and some new terror seemed to have gifted him with momentary strength.

"Yes, here's Lucy," I answered, hoping that by following the fancy I might quiet him, — for his face was damp with the clammy moisture, and his frame shaken with the nervous tremor that so often precedes death. His dull eye fixed upon me, dilating with a bewildered look of incredulity and wrath, till he broke out fiercely, —

"That's a lie! she's dead, — and so's Bob, damn him!"

Finding speech a failure, I began to sing the quiet tune that had often soothed delirium like this; but hardly had the line, —

"See gentle patience smile on pain,"

passed my lips, when he clutched me by the wrist, whispering like one in mortal fear, —

"Hush! she used to sing that way to Bob, but she never would to me. I swore I'd whip the devil out of her, and I did; but you know before she cut her throat she said she'd haunt me, and there she is!"

He pointed behind me with an aspect of such pale dismay, that I involuntarily glanced over my shoulder and started as if I had seen a veritable ghost; for, peering from the gloom of that inner room, I saw a shadowy face, with dark hair all about it, and a glimpse of scarlet at the throat. An instant showed me that it was only Robert leaning from his bed's foot, wrapped in a gray army-blanket, with his red shirt just visible above it, and his long hair disordered by sleep. But what a strange expression was on his face! The unmarred side was toward me, fixed and motionless as when I first observed it, — less absorbed now, but more intent. His eye glittered, his lips were apart like one who listened with every sense, and his whole aspect reminded me of a hound to which some wind had brought the scent of unsuspected prey.

"Do you know him, Robert? Does he mean you?"

"Laws, no, Missis; they all own half-a-dozen Bobs: but hearin' my name woke me; that's all."

He spoke quite naturally, and lay down again, while I returned to my charge, thinking that this paroxysm was probably his last. But by another hour I perceived a hopeful change; for the tremor had subsided, the cold dew was gone, his breathing was more regular, and Sleep, the healer, had descended to save or take him gently away. Doctor Franck looked in at midnight, bade me keep all cool and quiet, and not fail to administer a certain draught as soon as the captain woke. Very much relieved, I laid my head on my arms, uncomfortably folded on the little table, and fancied I was about to perform one of the feats which practice renders possible, — "sleeping with one eye open," as we say: a half-and-half doze, for all senses sleep but that of hearing; the faintest murmur, sigh, or motion will break it, and give one back one's wits much brightened by the brief permission to "stand at ease." On this night the experiment was a failure, for previous vigils, confinement, and much care had rendered naps a dangerous indulgence. Having roused half-a-dozen times in an hour to find all quiet, I dropped my heavy head on my arms, and, drowsily resolving to look up again in fifteen minutes, fell fast asleep.

The striking of a deep-voiced clock awoke me with a start. "That is one," thought I; but, to my dismay, two more strokes followed, and in remorseful haste I sprang up to see what harm my long oblivion had done. A strong hand put me back into my seat, and held me there. It was Robert. The instant my eye met his my heart began to beat, and all along my nerves tingled that electric flash which foretells a danger that we cannot see. He was very pale, his mouth grim, and both eyes full of sombre fire; for even the wounded one was open now, all the more sinister for the deep scar above and below. But his touch was steady, his voice quiet, as he said, —

"Sit still, Missis; I won't hurt yer, nor scare yer, ef I can help it, but yer waked too soon."

"Let me go, Robert, — the captain is stirring, — I must give him something."

"No, Missis, yer can't stir an inch. Look here!"

Holding me with one hand, with the other he took up the glass in which I had left the draught, and showed me it was empty.

"Has he taken it?" I asked, more and more bewildered.

"I flung it out o' winder, Missis; he'll have to do without."

"But why, Robert? why did you do it?"

"'Kase I hate him!"

Impossible to doubt the truth of that; his whole face showed it, as he spoke through his set teeth, and launched a fiery glance at the unconscious captain. I could only hold my breath and stare blankly at him, wondering what mad act was coming next. I suppose I shook and turned white, as women have a foolish habit of doing when sudden danger daunts them; for Robert released my arm, sat down upon the bedside just in front of me, and said, with the ominous quietude that made me cold to see and hear, —

"Don't yer be frightened, Missis; don't try to run away, fer the door's locked and the key in my pocket; don't yer cry out, fer yer'd have to scream a long while, with my hand on yer mouth, 'efore yer was heard. Be still, an' I'll tell yer what I'm gwine to do."

"Lord help us! he has taken the fever in some sudden, violent way, and is out of his head. I must humor him till some one comes"; in pursuance of which swift determination, I tried to say, quite composedly, —

"I will be still and hear you; but open the window. Why did you shut it?"

"I'm sorry I can't do it, Missis; but yer'd jump out, or call, if I did, an' I'm not ready yet. I shut it to make yer sleep, an' heat would do it quicker'n anything else I could do."

The captain moved, and feebly muttered "Water!" Instinctively I rose to give it to him, but the heavy hand came down upon my shoulder, and in the same decided tone Robert said, —

"The water went with the physic; let him call."

"Do let me go to him! he'll die without care!"

"I mean he shall; — don't yer meddle, if yer please, Missis."

In spite of his quiet tone and respectful manner, I saw murder in his eyes, and turned faint with fear; yet the fear excited me, and, hardly knowing what I did, I seized the hands that had seized me, crying, —

"No, no; you shall not kill him! It is base to hurt a helpless man. Why do you hate him? He is not your master."

"He's my brother."

I felt that answer from head to foot, and seemed to fathom what was coming, with a prescience vague, but unmistakable. One appeal was left to me, and I made it.

"Robert, tell me what it means? Do not commit a crime and make me accessory to it. There is a better way of righting wrong than by violence; — let me help you find it."

My voice trembled as I spoke, and I heard the frightened flutter of my heart; so did he, and if any little act of mine had ever won affection or respect from him, the memory of it served me then. He looked down, and seemed to put some question to himself; whatever it was, the answer was in my favor, for when his eyes rose again, they were gloomy, but not desperate.

"I *will* tell yer, Missis; but mind, this makes no difference; the boy is mine. I'll give the Lord a chance to take him fust: if He don't, I shall."

"Oh, no! remember he is your brother."

An unwise speech; I felt it as it passed my lips, for a black frown gathered on Robert's face, and his strong hands closed with an ugly sort of grip. But he did not touch the poor soul gasping there behind him, and seemed content to let the slow suffocation of that stifling room end his frail life.

"I'm not like to forgit dat, Missis, when I've been thinkin' of it all this week. I knew him when they fetched him in, an' would 'a' done it long 'fore this, but I wanted to ask where Lucy was; he knows, — he told to-night, — an' now he's done for."

"Who is Lucy?" I asked hurriedly, intent on keeping his mind busy with any thought but murder.

With one of the swift transitions of a mixed temperament like this, at my question Robert's deep eyes filled, the clenched hands were spread before his face, and all I heard were the broken words, —

"My wife, — he took her ——"

In that instant every thought of fear was swallowed up in burning indignation for the wrong, and a perfect passion of pity for the desperate man so tempted to avenge an injury for which there seemed no redress but this. He was no longer slave or contraband, no drop of black blood marred him in my sight, but an infinite compassion yearned to save, to help, to comfort him. Words seemed so powerless I offered none, only put my hand on his poor head, wounded, homeless, bowed down with grief for which I had no cure, and softly smoothed the long, neglected hair, pitifully wondering the while where was the wife who must have loved this tender-hearted man so well.

The captain moaned again, and faintly whispered, "Air!" but I never stirred. God forgive me! just then I hated him as only a woman thinking of a sister woman's wrong could hate. Robert looked up; his eyes were dry again, his mouth grim. I saw that, said, "Tell me more," and he did; for sympathy is a gift the poorest may give, the proudest stoop to receive.

"Yer see, Missis, his father, — I might say ours, ef I warn't ashamed of both of 'em, — his father died two years ago, an' left us all to Marster Ned, — that's him here, eighteen then. He always hated me, I looked so like old Marster: he don't, — only the light skin an' hair. Old Marster was kind to all of us, me 'specially, an' bought Lucy off the next plantation down there in South Car'lina, when he found I liked her. I married her, all I could; it warn't much, but we was true to one another till Marster Ned come home a year after an' made hell, fer both of us. He sent my old mother to be used up in his rice-swamp in Georgy; he found me with my pretty Lucy, an' though young Miss cried, an' I prayed to him on my knees, an' Lucy run away, he wouldn't have no mercy; he brought her back, an' — took her."

"Oh, what did you do?" I cried, hot with helpless pain and passion.

How the man's outraged heart sent the blood flaming up into his face and deepened the tones of his impetuous voice, as he stretched his arm across the bed, saying, with a terribly expressive gesture, —

"I half murdered him, an' to-night I'll finish."

"Yes, yes, — but go on now; what came next?"

He gave me a look that showed no white man could have felt a deeper degradation in remembering and confessing these last acts of brotherly oppression.

"They whipped me till I couldn't stand, an' then they sold me further South. Yer thought I was a white man once, — look here!"

With a sudden wrench he tore the shirt from neck to waist, and on his strong, brown shoulders showed me furrows deeply ploughed, wounds which, though healed, were ghastlier to me than any in that house. I could not speak to him, and, with the pathetic dignity a great grief lends the humblest sufferer, he ended his brief tragedy by simply saying, —

"That's all, Missis. I'se never seen her since, an' now I never shall in this world, — maybe not in t'other."

"But, Robert, why think her dead? The captain was wandering when he said those sad things; perhaps he will retract them when he is sane. Don't despair; don't give up yet."

"No, Missis, I 'spect he's right; she was too proud to bear that long. It's like her to kill herself. I told her to, if there was no other way; an' she always minded me, Lucy did. My poor girl! Oh, it warn't right! No, by God, it warn't!"

As the memory of this bitter wrong, this double bereavement, burned in his sore heart, the devil that lurks in every strong man's blood leaped up; he put his hand upon his brother's throat, and, watching the white face before him, muttered low between his teeth, —

"I'm lettin' him go too easy; there's no pain in this; we a'n't even yet. I wish he knew me. Marster Ned! it's Bob; where's Lucy?"

From the captain's lips there came a long faint sigh, and nothing but a flutter of the eyelids showed that he still lived. A strange stillness filled the room as the elder brother held the younger's life suspended in his hand, while wavering between a dim hope and a deadly hate. In the whirl of thoughts that went on in my brain, only one was clear enough to act upon. I must prevent murder, if I could, — but how? What could I do up there alone, locked in with a dying man and a lunatic? — for any mind yielded utterly to any unrighteous impulse is mad while the impulse rules it. Strength I had not, nor much courage, neither time nor wit for stratagem, and chance only could bring me help before it was too late. But one weapon I possessed, — a tongue, — often a woman's best defence; and sympathy, stronger than fear, gave me power to use it. What I said Heaven only knows, but surely Heaven helped me; words burned on my lips, tears streamed from my eyes, and some good angel prompted me to use the one name that had power to arrest my hearer's hand and touch his heart. For at that moment I heartily believed that Lucy lived, and this earnest faith roused in him a like belief.

He listened with the lowering look of one in whom brute instinct was sovereign for the time, — a look that makes the noblest countenance base. He was but a man, — a poor, untaught, outcast, outraged man. Life had few joys for him; the world offered him no honors, no success, no home, no love. What future would this crime mar? and why should he deny himself that sweet, yet bitter morsel called revenge? How many white men, with all New England's freedom, culture, Christianity, would not have felt as he felt then? Should I have reproached him for a human anguish, a human longing for redress, all now left him from the ruin of his few poor hopes? Who had taught him that self-control, self-sacrifice, are attributes that make men masters of the earth, and lift them nearer heaven? Should I have urged the beauty of forgiveness, the duty of devout submission? He had no religion, for he was no saintly "Uncle Tom," and Slavery's black shadow seemed to darken all the world to him, and shut out God. Should I have warned him of penalties, of judgments, and the potency of law? What did he know of justice, or the mercy that should temper that stern virtue, when every law, human and divine, had been broken on his hearthstone? Should I have tried to touch him by appeals to filial duty, to brotherly love? How had his appeals been answered? What memories had father and brother stored up in his heart to plead for either now? No,— all these influences, these associations, would have proved worse than useless, had I been calm enough to try them. I was not; but instinct, subtler than reason, showed me the one safe clue by which to lead this troubled soul from the labyrinth in which it groped and nearly fell. When I paused, breathless, Robert turned to me, asking, as if human assurances could strengthen his faith in Divine Omnipotence, —

"Do you believe, if I let Marster Ned live, the Lord will give me back my Lucy?"

"As surely as there is a Lord, you will find her here or in the beautiful hereafter, where there is no black or white, no master and no slave."

He took his hand from his brother's throat, lifted his eyes from my face to the wintry sky beyond, as if searching for that blessed country, happier even than the happy North. Alas, it was the darkest hour before the dawn! — there was no star above, no light below but the pale glimmer of the lamp that showed the brother who had made him desolate. Like a blind man who believes there is a sun, yet cannot see it, he shook his head, let his arms drop nervelessly upon his knees, and sat there dumbly asking that question which many a soul whose faith is firmer fixed than his has asked in hours less dark than this, — "Where is God?" I saw the tide had turned, and strenuously tried to keep this rudderless life-boat from slipping back into the whirlpool wherein it had been so nearly lost.

"I have listened to you, Robert; now hear me, and heed what I say, because my heart is full of pity for you, full of hope for your future, and a desire to help you now. I want you to go away from here, from the temptation of this place, and the sad thoughts that haunt it. You have conquered yourself once, and I honor you for it, because, the harder the battle, the more glorious the victory; but it is safer to put a greater distance between you and this man. I will write you letters, give you money, and send you to good old Massachusetts to begin your new life a freeman, — yes, and a happy man; for when the captain is himself again, I will learn where Lucy is, and move heaven and earth to find and give her back to you. Will you do this, Robert?"

Slowly, very slowly, the answer came; for the purpose of a week, perhaps a year, was hard to relinquish in an hour.

"Yes, Missis, I will."

"Good! Now you are the man I thought you, and I'll work for you with all my heart. You need sleep, my poor fellow; go, and try to forget. The captain is alive, and as yet you are spared that sin. No, don't look there; I'll care for him. Come, Robert, for Lucy's sake."

Thank Heaven for the immortality of love! for when all other means of salvation failed, a spark of this vital fire softened the man's iron will, until a woman's hand could bend it. He let me take from him the key, let me draw him gently away, and lead him to the solitude which now was the most healing balm I could bestow.

Once in his little room, he fell down on his bed and lay there, as if spent with the sharpest conflict of his life. I slipped the bolt across his door, and unlocked my own, flung up the window, steadied myself with a breath of air, then rushed to Doctor Franck. He came; and till dawn we worked together, saving one brother's life, and taking earnest thought how best to secure the other's liberty. When the sun came up as blithely as if it shone only upon happy homes, the Doctor went to Robert. For an hour I heard the murmur of their voices; once I caught the sound of heavy sobs, and for a time a reverent hush, as if in the silence that good man were ministering to soul as well as body. When he departed he took Robert with him, pausing to tell me he should get him off as soon as possible, but not before we met again.

Nothing more was seen of them all day; another surgeon came to see the captain, and another attendant came to fill the empty place. I tried to rest, but could not, with the thought of poor Lucy tugging at my heart, and was soon back at my post again, anxiously hoping that my contraband had not been too hastily spirited away. Just as night fell there came a tap, and, opening, I saw Robert literally " clothed, and in his right mind." The Doctor had replaced the ragged suit with tidy garments, and no trace of that tempestuous night remained but deeper lines upon the forehead, and the docile look of a repentant child. He did not cross the threshold, did not offer me his hand, — only took off his cap, saying, with a traitorous falter in his voice, —

" God bless yer, Missis! I'm gwine."

I put out both my hands, and held his fast.

"Good-by, Robert! Keep up good heart, and when I come home to Massachusetts we'll meet in a happier place than this. Are you quite ready, quite comfortable for your journey?"

"Yes, Missis, yes; the Doctor's fixed everything; I'se gwine with a friend of his; my papers are all right, an' I'm as happy as I can be till I find"——

He stopped there; then went on, with a glance into the room,—

"I'm glad I didn't do it, an' I thank yer, Missis, fer hinderin' me,—thank yer hearty; but I'm afraid I hate him jest the same."

Of course he did; and so did I; for these faulty hearts of ours cannot turn perfect in a night, but need frost and fire, wind and rain, to ripen and make them ready for the great harvest-home. Wishing to divert his mind, I put my poor mite into his hand, and, remembering the magic of a certain little book, I gave him mine, on whose dark cover whitely shone the Virgin Mother and the Child, the grand history of whose life the book contained. The money went into Robert's pocket with a grateful murmur, the book into his bosom, with a long look and a tremulous —

"I never saw *my* baby, Missis."

I broke down then; and though my eyes were too dim to see, I felt the touch of lips upon my hands, heard the sound of departing feet, and knew my contraband was gone.

When one feels an intense dislike, the less one says about the subject of it the better; therefore I shall merely record that the captain lived,—in time was exchanged; and that, whoever the other party was, I am convinced the Government got the best of the bargain. But long before this occurred, I had fulfilled my promise to Robert; for as soon as my patient recovered strength of memory enough to make his answer trustworthy, I asked, without any circumlocution, —

"Captain Fairfax, where is Lucy?"

And too feeble to be angry, surprised, or insincere, he straightway answered, —

"Dead, Miss Dane."

"And she killed herself when you sold Bob?"

"How the devil did you know that?" he muttered, with an expression half-remorseful, half-amazed; but I was satisfied, and said no more.

Of course this went to Robert, waiting far away there in a lonely home, — waiting, working, hoping for his Lucy. It almost broke my heart to do it; but delay was weak, deceit was wicked; so I sent the heavy tidings, and very soon the answer came, — only three lines; but I felt that the sustaining power of the man's life was gone.

"I tort I'd never see her any more; I'm glad to know she's out of trouble. I thank yer, Missis; an' if they let us, I'll fight fer yer till I'm killed, which I hope will be fore long."

Six months later he had his wish, and kept his word.

Every one knows the story of the attack on Fort Wagner; but we should not tire yet of recalling how our Fifty-Fourth, spent with three sleepless nights, a day's fast, and a march under the July sun, stormed the fort as night fell, facing death in many shapes, following their brave leaders through a fiery rain of shot and shell, fighting valiantly for "God and Governor Andrew," —

how the regiment that went into action seven hundred strong, came out having had nearly half its number captured, killed, or wounded, leaving their young commander to be buried, like a chief of earlier times, with his body-guard around him, faithful to the death. Surely, the insult turns to honor, and the wide grave needs no monument but the heroism that consecrates it in our sight; surely, the hearts that held him nearest, see through their tears a noble victory in the seeming sad defeat; and surely, God's benediction was bestowed, when this loyal soul answered, as Death called the roll, "Lord, here am I, with the brothers Thou hast given me!"

The future must show how well that fight was fought; for though Fort Wagner once defied us, public prejudice is down; and through the cannon-smoke of that black night, the manhood of the colored race shines before many eyes that would not see, rings in many ears that would not hear, wins many hearts that would not hitherto believe.

When the news came that we were needed, there was none so glad as I to leave teaching contrabands, the new work I had taken up, and go to nurse "our boys," as my dusky flock so proudly called the wounded of the Fifty-Fourth. Feeling more satisfaction, as I assumed my big apron and turned up my cuffs, than if dressing for the President's levee, I fell to work in Hospital No. 10 at Beaufort. The scene was most familiar, and yet strange; for only dark faces looked up at me from the pallets so thickly laid along the floor, and I missed the sharp accent of my Yankee boys in the slower, softer voices calling cheerily to one another, or answering my questions with a stout, "We'll never give it up, Missis, till the last Reb's dead," or, "If our people's free, we can afford to die."

Passing from bed to bed, intent on making one pair of hands do the work of three, at least, I gradually washed, fed, and bandaged my way down the long line of sallow heroes, and coming to the very last, found that he was my contraband. So old, so worn, so deathly weak and wan, I never should have known him but for the deep scar on his cheek. That side lay uppermost, and caught my eye at once; but even then I doubted, such an awful change had come upon him, when, turning to the ticket just above his head, I saw the name, "Robert Dane." That both assured and touched me, for, remembering that he had no name, I knew that he had taken mine. I longed for him to speak to me, to tell how he had fared since I lost sight of him, and let me perform some little service for him in return for many he had done for me; but he seemed asleep; and as I stood re-living that strange night again, a bright lad, who lay next him softly waving an old fan across both beds, looked up and said,—

"I guess you know him, Missis?"

"You are right. Do you?"

"As much as any one was able to, Missis."

"Why do you say 'was,' as if the man were dead and gone?"

"I s'pose because I know he'll have to go. He's got a bad jab in the breast, an' is bleedin' inside, the Doctor says. He don't suffer any, only gets weaker 'n' weaker every minute. I've been fannin' him this long while, an' he's talked a little; but he don't know me now, so he's most gone, I guess."

There was so much sorrow and affection in the boy's face, that I remembered something, and asked, with redoubled interest, —

"Are you the one that brought him off? I was told about a boy who nearly lost his life in saving that of his mate."

I dare say the young fellow blushed, as any modest lad might have done; I could not see it, but I heard the chuckle of satisfaction that escaped him, as he glanced from his shattered arm and bandaged side to the pale figure opposite.

"Lord, Missis, that's nothin'; we boys always stan' by one another, an' I warn't goin' to leave him to be tormented any more by them cussed Rebs. He's been a slave once, though he don't look half so much like it as me, an' I was born in Boston."

He did not; for the speaker was as black as the ace of spades, — being a sturdy specimen, the knave of clubs would perhaps be a fitter representative, — but the dark freeman looked at the white slave with the pitiful, yet puzzled expression I have so often seen on the faces of our wisest men, when this tangled question of Slavery presented itself, asking to be cut or patiently undone.

"Tell me what you know of this man; for, even if he were awake, he is too weak to talk."

"I never saw him till I joined the regiment, an' no one 'peared to have got much out of him. He was a shut-up sort of feller, an' didn't seem to care for anything but gettin' at the Rebs. Some say he was the fust man of us that enlisted; I know he fretted till we were off, an' when we pitched into old Wagner, he fought like the devil."

"Were you with him when he was wounded? How was it?"

"Yes, Missis. There was somethin' queer about it; for he 'peared to know the chap that killed him, an' the chap knew him. I don't dare to ask, but I rather guess one owned the other some time; for, when they clinched, the chap sung out, 'Bob!' an' Dane, 'Marster Ned!'— then they went at it."

I sat down suddenly, for the old anger and compassion struggled in my heart, and I both longed and feared to hear what was to follow.

"You see, when the Colonel,— Lord keep an' send him back to us!— it a'n't certain yet, you know, Missis, though it's two days ago we lost him,— well, when the Colonel shouted, 'Rush on, boys, rush on!' Dane tore away as if he was goin' to take the fort alone; I was next him, an' kept close as we went through the ditch an' up the wall. Hi! warn't that a rusher!" and the boy flung up his well arm with a whoop, as if the mere memory of that stirring moment came over him in a gust of irrepressible excitement.

"Were you afraid?" I said, asking the question women often put, and receiving the answer they seldom fail to get.

"No, Missis!"— emphasis on the "Missis"— "I never thought of anything but the damn' Rebs, that scalp, lash, an' cut our ears off, when they git us. I was bound to let daylight into one of 'em at least, an' I did. Hope he liked it!"

"It is evident that you did. Now go on about Robert, for I should be at work."

"He was one of the fust up; I was just behind, an' though the whole thing happened in a minute, I remember how it was, for all I was yellin' an' knockin' round like mad. Just where we were, some sort of an officer was wavin' his sword an' cheerin' on his men; Dane saw him by a big flash that come by; he flung away his gun, give a leap, an' went at that feller as if he was Jeff, Beauregard, an' Lee, all in one. I scrabbled after as quick as I could, but was only up in time to see him git the sword straight through him an' drop into the ditch. You needn't ask what I did next, Missis, for I don't quite know myself; all I'm clear about is, that I managed somehow to pitch that Reb into the fort as dead as Moses, git hold of Dane, an' bring him off. Poor old feller! we said we went in to live or die; he said he went in to die, an' he's done it."

I had been intently watching the excited speaker; but as he regretfully added those last words I turned again, and Robert's eyes met mine, — those melancholy eyes, so full of an intelligence that proved he had heard, remembered, and reflected with that preternatural power which often outlives all other faculties. He knew me, yet gave no greeting; was glad to see a woman's face, yet had no smile wherewith to welcome it; felt that he was dying, yet uttered no farewell. He was too far across the river to return or linger now; departing thought, strength, breath, were spent in one grateful look, one murmur of submission to the last pang he could ever feel. His lips moved, and, bending to them, a whisper chilled my cheek, as it shaped the broken words,—

"I'd 'a' done it,—but it's better so,—I'm satisfied."

Ah! well he might be,—for, as he turned his face from the shadow of the life that was, the sunshine of the life to be touched it with a beautiful content, and in the drawing of a breath my contraband found wife and home, eternal liberty and God.

LOVE AND LOYALTY.

"DO you mean it, Rose?"
"Yes."
"You set a high price on your love; I cannot pay it."
"I think you will."

She came a little nearer, this beautiful woman, whom the young man loved with all the ardor of a first affection, she laid her hand upon his arm, and looked up in his face, her own wearing its most persuasive aspect; for tenderness seemed to have conquered pride, and will was concealed under a winning softness which made her doubly dangerous, as she said, in the slow, sweet voice that betrayed her Southern birth, —

"Remember what you ask, — what I offer; then tell me which demands the highest price for love. You would have me give up friends, fortune, home, all the opinions, prejudices, and beliefs of birth and education, all the hopes and purposes of years, for your sake. I ask nothing of you but the relinquishment of a mistaken duty; I offer you all I possess: a life of luxury and power, and, — myself."

She paused there, with a gesture of proud humility, as if she would ignore the fact, yet could not quite conceal the consciousness, that she had much to bestow upon the lover who had far less to offer.

"Oh, Rose, you tempt me terribly," he said; "not

with your possessions or a life of luxury, but with yourself, because I love you more than a thousand fortunes or a century of ease and power. Yet, dear as you are to me, and barren as the world will be without you, I dare not turn traitor even for your sake."

"Yet you would have me do it for yours."

"No: treachery to the wrong is allegiance to the right, and I only ask you to love your country better than yourself, as I try to do."

"Who shall say which is right and which wrong? I am tired of the words. I want to forget the ills I cannot cure, and enjoy life while I may. Youth was made for happiness; why waste it in a quarrel which time alone can end? Robert, I do not ask you to turn traitor. I do not care what you believe. I only ask you to stay with me, now that I have owned how much you are to me."

"God knows I wish I could, Rose; but idleness is treason in times like these. What right have I to think of my own happiness when my country needs me? It is like deserting my old mother in extremest peril to stand idle now; and when you tempt me to forget this, I must deny your prayer, because it is the only one I cannot grant."

"But, Robert, you are little to the rest of the world, and everything to me. Your country does not need you half so much as I,—'a stranger in a strange land'; for, in a great struggle like this, what can one man do?"

"His duty, Rose."

She pleaded eloquently with voice, and eyes, and hands; but something in the sad gravity of the young man's face was a keener reproach than his words. She felt that she could not win him so, and, with a swift and subtle change of countenance and manner, she put him from her, saying reproachfully, —

"Then do yours, and make some reparation for the peace of mind you have destroyed. I have a right to ask this. I came here as to a refuge, hoping to live unknown till the storm was over. Why did you find me out, protect me by your influence, lighten my exile by your society, and, under the guise of friendship, teach me to love you?"

Robert Stirling watched her with lover's eyes, listened with lover's ears, and answered like a lover, finding her the fairer and dearer for the growing fear that a hard test was in store for him.

"I found you out, because your beauty would not be concealed; I protected you, because you were a woman, and alone; I gave you friendship, because I wished to prove that we of the North hold sacred the faith our enemies place in us by sending to our keeping the treasure they most value; and, Rose, I loved you because I could not help it."

She smiled then, and the color deepened beautifully in the half-averted face, but she did not speak, and Robert took heart from the sign.

"I never meant to tell you this, fearing what has now happened, and I resolved to go away. But, coming here to say good-by, your grief melted my resolve, and I told you what I could no longer hide. Have I been ungenerous and unjust? If you believe so, tell me what reparation I can make, and, if it is anything an honest man may do, I will do it."

She knew that, was glad to know it; yet, with the exacting affection of a selfish woman, she felt a jealous fear that she loved more than she was beloved, and must assure herself by some trial that she was all in all to her young lover. He waited for her answer with such keen anxiety, such wistful tenderness, that she felt confident of success; and, yielding to the love of power so strong within her, she could not resist the desire of exercising it over this new subject, finding her excuse in the fond yet wayward wish to keep from danger that which was now so dear to her.

"I have lost enough by this costly war: I will lose no more," she said. "It is easier to part at once than later, when time has more endeared us to each other. Choose between the country which you love and the woman who loves you, and by that choice we will both abide."

"Rose, this is cruel, this is hard! Let me choose both, and be the better man for that double service."

"It is impossible. No one can serve two mistresses I will have all or nothing."

As she spoke she gently, but decidedly, freed herself from his detaining hold, and stood away from him, as if to prove both her strength and her sincerity. The act changed the words of separation trembling on Robert's lips to words of entreaty; for, though his upright nature owned the hard duty, his heart clung to its idol, feeling that it must be wrenched away.

"Wait a little, Rose. Give me time to think. Let me prove that I am no coward; then I will serve you, and you alone."

"No, Robert; if you truly loved me, you would be eager and glad to make any sacrifice for me. I would willingly make many for you; but this one I cannot, because it robs me of you in a double sense. If you fall, I lose you; if you come back alive, I lose you no less, for how can I accept a hand reddened with the blood of those I love?"

He had no answer, and stood silent. She saw that this moment of keen suffering and conflicting passions was the turning-point in the young man's life, yet, nothing doubting her power, she hardened herself to his pain that she might gain her point now and repay his submission by greater affection hereafter. Her voice broke the brief silence, steady, sweet, and sad:

"I see that you have chosen; I submit. But go at once, while I can part as I should; and remember, we must never meet again."

He had dropped his face into his hands, struggling dumbly with honest conscience and rebellious heart. Standing so, he felt a light touch on his bent head, heard the sound of a departing step, and looked up to see Rose passing from his sight, perhaps forever. An exclamation of love and longing broke from his lips; at the sound she paused, and, turning, let him see that her face was bathed in tears. At that sight duty seemed doubly stern and cruel, the sacrifice of integrity grew an easy thing, and separation an impossibility. The tender eyes were on him, the imploring hands outstretched to him, and the beloved voice cried, brokenly,—

"Oh, Robert, stay!"

"I will!"

He spoke out defiantly, as if to silence the inward monitor that would not yield consent; he offered his hand to seal the promise, and took one step toward the fair temptation,— no more; for, at the instant, up from below rose a voice, clear and mellow as a silver horn, singing, —

> "He has sounded forth the trumpet
> That shall never call retreat;
> He is sifting out the hearts of men
> Before his judgment-seat;
> Oh, be swift, my soul, to answer him;
> Be jubilant, my feet!
> For God is marching on."

The song broke the troubled silence with a martial ring that, to one listener, sounded like a bugle-call, banishing with its magic breath the weakness that had nearly made a recreant of him; for the opportune outbreak of the familiar voice, the memories it woke, the nobler spirit it recalled, all made that sweet and stirring strain the young man's salvation. Both stood motionless, and so still that every word came clearly through the sunny hush that filled the room. Rose's face grew anxious, a flash of anger dried the tears, and the expression which had been so tender changed to one of petulant annoyance. But Robert did not see it; he no longer watched her; he had turned towards the open window, and was looking far away into the distance, where seemed to lie the future this moment was to make or mar, while his whole aspect grew calm and steady, as if with the sense of self-control came the power of self-sacrifice.

As the song ended, he turned, gave one parting look at the woman whom he loved, said, "I have chosen! Rose, good-by," and was gone.

Out into the beautiful spring world he went, blind to its beauty, deaf to its music, unconscious of its peace.

Before him went the blithe singer, — a young man, with uncovered head, brown hair blowing in the wind, thoughtful eyes bent on the ground, and lips still softly singing, as he walked. This brother, always just and gentle, always ready with sympathy and counsel, now seemed doubly dear to the sore heart of Robert, as, hurrying to him, he grasped his arm as a drowning man might clutch at sudden help; for, though the victory seemed won, he dared not trust himself alone, with that great longing tugging at his heart.

"Why, Rob! what is it?" asked his brother, pausing to wonder at the change which had befallen him since they parted but a little while ago.

"Ask no questions, Richard; but sing on, sing on, and, if you love me, keep me fast till we get home," answered Robert, excitedly.

Something in his manner, and the glance he cast over his shoulder, seemed to enlighten his brother. Richard's face darkened ominously for a moment, then softened with sincerest pity as he drew the hand closer through his arm, and answered, with an almost womanly compassion, —

"Poor lad, I knew it would be so! but I had no fear that you would become a slave to that beautiful tyrant. The bitter draught is often more wholesome than the sweet, and you are wise to *let* her go before it is too late. Tell me your trouble, Rob, and let me help you bear it."

"Not now! not here! Sing, Rick, if you would not have me break away and go back to her again."

His brother obeyed him, not with the war-song, but with the simpler air their mother's voice had made a lullaby, beloved by them as babies, boys, and men.

Now, as of old, it soothed and comforted; and, though poor Robert turned his face away and let his brother lead him where he would, the first sharpness of his pain was eased by a recollection born of the song; for he remembered that though one woman had failed him, there still remained another whose faithful love would know no shadow of a change.

As they came into the familiar room, where every object spoke of the dear household league lasting unbroken for so many years, a softer mood replaced the pain and passion that had struggled in the lover's heart; and, throwing himself into the ancient chair where so many boyish griefs had been consoled, he laid his head upon his arms, and forgot his manhood for a little while. Richard stood beside him, with a kind hand on his shoulder, to assure him of a sympathy too deep and wise for words, till the fitting moment should appear. It soon came; and when the younger brother had made known his trouble, and the elder given what cheer he could, he tried to lead Robert's thoughts to other things, that he might forget disappointment in action.

"Nothing need detain you now, Rob," he said; "for the loss of one hope opens the way to the attainment of another. You shall enlist at once, and march away to fight the good fight."

"And you, Rick? We have both longed to go, but could not decide which it should be. Why should not you march away, and let me stay with mother till my turn comes?"

"Need I tell you why? We did delay at first, because we could not choose which should stay with the dear old lady who has only us left now. But lately you have lingered because of Rose, and I because I would not leave you till I knew how you fared. That is all over now; and surely it is best for you to put States between you, and let absence teach you to forget."

"You are right, and I am a weak fool to dream of staying. I ought to go; but the spirit that once would have made the duty easy has deserted me. Richard, I have lost faith in myself, and am afraid to go alone. Come with me, to comfort and keep me steady, as you have done all my life."

"I wish I could. Never doubt nor despond, no; but remember that *we* trust you, *we* expect great things of you, and are sure you never will disgrace the name father gave into our keeping."

"I'll do my best, Rick; but I shall need you more than ever: and if mother only knew how it is with me, I think she would say, 'Go.'"

"Mother does say it, heartily!"

Both started, and turned to see their mother watching them with an untroubled face. A right noble old woman, carrying her sixty years gracefully and well, — for her tall figure was unbent; below the gray hair shone eyes clear as any girl's, and her voice had a cheery ring to it that roused energy and hope in those who heard it; while the benignant power of her glance, the motherly compassion of her touch, brought confirmation to the wavering resolve and comfort to the wounded heart.

With the filial instinct which outlives childhood, Robert leaned against her as she drew his head to the bosom that could always give it rest, and told his sorrow in one broken exclamation, —

"Oh, mother, I loved her so!"

"I know it, dear: I saw it, and I warned you. But [yo]u thought me unjust. I desired to be proved so, and [it] has ended here. You have loved like a man, have [w]ithstood temptation like a man; now bear your loss like [a ma]n, and do not mar your sacrifice to principle by any [va]in regrets."

"Ah, mother, all the courage, energy, and strength [se]em to have gone out of me, and I am tired of my life."

"Not yet, Rob; wait a little, and you will find that [li]fe has gained a new significance. This trouble will [ch]ange the boy into a man, braver and better for the [p]ast, because, if I know my son, he will never let his life [be] thwarted by a selfish woman's folly or caprice."

She spoke proudly, and Robert lifted his head with an [ai]r as proud.

"You are right. I will not. But you must let me go! [I] cannot answer for myself if I stay here."

"You shall go, and Rick with you."

"But, mother, can we, — ought we, — to leave you [al]one?" began Richard, longing, yet loath, to go.

"No, my boys, you neither can nor will; for I go [w]ith you."

"With us?" cried both brothers, in a breath.

"Ay, lads, that I will!" she answered, heartily. [.] There is work for the old hands as well as for the [yo]ung; and while my boys fight for me, I will both nurse [an]d pray for them."

"But, mother, the distance and danger, the hardships [an]d horrors of such a life, will be too much for you. Let [on]e of us stay, and keep you safely here at home."

"Not while you are needed elsewhere. Other mothers [g]ive their boys; why should not I give mine? Other women endure the hardships and horrors of camps and hospitals; can I not do as much? You offer your young lives; surely I may offer the remains of mine. Say no more: I must enlist with my boys. I could never sit with folded hands at home, tormenting myself with fears for you, although God knows I send you willingly."

"You should have been a Roman matron, mother, with many sons to give for your country and few tears for yourself," said Richard, watching the fire of her glance, and listening to the steady voice that talked so cheerfully of danger and of death.

"Ah, Rob, the ancient legends preserved the brave words of the Roman matrons, but they left no record of the Roman mothers' tears, because they kept them for the bitter hours that came when the sacrifices had been made." And, as she spoke, two great drops rolled down to glitter upon Robert's hair.

For a moment no one stirred, as the three looked their new future in the face, and, seeing all its perils, owned its wisdom, accepted its duties, and stood ready to fulfil them to the last.

Mrs. Stirling spoke first:

"My sons, these are times to try the metal of all souls; and if we would have ours ring clear, we must follow with devout obedience the strong convictions that prompt and lead us to the right. Go, lads, and do your best, remembering that mother follows you, to rejoice if you win, to comfort you if you fail, to nurse you if you need it, and if you fall to lay you tenderly into your graves, with the proud thought, 'They did their duty: God will remember that, and comfort me.'"

The faces of the brothers kindled as she spoke; their

hearts answered her with a nobler fervor than the chivalrous enthusiasm of young blood, and both made a silent vow of loyalty, to last inviolate through all their lives, as, laying a hand on either head, that brave old mother dedicated sons and self to the service of the liberties she loved.

II.

The Army of the Potomac was on its march northward, to defeat Lee's daring raid and make a little Pennsylvania village forever memorable. The heights above the town were already darkened by opposing troops; the quiet valley was already tumultuous with the tramp of gathering thousands, and the fruitful fields already re-ploughed for the awful human harvest soon to be gathered in. Every road swarmed with blue coats, every hill-side was a camp, every grove a bivouac, every wayside stream a fountain of refreshment to hundreds of weary men spent with the privations and fatigues of those forced marches through midsummer heats.

By one of these little brooks a dusty regiment was halted for brief repose. At the welcome order, many of the exhausted men dropped down where they stood, to snatch an hour's sleep; some sought the grateful shade of an orchard already robbed of its early fruit, and ate their scanty fare with a cheerful content that made it sweet; others stretched themselves along the trampled borders of the brook, bathing their swollen feet, or drinking long draughts of the turbid water, which, to their parched lips, was a better cordial than the costliest wine. Apart from all these groups, two comrades lay side by side in the shadow of the orchard-wall. Both were young and comely men, stalwart, keen-eyed, and already bronzed by a Southern sun, although this was their first campaign. Both were silent, yet neither slept, and in their silence there was a marked difference, — one lay looking straight up through the waving boughs at the clear blue overhead, with an expression as serene; the other half leaned on his folded arm, moodily plucking at the turf which was his pillow, with now and then an impatient sigh, a restless gesture. One of these demonstrations of discontent presently roused his comrade from a waking dream. He sat up, laid a cool hand on the other's hot forehead, and said, with brotherly solicitude, —

"Not asleep yet, Rob? I hope you've not had a sunstroke, like poor Blake; for, if you are left behind, we shall both lose our share of the fight."

"As well die that way as with a rebel bullet through your head; though, if I had my choice, I'd try the last, as being the quickest," replied the other, gloomily.

"That doesn't sound like you, Rob, — you'll think better of it to-morrow, when you've had a night's sound sleep. This has been a hard march for a young soldier's first."

"How much older are you than I, either as man or soldier, Rick?" asked Robert, half petulantly, half proudly.

"Three hours older as a man, ten minutes as a soldier, you know I enlisted first. Yet I'm much the elder in many things, as you often tell me," said Richard, with the smile that always soothed his brother's more fiery spirit. "One of the privileges of my seniority is the care of you; so tell me what harasses you and scares rest away?"

"The old pain, Rick. All these weeks of absence have not lessened it; and the thought of going into a battle out of which I may never come alive, without seeing her once more, makes me almost resolve to desert, and satisfy myself at any cost. You cannot understand this, for you don't know what it is to love — to have a woman's face haunting you day and night, to hear a woman's voice always sounding in your ears with a distinctness that will not let you rest."

"I know it all, Rob!"

The words seemed to slip involuntarily from the young man's lips, for he checked himself sharply, and cast an anxious look at his brother. But Robert was too absorbed in his own emotions to read those of another, and only answered, in a cheerier tone, —

"You mean mother. God bless her, wherever she is, and send us safely home to her!"

An almost pathetic patience replaced the momentary agitation Richard's face betrayed, and his eyes turned wistfully towards the green hills that lay between the mother and her boys, as he answered, with a smile of sorrowful significance, —

"Every man is better and braver for a woman's love; so, as I have no younger sweetheart, I shall take the dear old lady for my mistress, and try to serve her like a loyal knight."

"Rick!" exclaimed his brother, earnestly, "if the coming battle proves my last as well as my first, promise that for my sake you'll befriend poor Rose, — that you will forgive her, love her, care for her, as if in truth she were my widow."

Richard grasped the hand outstretched to him, and

answered, with a fervor that fully satisfied his brother, "I promise, Rob!" then added quickly, "But there will be no need of that; for, if mortal man can do it, I will keep you, to care for Rose yourself."

Through the momentary pause that followed came the pleasant sound of falling water.

"Hark, Rob! do you hear it? Give me your canteen, and I'll bring you a cool draught that shall remind you of the old well at home."

Rising as he spoke, Richard went to the low wall that rose behind them, swung himself over, and, plunging down a ferny slope, found a hidden spring dripping musically from mossy crevices among the rocks into a little pool below. Pausing a moment to let the shadowy solitude of the green nook bathe his weary spirit in its peace, he turned to catch the coolest drops that fell; but, as he bent, the canteen slipped from his hand and splashed unheeded into the pool, for, just opposite, through thickly-growing brakes, he caught the glitter of a pair of human eyes fixed full upon his face. An instant he stood motionless, conscious of that subtle thrill through blood and nerves which sudden danger or surprise can bring to the stoutest heart. Before he could move or speak, the brakes were parted, and the weird, withered face of an old woman was lifted to the light. One of the despised race, clothed in rags, covered with dust, spent with weariness and pain, she lay there, such a wild and woful object that the lonely spot seemed chosen not as a resting-place, but as a grave. Leaning on one arm, she stretched the other trembling hand towards the young man, whispering, with an assuring nod, —

"Don't be skeered, honey; I'se only a pore ole conty

ban', gwine up ter de lan' ob freedum, ef I doesn't drap down by de way."

"Are you sick, or hurt, or only tired, my poor soul?" asked Richard, with such visible compassion in his face that the woman's brightened as she answered, with a cheerfulness which made her utter destitution more pathetic, —

"I'se all dem, and starved inter de bargain; but, bress yer, chile, I'se done got used ter dat, and don't mind em much ef I kin jes git on a piece ter-day. I'se ben porely fer a spell, and layin' by; but I'se mendin' fas', and de sight ob de blue-coats and de kine face is mos' as relishin' as vittles."

"You shall have all three, as far as I can give them to you," said Richard, offering the last of his day's ration, and sitting down opposite the poor old creature, who, muttering hasty thanks, seized and devoured the food with an almost animal voracity, which proved how great her need had been. As the last morsel vanished, she drew a long breath, uttered a sigh of satisfaction, and, sitting more erect, said, with a deprecating gesture and a grateful glance, —

"Massa, I couldn't help forgittin' manners, kase I'se ben widout a mouffle sence yisterday, scept two green apples and de mint growin' ober dar."

"Have you been lying here all night? Where do you come from, and where are you going? Tell me, without fear, and let me help you if I can."

"De Lord lub yer kine heart, chile, and keep yer fer yer mudder. My boys is all gone now; but I knows de feelin', and I'll trus' yer, fer's I dares. Yer see, I'se come from Souf Car'liny, and I'se gwine to de bressed

Norf to fine my ole man, what missis tuk wid her when she lef' us bery suddin."

"What part of the North do you want to find?" asked Richard, eager to offer the desolate being such help as lay in his power. She saw the friendly impulse, and thanked him for it with a look; but the distrust born of many wrongs was stronger than the desire for sympathy, and cautiously, yet humbly, she said, —

"Massa mus' please ter 'scuse me ef I doesn't tell jes' whar I'se gwine. My pore old man is all dey's lef me; and ef missis knowed any ways dat I was lookin' fer him, she'd tote him some place whar I couldn't come. It's way off bery fur; but de name of de town is wrote down in my heart, and, ef I lives, I'll fine it, shore."

"Where are your boys?" asked Richard, interested in spite of the woman's uninviting aspect.

"I'se had seven chil'en, honey, but dey's ben sent eberywhich way, and I doesn't know whar dey is now, scept de dead ones. My darters was sole off years ago; one ob my boys was whipped to def, and one tore so wid de houn's it was a mercy de dear Lord tuk him. Two was put to work on de fortycations down dar; and the las' one, my little Mose, starved in my arms as we was wadin' fru de big swamps, where we runned when word come dat de Yanks was comin' and we'd be free ef we got to um. It was bery hard to leave de pore chile dar, but dere was two or free more little grabes to keep him comp'ny; so I come on alone, and, Glory Halleluyer! here I is."

"Now, how can I help you, ma'am?" said Richard, involuntarily adding respect to pity, as he heard the short, sad story of the losses now past help.

"Ef yer has a bit of money dat yer could spar, chile. dat would 'sist me a heap: I kin hide it handy, and git vittles or a lif' when de roads is bery bad. I'se mos' wore out, fer I'se ben weeks a comin', kase I dunno de way, and can't trus' folks much. Now the Yanks is gwine my road, I wants to foller fas' as I kin, fer I'se shore dey's right."

While she rambled on, Richard had taken out his purse, and halving the small store it contained, offered it, saying, kindly, —

"There old friend; I'd gladly do more for you if I could. I may be going where I shall never need money any more; and, you know, they who give to the poor lend to the Lord: so this much will be saved up for me."

The woman rose to her knees, and, taking the generous hand in both her dusky ones, kissed it with trembling lips, wet it with grateful tears, as she cried, brokenly, —

"Bress yer, chile! bress yer! I'se no words white 'nuff to tank yer in, but I'll 'member yer all my days, and pray de Lord to hold yer safe in de holler ob His han'."

"Thank you, ma'am. What else can I do for you before I go?"

"Jes' tell me yer name, honey, so I kin 'mind de Lord ob yer tickerlally; fer dere's such a heap ob prayers gwine up to Him dese bitter times, He mightn't mine sech pore ones as ole June's ef de good name warn't in um."

"Richard Stirling," answered the young man, smiling at the poor soul's eagerness. "Good-by, old mother. Keep up a stout heart, and trust the blue-coats when you see them, till you find your husband and the happy North."

While he refilled the canteen, the contraband, with the fine sentiment so often found in the least promising of this affectionate race, hastily gathered a delicate fern or two, and, adding the one wild rose that blossomed in that shady spot, offered her little nosegay, with a humility as touching as her earnestness.

"It's a pore give, chile; but I'se nuffin' else sceptin' de wish dat yer'll hab all yer want in dis world and de nex'."

As Richard took it, through his mind flashed the memory of old romantic legends, wherein weird women foretold happy fortunes to young knights pausing at some wayside well, — fortunes to be won only by unshaken loyalty to virtue, love, and honor. Looking down upon the flower, whose name lent it a double charm to him, he said low, to himself, with quickened breath and kindling eyes, —

"A propitious wish! May it be fulfilled, if I deserve it!"

Then, as the first drum-beat sounded, he pressed the hard hand that gave the gift, and sprang up the bank, little dreaming how well the grateful heart he left behind him would one day remember and repay his charity.

Three days later, the brothers stood side by side in the ranks at Gettysburg, impatiently awaiting their turn to attack a rebel battery that must be silenced. From height to height thundered the cannon; up and down the long slopes surged a sea of struggling humanity; all the air was darkened by wavering clouds of smoke and dust, which lifted only when iron messengers of death tore their way through with deafening reports and sheets of flame; while, in the brief pauses that sometimes fell, the bands crashed out with dance-music, as if the wild excitement of the hour had made them fitting minstrels for an awful "dance of death."

"Remember, Rob, where that goes, we follow while we can," whispered Richard, glancing up at the torn flag streaming overhead.

"I'm ready, Rick," returned his brother, with flashing eyes, set teeth, and in every lineament such visible resolve to do and dare, that one hour seemed to have made the boy a hero and a man.

As the words left his lips, down the long line rang the welcome order, "Forward! charge!" and, with a shout that rose sharp and shrill above the din of arms, the brave —th dashed into the rain of shot and shell. Stirred by one impulse, the brothers followed wherever through the smoke they caught the flutter of the flag, as it was borne before them up the hill. More than once it dropped from a dead hand, to be caught up by a living one before it touched the ground. Robert Stirling's was one of these; and, as he seized the staff, the battle-madness seemed to fall upon him, for, waving the banner, with a ringing shout he sprang upon the wall, behind which rebel riflemen were lying. The sharp sting of a ball in the right arm reminded him that he was mortal, and at the same instant his brother's hand clutched him, his brother's voice called through the din, —

"You're wounded, Rob! For God's sake fall back." But, with a grim smile, Robert passed the banner into the keeping of his other hand, saying, as his arm dropped useless at his side, —

"Not yet. Clear the way for me, Rick, and let the old flag be the first up."

A loyal cheer from behind drowned the rebel yell that rose in front, as a blue wave rolled up and broke over the wall, carrying the brothers with it. Above the deadly conflict that went on below, the Stars and Stripes tossed wildly to and fro; but steadily the color-bearer struggled higher, and steadily his body-guard of one went on before him, forcing a passage through the press, till, in a single instant, there came a hurtling sound, a deafening crash, a fiery rain of death-dealing fragments, and, with an awful vision of dismembered bodies, wrathful faces panic-stricken in the drawing of a breath, and a wide gap in the swaying mass before him, Robert Stirling was flung, stunned and bleeding, against the wall so lately left.

Cries of mortal anguish roused him from a moment's merciful oblivion, and showed him that, for his brother and himself, the battle was already done. Not far away, half hidden under a pile of mingled blue and gray, Richard lay quiet on the bloody grass, and, as Robert's dizzy eyes wandered up and down his own bruised body to discover whence came the sharp agony that wrung his nerves, he saw that but one arm now hung shattered at his side; the left was gone, and a single glance at the ghastly wound sent such a pang of horror through him that he closed his eyes, muttering, with white lips, —

"Poor mother! it will be hard to lose us both."

Something silken-soft swept across his face, and, looking up, he saw that the flag had fallen with him, and lay half upright against the wall, still fluttering bravely where many eyes could see it, many willing hearts press on to defend it. Faithful to the last, he leaned across the staff, and, making a shield of his maimed body, waited patiently for the coming of friend or foe. How the battle went he no longer knew; he scarcely cared; for now to him the victories and defeats of life seemed over, and Death standing ready to bestow the pale cross of the legion of honor, laid on so many quiet breasts as the loyal souls depart to their reward.

With strange distinctness came the roar of cannon, the sharp, shrill ringing of the minie-balls, the crash of bursting shells, the shouts, the groans, even the slow drip of his blood, as it plashed down upon the stones; yet neither hope nor fear disturbed him now, as all the past flashed through his mind and faded, leaving three memories, — his love for Rose, his brother's death, his mother's desolation, — to embitter the memorable moment when, with a deathly coldness creeping to his heart, he leaned there bleeding his young life away.

To him it seemed hours, yet but a few short minutes passed before he became conscious of a friendly atmosphere about him, and, through the trance of suffering fast reaching its climax, heard a commanding voice exclaim, —

"It is Stirling: I shall remember this. Take him to the rear, and see that he is cared for."

Robert knew his Colonel's voice, and, gathering up both failing strength and sense, he tried to stand erect, tried to salute with his one arm, and, failing, said, with a piteous look at either wound, —

"I have done my best, sir."

"My brave fellow, you have! What more *could* you do for the old flag?"

Something in the glance, the tone, the words of the

commander whom he so loved and honored, seemed to send new life through the fainting man. His dim eye kindled, his voice grew strong and steady, as, forgetful of the maimed body it inhabited, the unconquerable spirit answered, fervently, —

"I could die for it."

Then, as if in truth he *had* done his best, *had* died for it, Robert Stirling fell forward in the shadow of the flag, his head upon the same green pillow where his brother's lay.

III.

"HERE's the paper, and Fisher to read it for us, boys. Hush, there, and let's hear what's up!"

An instant silence reigned through the crowded ward as the chief attendant entered with the morning sheet that daily went the rounds. The convalescents gathered about him; the least disabled propped themselves upon their arms to listen; even the weakest turned wistful eyes that way, and ceased their moaning, that they might hear, as Fisher slowly read out the brief despatches, and then the mournful lists of wounded, dead, and missing.

Among the many faces in the room, one female one appeared; a strong, calm face, with steadfast eyes, and lips grown infinitely tender with the daily gospel of patience, hope, and consolation which they preached in words of motherly compassion. Still bathing and binding up a shattered limb, she listened to the reading, though her heart stood still to hear, and her face flushed and paled with the rapid alternations of hope and fear. Presently the one audible voice paused suddenly, and a little stir ran through the group as the reader stole an anxious glance at the woman. She saw it, divined its meaning, and in an instant seemed to have nerved herself for anything. Sponge and bandage dropped from her hands, a quick breath escaped her, and an expression of sharp anguish for a moment marred the composure of her countenance; but she fixed a tearless eye on Fisher, asking, steadily, —

"Are my boys' names there?"

"Only one, ma'am, — only one, I do assure you; and he's merely lost an arm. That's better luck than half of 'em have; and now it's got to be a kind of an honor to wear an empty sleeve, you know," replied the old man, with a half-encouraging, half-remorseful look, as he considerately omitted to add the words, "and seriously wounded in the right," to the line, "R. Stirling, left arm gone."

A long sigh of thanksgiving left the mother's lips; then, with one of the natural impulses of a strong character, which found relief in action, she took up the roller and resumed her work more tenderly than ever, — for in her sight that shattered arm was her boy's arm now, — only saying, with a face of pale expectancy, —

"Read on, Fisher: I have another son to keep or lose."

So swift, so subtle, is the magnetism of human sympathy, that not a man in all that room but instantly forgot himself, his own anxieties, hopes, fears, and waited breathlessly for the utterance of that other name. Several sat upright in their beds to catch the good or evil tidings in the reader's face; one dying man sighed softly, from the depths of a homesick heart, "Lord, keep him for his mother!" and the standing group drew closer about Fisher, peering over his shoulder, that younger, keener eyes might read the words, and warn him lest they left his lips too suddenly for one listener's ear.

Slowly name after name was read, and the long list drew near its end. A look of relief already settled upon some countenances, and one friendly fellow had turned to nod reassuringly at the mother, when a hand clutched Fisher's shoulder, and with a start he stopped short in the middle of a word. Mrs. Stirling rose up to receive the coming blow, and stood there mute and motionless, a figure so full of pathetic dignity that many eyes grew very dim. A gesture signified her wish, and, with choked voice and trembling lips, poor Fisher softly read the brief record that one word made so terrible, —

"R. Stirling, dead."

"Give me the paper."

A dozen hands were outstretched to serve her; and, as she took it, trying to teach herself that the heavy tidings were not false, several caps were silently swept off, — an involuntary tribute of respect to that great grief from rough yet tender-hearted men who had no words to offer.

The hurried entrance of a surgeon broke the heavy silence; and his brisk voice jarred on every ear, as he exclaimed, —

"Good-by, boys! I'm off to the front. God bless me! what's the matter?"

"Bad news for Mrs. Stirling, sir. Do speak to her: I can't," whispered Fisher, with two great tears running down his waistcoat.

There was no time to speak; three words had roused her from the first stupor of her sorrow, and down the long room she went, steady and strong again, straight to the surgeon, saying, briefly, —

"To the front? When do you go?"

"In half an hour. What can I do for you?"

"Take me with you."

"Mrs. Stirling, it is impossible," began the astonished gentleman.

"Nothing is impossible to me. I must find my boys, — one living and one dead. For God's sake don't deny me this!"

She stretched her hands to him imploringly; she made as though she would kneel down before him; and her stricken face pleaded for her more eloquently than her broken words.

Dr. Hyde was an army surgeon; but a man's heart beat warm behind his bright buttons, unhardened by all the scenes of suffering, want, and woe through which he had been passing for three memorable years. Now it yearned over this poor mother with an almost filial pity and affection, as he took the trembling hands into his own and answered, earnestly, —

"Heaven knows I would not deny you if it were safe and wise to grant your wish. My dear lady, you have no conception of the horrors of a battle-field, or the awful scenes you must witness in going to the front. These hasty lists are not to be relied upon. Wait a little, and let me look for your sons. On my soul, I promise to do it as faithfully as a brother."

"I cannot wait. Another week of such suspense would kill me. You never saw my boys. I do not even know which is living and which is dead. Then how can you look for them as well as I? You would not know the poor dead face among a hundred; you would not recognize the familiar voice even in the ravings of pain or the din and darkness of those dreadful transports. I can bear anything, do anything, go anywhere, to find my boys. Oh, sir, by the love you bear your mother, I implore you to let me go!"

The look, the tone, the agony of supplication, made her appeal irresistible.

"You shall," replied the doctor, decidedly, putting all objections, obstacles and dangers out of sight. "I'll delay one hour for you, Mrs. Stirling."

Up she sprang, as if endowed with the spirit and activity of a girl; hope, courage, gratitude, shone in her eyes, flushed warm across her face, and sounded in her eager voice, as she said, hurrying from the room, —

"Not an instant for me. Go as you first proposed. I shall be ready long before the time."

She was: for all her thought, her care, was for her boys, not for herself; and, when Dr. Hyde went to seek her in the matron's room, that busy woman looked up from the case of stores she was unpacking, and answered, with a sob, —

"Poor soul! she's waiting for you in the hall."

News of her loss and her departure had flown through the house; for no nurse there was so beloved and honored as "Madam Stirling," as the stately old lady was called among the boys; and when the doctor led her to the ambulance, it was through a crowd of wan and crippled creatures gathered there to see her off. Many eyes followed her, many lips blessed her, many hands were outstretched for a farewell grasp; and, as the ambulance went clattering away, old Fisher gave expression to the general feeling, when he said, with an air of solemn con viction in almost ludicrous contrast to the emotional contortions of his brown countenance, —

"She'll find 'em! It's borne in upon me uncommon strong that the Lord won't rob such a woman of her sons, — bless her stout heart! so give her a cheer, boys, and then clear the way!"

They did give her a cheer, a right hearty one, — though the voices were none of the strongest, and nearly as many crutches as caps were waved in answer to the smile she sent them as she passed from sight.

It was not a long journey that lay before her, yet to Mrs. Stirling it seemed interminable; for a heavy heart went with her, and, through all the hopeful or despondent thoughts that haunted her, one unanswerable question continually sounded, like a sorrowful refrain, — "One killed, one wounded. Which is living? which is dead?"

All along the road they went two streams of life continually flowed, in opposite directions: one, a sad procession of suffering humanity passing hospital, or homeward, to live or die, as Heaven willed; the other, an almost equally sad procession of pilgrims journeying to the battle-field, to find their wounded or to weep their dead, — men and women, old and young, rich and poor, all animated by a spirit which made them as one great family, through the same costly sacrifice, the same sore affliction. It was well for Mrs. Stirling that the weary way was a little shortened, the heavy hours a little lightened, for her, by the companionship of others bent on a like errand. In this atmosphere of general anxiety and excitement, accustomed formalities and reserves were forgotten or set aside; strangers spoke freely to each other; women confidingly asked and gratefully received the chivalrous protection of men, and men yearning for sympathy always found it ready in the hearts and eyes of women as they told their sorrows and were comforted. Many brief tragedies were poured into Mrs. Stirling's ear; more than one weaker nature leaned upon her strength; more than one troubled soul felt itself calmed by the pious patience which touched that worn and venerable countenance with an expression which made it an unconscious comfort to many eyes; and in seeing, solacing the woes of others, she found fresh courage to sustain her own.

They came at last, with much difficulty and many delays, to the little town in and along which lay nine thousand dead, and nearly twenty thousand wounded men. Although a week had not yet passed since the thunder of the cannon ceased, the place already looked like the vast cemetery which it was soon to become; for, in groves and fields, by the roadside and along the slopes, wherever they fell, lay loyal and rebel soldiers in the shallow graves that now are green. The long labor of interment was but just begun; for the living appealed more urgently to both friend and stranger, and no heart was closed, no hand grew weary, while strength and power to aid remained. All day supply wagons and cars came full and departed empty; all day ambulances rolled to and fro, bringing the wounded from remoter parts of the wide battle-field to the railroad for removal to fixed hospitals elsewhere; all day the relief-stations, bearing the blessed sign, "U. S. San. Com.," received hundreds of sufferers into the shelter of their tents, who must else have laid waiting their turn for transportation in the burning July sun; all day, and far into the night, red-handed surgeons stood at the rude tables, heart-sick and weary with their hard yet merciful labors, as shattered body after body was laid before them, while many more patiently, even cheerfully, awaited their turn; and all day mothers, wives, and widows, fathers, friends, and lovers, roamed the hills and valleys, or haunted the field-hospitals, searching for the loved and lost.

Dr. Hyde was under orders; but for many hours he neglected everything but Mrs. Stirling, going with her from houses, tents, and churches, to barns, streets, and crowded yards; for everywhere the wounded lay thick as autumn leaves, — some on bloody blankets, some on scattered straw, a few in cleanly beds, many on the bare ground; and if anything could have added to the bitter pain of hope deferred, it would have been the wistful glances turned on the new-comers from eyes that, seeing no familiar face, closed again with a pathetic patience that wrung the heart. All day they searched; but nowhere did the mother find her boys, nor any tidings of them; and, as night fell, her companion besought her to rest from the vain search, and accept the hospitality of a friendly citizen.

"Dear Mrs. Stirling, wait here till morning," the doctor said. "I must go to my work, but will not till I know that you are safe; for you can never wander here alone. I will send a faithful messenger far and wide, to make inquiries through the night, and hope to greet you in the morning with the happiest news."

She scarcely seemed to hear him, so intent was her mind upon the one hope that absorbed it.

"Go to your work, kind friend," she said; "the poor souls need you more than I. Have no fears for me. I want neither rest nor food; I only want my boys; and I must look for them both day and night, lest one hour of idleness should make my coming one hour too late. I shall go back to the station. A constant stream of wounded men is passing there; and, while I help and comfort them, I can see that my boys are not hurried away while I am waiting for them here."

He let her have her will, well knowing that for such as she there was no rest till hope came, or exhausted nature forced her to pause. Back to the relief-station they went, and, while Dr. Hyde dressed wounds, issued orders, and made diligent inquiry among the throngs that came and went, Mrs. Stirling, with other anxious yet hopeful, helpful women, moved about the tents, preparing nourishment for the men, who came in faster than they could be served. Through the whole night she worked, lifting water to lips too parched to syllable the word, wetting wounds unbandaged for days, feeding famished creatures who had lain suffering in solitary places till some minister of mercy found and succored them, whispering words of good cheer, and, by the cordial comfort of her presence, sending many a poor soul on his way rejoicing. But, while she worked so tirelessly for others, she still hungered for her children, and would not be comforted. No ambulance came rumbling from the field that she did not hurry out to scan the new-comers with an eye that neither darkness nor disguise could deceive; not a stretcher with its helpless burden was brought in that she did not bend over it with the blessed cup of water in her hand, and her poor heart fluttering in her breast; and often, among the groups of sleepers that lay everywhere, there went a shadowy figure through the night, turning the lantern's glimmer on each pallid face; but nowhere did Rick or Rob look back at her with the glad cry, "Mother!"

At dawn, Dr. Hyde came to her. With difficulty did he prevail upon her to eat a morsel and rest a little, while he told her of his night's attempts, and spoke cheerfully of the many mishaps, the unavoidable disappointments and delay, of such a quest at such a time and place.

"We have searched the town; and Blake and Snow will see that no Stirling leaves by any of the trains to-day. But the hospitals on the outskirts still remain for us, — besides the heights and hollows; for, on a battle-field like this, many men might lie unfound for days while search was going on about them. I have a wagon here, — a rough affair, but the best I can get; and, if you will not rest, let us go together, and look again for these lost sons of yours."

They went; and for another long, hot, summer day looked on sights that haunted their memories for years, listened to sounds that pierced their souls, and with each hour felt the weight of impotent compassion weigh heavier and heavier upon their hearts. Various and conflicting rumors, conjectures, and relations from the comrades of the brothers perplexed the seekers, and augmented the difficulties of their task. One man affirmed that he saw both Stirlings fall; a second, that both were taken prisoners; a third, that he had seen both march safely away; and a fourth, that Richard was mortally wounded and Robert missing. But all agreed in their admiration for the virtue and the valor of the brothers, heartily wishing their mother success, and unconsciously applying, by their commendations, the only balm that could mitigate her pain. Up and down, from dawn till dusk, went the heavy-hearted pair; but evening came again, and still no sure intelligence, no confirmed fear or happy meeting, lightened the terrible uncertainty that tortured them.

"Dear madam, we have done all that human patience and perseverance can do. Now, leave your boys in God's hand, and let me care for you as if you were my mother," said the compassionate doctor, as they paused, dusty, jaded, and dejected, at the good citizen's hospitable door.

Mrs. Stirling did not answer him. She sat there, an image of maternal desolation, her hands locked together on her knee, her eyes fixed and unseeing, and in her face a still, white anguish piteous to see. With gentlest constraint, her friend led her in, laid the gray head down upon a woman's breast, and left her to the tender care of one who had known a grief like hers.

For hours she lay where kind hands placed her, physically spent, yet mentally alert as ever. No passing face escaped her, no sound fell unheeded on her ear, no movement of those about her was unobserved: yet she neither spoke, nor stirred, nor slept, till midnight gathered cool and dark above a weary world. Then a brief lapse into unconsciousness partially repaired the ravages those two hard days had wrought. But even when the exhausted body rested, the unwearied soul continued its sad quest, and in her dreams the mother found her boys. So vivid was the vision, that she suddenly awoke to find herself thrilled with a strange joy, trembling with a strange expectancy. She rose up in her bed, she put away her fallen hair, fast whitening with sorrow's frost, and held her breath to listen; for a cry, urgent, imploring, distant, yet near, seemed ringing through the room.

From without came the ceaseless rumble of ambulances and the tread of hurrying feet; from within, the sound of women weeping for their dead, and the low moaning of a brave officer fast breathing his life away upon his young wife's bosom. No voice spoke, that human ear could hear; yet through the mysterious hush that fell upon her in that hour, her spirit heard an exceeding bitter cry, —

"Mother! mother! come to me!"

Like one possessed by an impulse past control, she left her bed, flung on her garments, seized the little store of comforts untouched till now, and, without sign or sound, glided like a shadow from the house.

The solemn peace of night could not so soon descend upon those hills again; nature's tranquillity had been rudely broken; and, like the suffering humanity that cumbered her wounded breast, she seemed to moan in her troubled sleep. Lights flashed from hill and hollow, some fixed, some wandering, — all beacons of hope to the living or funeral torches for the dead. Many feet went to and fro along the newly-trodden paths; dusky figures flitted everywhere, and sounds of suffering filled the night-wind with a sad lament. But, upheld by a power beyond herself, led by an instinct in which she placed blind faith, and unconscious of doubt, or weariness, or fear, the solitary woman walked undaunted and unscathed through that Valley of the Shadow of Death.

Out from the crowded town she went, turning neither to the right nor left, up a steep path her feet had trodden once that day, straight to the ruined breastworks formed of loose fragments of stone, piled there by many hands whose earthly labor was already done. There, gathered from among the thickly-strewn dead, and sheltered by an awning till they could be taken lower, lay a score of men, blue coats and gray, side by side on the bare earth, equals now in courage, suffering, and patience. The one faithful attendant who kept his watch alone was gone for water, that first, greatest need and comfort in hours like those, and the dim light of a single lantern flickered through the gloom. Utter silence filled the dreary place, till from the remotest corner came a faint, imploring cry, the more plaintive and piteous for being a man's voice grown childlike in its weak wandering: —

"Mother! mother! come to me!"

"Who spoke?"

A woman's voice, breathless and broken, put the question; a woman's figure stood at the entrance of the rude shelter; and when a wakeful sufferer answered, eagerly, "Robert Stirling, just brought in dying. For God's sake help him if you can,"— a woman's face, transfigured with a sudden joy, flashed swiftly, silently before his startled eyes, to bend over one low bed, whence came the sound of tender speech, prayerful thanksgiving, and the strong sobbing of a man who in his hour of extremest need found solace and salvation in the dear refuge of his mother's arms.

IV.

They were alone together, the mother and her one son, after weeks of suffering and a long, slow journey, safely at home at last. Poor Rob was a piteous sight now, for both arms were gone, one at the shoulder, the other at the elbow; yet sadder than the maimed body was the altered face, for, though wan and wasted by much suffering, a strong soul seemed to look out at the despairing eyes, as if the captivity of helplessness were more than he could bear. A still deeper grief cast its shadow over him, making the young man old before his time, for day and night his heart cried out for his brother, as if the tie between the twin-born could not be divided even by death. This longing, which the consolations of neither tenderness nor time could appease, was now the only barrier to his recovery. Vainly his mother assured him that Richard's death had been confirmed by more than one account; vainly she tried to comfort him by hopeful reminders of a glad reunion hereafter, and endeavored to rouse him by appeals to his filial love, telling him that he was her all now, and imploring him to live for his old mother's sake. He listened, promised, and tried to be resigned, but still cherished an unconquerable belief that Richard lived, in spite of all reports, appearances, or seeming certainties. Asleep, he dreamed of him; awake, he talked of him; and the hope of seeing him again in this world seemed the only thing that gave Rob patience and courage to sustain the burden which life had now become to him.

"Mother, when shall I be freed from this dreadful bed?" he broke out, suddenly, as she laid down the book she had been reading to deaf ears; and brushed away a lock of hair the wind had blown across his forehead, for her watchful eye and tireless hand spared him the pain of asking any service that recalled his loss.

"Weeks yet, dear. It takes nature long to repair

such rents in her fine handiwork; but the wounds are healing rapidly, thanks to your temperate life and hardy frame."

"And your devoted care, most faithful of nurses," added Robert, turning his lips to the hand that had strayed caressingly from forehead to cheek. "Do your best for me, mother, — and you can do more than any other in the world; get me on my feet again as soon as may be, and then, God willing, I'll find Rick if he's above the sod."

Mrs. Stirling opened her lips to remonstrate against the vain purpose, but, seeing the sudden color that lent the wan face a semblance of health, hearing the tone of energy that strengthened the feeble voice, and remembering how deep a root the hope had taken in the brother's heart, she silently resolved to let it sustain him if it could, undisturbed by a look or word of unbelief.

"We will go together, Rob. My first search was successful; Heaven grant my second may be so likewise. I will do my best; and when I see you your old self again I shall be ready to follow anywhere."

"My old self again! I never can be that, and why I was spared to be a burden to you while Rick was taken — no, not taken — I'll neither say nor think that. If he were dead I should either follow him or find comfort in the thought that he was at peace; but he is alive, for day and night his spirit calls to mine, and I must answer it as you answered me when I cried to you in what I thought to be my dying hour. Remember, mother, how many of our men were found after they were believed to to have been killed or taken. John King's grave was pointed out to his wife, you know; and, when she had almost broken her poor heart over it, she went home, to find him waiting for her there. Why should not some such happy chance befall us? Let us believe and hope till we can do so no longer, and then I will learn submission."

His mother only answered with a gentler touch upon his head, for in her heart she believed that her son was dead. Perhaps the great fear of losing both had made the loss seem less when one was spared, or perhaps she thought that if either must go Richard was fittest for the change, and the nearness she still felt to him made the absence of his visible presence less keenly felt than that of Robert would have been; for, though as dear, he was not so spiritually akin to her as that stronger, gentler son.

"Is Rose in town, mother?" was the abrupt question that broke a momentary silence.

"Yes, she is still here."

"Does she know we have come?"

"She cannot help knowing, when half the town has been trooping by with welcomes, messages, and gifts for you."

"Do you think she will come to welcome us?"

"Not yet, dear."

"Ah! her pride will keep her away, you think?"

"Her pity, rather. Rose has generous impulses, and, but for her mistaken education, would have been a right noble woman. She may be yet, if love proves strong enough to teach her the hard, though happy lesson, that shall give her back to you again."

"That can never be, mother. What woman could love such a wreck; and what right have I to expect or hope it, least of all from Rose? No, I am done with love; my dream has had a stern awakening; do not talk of the impossible to me."

His mother smiled the wise smile of one who understood the workings of a woman's heart, and, knowing both its weakness and its strength, believed that all things are possible to love. Perhaps some village gossip had breathed a hint into her ear which confirmed her hope; or, judging another by herself, she ventured to comfort her son by prophesying the return of the dream which he believed forever ended.

"I will leave that theme for a younger, more persuasive woman to discourse upon, when the hour comes in which you find that hearts do not always change with changing fortunes, that affliction often deepens affection, and when one asks a little pity one sometimes receives much love."

"I shall never ask either of Rose."

"If she truly loves you there will be no need of asking, Rob."

His face brightened beautifully as he listened; his eyes shone, and he moved impetuously, as if the mere thought had power to lift and set him on his feet, a hale and happy man again. But weakness and helplessness held him down; and, with a sharper pang than that of the half-healed wounds, he lay back, exclaiming with a bitter sigh, —

"No hope of such a fate for me! I must be content with the fulfilment of my other longing, and think of poor Rick all the more because I must not think of Rose. Oh! if my worst enemy should bring the dear lad home to me, I'd joyfully forgive, love, honor him for that one act."

As Robert spoke with almost passionate earnestness, a shadow that had lain across the sunny threshold of the door vanished as noiselessly as it had come; and unseen, unheard, Rose glided back into the green covert of the lane, saying within herself, as she hurried on, agitated by the mingled pain, pride and passion of the new-born purpose at her heart, —

"Yes, Mrs. Stirling, love *shall* prove strong enough to make me what I should be, and Robert shall yet forgive and honor me; for, if human power can do it, I will bring his brother home to him."

Completely absorbed by the design that had taken possession of her, she hastened back, thinking intently as she went; and, when she called her one faithful servant to her, all her plans were laid, her resolution fixed, and every moment seemed wasted till the first step was taken, for now her impetuous spirit could not brook delay.

"Jupiter, I am going to Washington in the morning, and shall take you with me — so be ready," was the rapid order issued to the astonished old man, who had no answer to make, but the usual obedient — "Yes, missis."

"I am going to look for Mrs. Stirling's son, the one who is supposed to be dead."

"Lors, missis, he is dead, shore, — ain't he?"

"I intend to satisfy myself on that point, if I search the prisons, camps, hospitals, and graveyards, from Gettysburg to Richmond. I have strength, courage, money, and some power, and what better use can I make of them than to look for this good neighbor, and ease the hearts of those who love him best. Go, Jupe, tell no one of my purpose, make ready in all haste, and be sure I will reward you well if you serve me faithfully now."

"Yes, missis, — you may 'pend on me."

At dawn they were away, the young mistress and her old slave. No one knew why they had gone, nor whither; and village rumor said Miss Rose had left so suddenly because young Stirling and his mother had come home. When Mrs. Stirling heard of the departure, her old eyes kindled with indignation, while her voice trembled with grief, as she said to her son, —

"I am bitterly disappointed in her; think of her no more, Rob."

But Robert turned his face to the wall, and neither spoke nor stirred for many hours.

In ancient times, young knights went out to defend distressed dames and free imprisoned damsels; but, in our day, the errantry is reversed, and many a strong-hearted woman goes journeying up and down the land, bent on delivering some beloved hero from a captivity more terrible than any the old legends tell. Rose was now one of these; and, though neither a meek Una nor a dauntless Britomart, she resolutely began the long quest which was to teach her a memorable lesson, and make a loyal woman of the rebel beauty.

At first she haunted hospitals; and, while her heart was wrung by the sight of every form of suffering, she marked many things that sunk deep into her memory, and forced it to bear testimony to the truth. She saw Confederate soldiers lying side by side with Union men, as kindly treated, almost as willingly served, and twice conquered by those who could smite hard like valiant soldiers, and then lift up their fallen enemy like Christian gentlemen. This sight caused her to recall other scenes in other hospitals, where loyal prisoners lay perishing for help, while rebels close by were cherished with every demonstration of indulgent care by men and women, who not only hardened their hearts against the sadder sufferers, but found a cruel pleasure in tormenting them by every deprivation and indignity their hatred could devise. She had seen a woman, beautiful and young, go through a ward leaving fruit, flowers, delicate food and kind words behind her, for every Southern man that lay there; then offer a cup of water to a Northern soldier, and as the parched lips opened eagerly to receive the blessed draught, she flung it on the ground and went her way with a scornful taunt. This picture was in Rose's mind as she stood in a Washington hospital, by the death-bed of a former neighbor of her own, hearing the fervent thanks uttered with the last breath he drew, watching the sweet-faced nurse close the weary eyes, fold the pale hands, and then forgetting everything but the one fact, that some woman loved and mourned the lost rebel, she "kissed him for his mother," while Rose turned away with full heart and eyes, never again to speak contemptuously of Northern men and women.

She visited many battle-fields and graveyards, where the low mounds rose thickly everywhere, and an army of brave sleepers lay awaiting the call to God's great review. Here, too, despite the dreary task before her, and the daily disappointment that befell her, she could not but contrast the decent burial given to dead enemies with the sacrilegious brutality with which her friends often tried to rob death of its sanctity by mutilation, burning, butchery, and the denial of a few feet of earth to cover some poor body which a brave soul had ennobled by its martyrdom. Seeing these things, she could not but blush for those whom she once had blindly honored; could not but heartily respect those whom she once had as blindly distrusted and despised.

She searched many prisons; for, when neither eloquence nor beauty could win its way, money proved a golden key, and let her in. Here, as elsewhere, the same strong contrast was forced upon her; for, while one side fed, clothed, and treated their conquered with courteous forbearance, often sending them back the richer and better for their sojourn, the other side robbed, starved, tormented, and often wantonly murdered the helpless victims of the chances of war, or returned them worn out with privation and neglect to die at home, or to endure the longer captivity of strong souls pent in ruined bodies. And Rose felt her heart swell with indignant grief and shame, as she came out into the free world again, finding the shadow of prison-bars across its sunshine, hearing the sighs of long-suffering men in every summer wind, and fully seeing at last how black a blight slavery and treason had brought upon the land she loved.

She went to Hospital Directories, those kindly instituted intelligence offices for anxious hearts, and there she saw such sorrowful scenes, yet heard such cheerful, courageous words, that sympathy and admiration contended for the mastery in the Southern woman's breast. She heard an old mother say proudly, as she applied for a pass, "I have had seven sons in the army; three are dead, and two are wounded, but I'm glad my boys went." She saw a young wife come to meet her husband, and learn that he was waiting for her in his coffin; but though her heart was broken, there was no murmuring at the heavy loss, no bitter denunciation of those who had made her life so desolate, only a sweet submission, and sustaining consolation in the knowledge that the great sacrifice had been freely made, and the legacy of an honorable name had been bequeathed to the baby at her breast. Lads came asking for fathers, and whether they found them dead or wounded, the spirit of patriotism burned undiminished in their enthusiastic hearts, and each was eager to fill the empty place, undaunted by pain and peril of the life. Old men mingled, with their tearless lamentations for lost sons, their own regrets that they too could not shoulder guns, and fight the good fight to the end.

All these loyal demonstrations sunk deeply into Rose's softened heart, and in good time bore fruit; for now she began to think within herself, "Surely, a war which does so much for a people, making women glad to give their best and dearest, men eager to lay down their lives, strengthening, purifying, and sustaining all, must be a holy war, approved by God, and sure of victory in the end." The last touch needed to complete the work of regeneration was yet to come; but slowly, surely this long discipline made her ready to receive it.

Her search, meanwhile, had not proved fruitless, for after many disappointments one fact was established beyond doubt: Richard Stirling was not killed at Gettysburg. By the merest chance she met, in one of the Union hospitals which she visited, a rebel lieutenant who told her that the same shell wounded both Stirling and himself, and when the first attack was repulsed, that Richard was taken prisoner, and sent to the rear with others of his regiment. An hour later, the lieutenant himself was taken by our men when they returned to the charge; but whether Stirling lived or died he could not tell: probably the latter, being severely wounded in head and chest.

The smile, the thanks Rose gave in return for these good tidings, and the comforts she gratefully provided, would have made captivity dangerously alluring to the young lieutenant had she remained. But armed with this intelligence she went on her way rejoicing, eager to trace and follow the army of prisoners that had gone southward. Weeks had been consumed in her search, and already rumors of the horrors of the Libby Prison-house and Belle Island had disturbed and shocked the North. Haunted with woful recollections of all the varied sufferings she had seen, her imagination pictured Richard weak and wounded, shivering and starving, while she waited with full hands and eager heart to save, and heal, and lead him home. Intent on reaching Richmond, she besieged officials in high places as well as low, money flowed like water, and every faculty was given to the work. It seemed as if she had undertaken an impossibilty; for though all pitied, tried to help, and heartily admired the beautiful brave woman, no one could serve her as she would be served; and she began to exercise her fertile wit in devising some way in which she could attain her object by stratagem, if all other means should fail.

Waiting in her carriage, one day, at the door of a helpful friend's office, while Jupe carried up a message, she was startled from an anxious reverie by the sudden appearance of an agitated black countenance at the window, and the sound of an incoherent voice, exclaiming, between laughter and tears, —

"Oh, bress de Lord, and sing hallyluyer! I'se foun' her! I'se foun' her! Doesn't yer know me, Missy Rose? I'se old June, and I'se run away; but I doesn't kere nuffin what comes ob me ef missy'll jes' lem me see my pore ole man once more."

To Juno's infinite surprise, no frown appeared upon the face of her young mistress, and no haughty reprimand followed the recognition of the half-ludicrous, half-pathetic tatterdemalion who addressed her, but a white hand was put forth to draw the new-comer in, and the familiar voice answered with a friendliness never heard before, —

"Jupe is safe, and you shall see him soon. Come in, you poor old soul, come in."

In bundled the delighted creature, and began to tell her story, but stopped in the middle to dart out again, and fall upon the neck of the bewildered Jupiter, as he came soberly up to deliver his message. Fortunately it was a quiet street, else that tumultuous meeting might have been productive of discomfort to all parties; for the old couple wept, laughed, and sung, — went down upon their knees to thank Heaven, — got up to embrace, and dance, and weep again, in a perfect abandonment of gratitude, affection and delight. When Rose could make herself heard, she bade them both enter the carriage; then drawing down the curtains, and ordering the coachman to drive slowly round the square, she let the reunited husband and wife give free vent to their emotions, till from sheer weariness they grew calm again.

"We hopes missis will 'scuse us actin' so wild, but

'pears like we couldn't help it, comin' so bery sudden an' undispected," apologized Jupe, wiping away the last of his own and Juno's tears with the same handkerchief, which, very properly, was a miniature star-spangled banner."

But Rose's own eyes were wet; and in her sight there was nothing unlovely or unmannerly in that natural outbreak of affection, for she had learned to feel for others now, and the same stern discipline which made her both strong and humble, taught her to see much that was true and touching in the spectacle of the gray heads bent towards each other; the wrinkled faces shining with joy; the hard hands locked together, as the childless, friendless old pair found freedom, happiness, and rest for a moment in each other's arms. Like a true woman, Juno calmed herself first, that she might talk; and, emboldened by the gracious change in her once imperious mistress, she told the story of her wanderings at length, not forgetting the chief incident of her long and lonely flight, the meeting with Robert Stirling. At the sound of his name, both Rose and Jupe exclaimed, and Juno was rapidly made acquainted with the mission which had brought them there. Deeply impressed with the circumstance, and a sense of her own importance, the good soul entered heartily into the matter, saying, with the pious simplicity of her race,—

"De ways ob de Lord is 'mazing 'sterious! but we's boun' to b'lieve dat He'll take special kere ob dat dear chile, elseways we shouldn't hab ben brung togedder so cur'us. I tole de blessed gen'l'man I'd 'member him, and I has; I prayed ter be spared ter see his kine face agin, an' I was."

"Where? wher? Oh, Juno, you were surely sent to me in my last extremity," cried Rose, now trembling with interest and impatience.

"It was dis way, missy. When dat dear gen'l'man lef me I creeped on a piece, but was tuk sick, an' a kind fam'ly kep' me a long time. Den I come on agin bery slow, an' one day as I was gwine fru a town, — I'se los' de name, but it don't matter, — as I was gwine fru dat town, dere come a lot ob pris'ners frum Gettysbury, or some place like dat, a gwine to Richmun. Dear heart, honey, dey was an orfle sight, all lame, an' rags, an' hungry, an' de folks run out into de street wid bread ter feed um. De guard was bery ugly, and wouldn't let de folks come nigh ter do it, so dey jes' fell back and frowed de vittles ober de heads of dem rebs, and de pore souls cotched it as ef it was de manny dey tells of in de Bible. I helped um; yes, missy, I couldn't stay still noways, so I runned into a bake-shop wid some more women, and we stood in de winders and hev de bread down to de starvin' creeters in de street mighty hearty, you'm be shore ob dat. I had a big loaf in my han', and was lookin' roun' for de starvinest man dar, when I saw de bery face dat looked so kine inter mine yonder by de spring. I tank de Lord I'd kep de name handy, fer I screeched right out, 'Oh, Massa Stirlin'! Massa Stirlin'! dis yere's for you wid my lub.' He looked up, he 'membered me, he larfed all over his pore thin face, jes' as he done de day I gib him de rose. Oh, missy! he was hurted bad; dey had tuk away his hat, and coat, and shoes, and I saw his head was tied up, and dere was a great red stain on de bosom ob his shirt, and he looked so weak and wore down dat I jes bus out cryin', and forgot all 'bout de bread till I was gwine to wipe my eyes wid it. Den I got my wits togedder and gib de loaf such a great chuck dat I mos' fell out a winder, but he got it; I sawed him break it in bits and gib em roun' to de pore boys side ob him, some wid no arms to grab wid, some too hurted to fight and run for it like de res. Den I'se fraid he won't had nuf for his self, so I gets more and fros it far, and he larfs out hearty like a boy, and calls to me, 'I tank yer, ma'am. God bless yer!' Dat set me cryin' agin, like a ole fool as I is, and when I come to dey was movin' on agin, and de las I see ob dat dear soul he was marchin' brave, wid de sun beatin' down on his pore head, de hot sand burnin' his pore feet, and a sick boy hangin' on his arm. But fer all dat he kep lookin' back, noddin' and smilin' till dey was clean gone, and dere was nuffin left but prayers and sobbin' all dat day fer me."

"It is certain then that he has gone to Richmond; I must follow. Jupe, what message did Mr. Norton send me?" asked Rose, remembering her unanswered inquiry at last.

"He bery busy, Missis, elseways he come down and see yer; but he says dere's no gittin' any passes, and de only 'vice he can gib, is dat you goes to 'Napolis and looks dere, kase dere's ben some pris'ners fetched dere frum Belle Island, and dere's jes one chance dat Massa Stirlin' mought be 'mong em."

"I'll go! Jupe, order the man back to the hotel. There's not a moment to be lost," said Rose.

"Oh, missy, lem me go wid you!" implored Juno. "I knows I don't look bery spectable, but I'll follow on hind yer some ways: I'se good at nussin', I can pry roun' in places whar a lady couldn't, and ef dat bressed gen'l'man ain't dar, I'll jes go back and try to fetch him out ob de lan' ob bondage like I did myself."

"You shall go, Juno, for without you I should still be groping in the dark. Surely Heaven helps me, and I feel that I shall find him now."

She did find him, but how? She went to Annapolis, where a hundred and eighty exchanged prisoners had just arrived, and entering the hospital, stood aghast at the sight before her. Men who for weeks had been confined on that desert waste, Belle Island, without shelter or clothing, almost without food, and no help, sick or well, lay there dead or dying from starvation and neglect. Nurses, inured to many forms of suffering, seemed dismayed at the awful spectacle of living skeletons famishing for food, yet too weak to taste when eager hands tried to minister to them. Some were raving in the last stage of their long agony; some were hopelessly insane; many had died unconscious that they were among friends; and others were too far gone to speak, yet dumbly grateful for the help that came too late.

Heart-wrung and horror-stricken, Rose could only pray that she might not find Richard among these victims of a barbarous revenge which made her disown and denounce the cause she had clung to until then, and oppressed her with a bitter sense of remorse for ever giving it her allegiance. As she stood struggling with a flood of thoughts and feelings too strong for utterance, old Juno, who had pressed on before her, beckoned with an eager hand. Going to her, Rose found her bending over the mournful ghost of a man who lay there like one dead, with hollow eyes fast shut, the pinched mouth breathless, the wasted limbs stiff and cold, and no trace of Richard Stirling visible, for the frightful emaciation, the long, neglected hair and beard, so changed him that his own mother might have passed by without a glance of recognition.

"It is not he, Juno. Poor soul, poor soul! cover his face, and let him rest," sighed Rose, with tremulous lips, bending to lay her delicate handkerchief over the piteous face, one glance at which had made her eyes too dim for seeing, and seemed to utter a mute reproach, as if the loss of this life lay at her door.

"It *is* de dear boy, missy; I'se shore ob it, fer see what I foun' in dis faded little bag dat lay on his heart, when I feeled to see if dere was any beat lef. Here's a bit ob gray har in a paper wid somefin wrote on it, an' here's de flower I gib him. I knows it by de red string I pulled out ob my old shawl to tie de posy wid. Ah, honey, I specks he smiled so when he tuk de rose, an' kep it, kase he tort ob you, and lubbed you bery dear."

The little case and the dead flower fell from Rose's hand, as she read these words upon the worn paper that held the gray curl: "For Rick from mother, May 10, 1863"; and she laid her warm cheek down beside that chilly one, crying through the heartiest, happiest tears she ever shed.

"Oh, Richard, have I come too late?"

Something in the touch of tender lips, the magnetism of a living, loving heart, seemed to arrest the weary spirit in its flight, and call it back to life by the power of that passion which outlives death.

"De heart's a beatin', and de bref's a comin', shore. Lif' up his head, honey! Jupe, fan him bery kereful, while I gets a drop ob brandy down his frote, an' rubs dese pore hans dat is all bones. Dear boy, we's got yer Def may go 'way now!"

Juno both worked and spoke as if the young man were her son; for she forgot all differences of rank, color, and condition, in her glad gratitude to nurse him like a mother. Rose laid the unconscious head upon her bosom, and, brushing back the tangled hair, watched the faint flutter of the eyelids, as life came creeping back, and hope dawned again for both of them; for she felt that Richard's restoration would win Robert's pardon, and be her best atonement for the past.

It was long before he was himself again, but Juno never left him, day or night; Jupe was a sleepless, tireless guard, and Rose ministered to him with heart as well as hand, seeming to hold death at bay by the sheer force of an indomitable will. He knew the forms about him, at last; and the happiest moment of Rose's life was that in which he looked up in her face with eyes that blessed her for her care, and whispered feebly, —

"I thought I had suffered much, but this atones for all!"

After that, every hour brought fresh strength, and renewed assurances that the danger had gone by. At this point Juno discovered that her soul was stronger than her body, for the latter gave out, and Rose commanded her to rest.

"I need you no longer, for my work is nearly done," she said. "Jupe, I told you that if you served me well you should be rewarded, and I will keep my word. This paper assures your freedom, and your wife's, forever; this purse contains a little fortune, to keep you above want while you live. Take the late gift, my good old friends, and forgive me for the wrong I have done you all these years."

Rose's subdued yet earnest manner, and the magnitude of the gift, restrained the rapture of the old pair, which found vent only in a demonstration that touched Rose more than a stream of thanks and blessings. Holding fast the precious paper that gave them freedom only at life's close, they put back the money, feeling too rich in that other gift to fear want, and, taking one of the white hands in their black ones, they kissed them, wet them with grateful tears, and clung to them, imploring to be allowed to stay with her, to serve her, love her, and be her faithful followers to the end.

Much moved, she gave the promise; and happier than any fabled king and queen of Olympus were the old freedman and his wife, when they went away to nurse each other for a little while, at their mistress's desire, leaving her to tend the "General," as Jupe insisted upon calling Richard, laboring under a delusion that, because he had suffered much, he must have received honor and promotion.

Very quiet, useful hours were those that followed, and these proved the sincerity of her amendment, by the zeal with which she performed many a distasteful duty for Richard and his companions in misfortune, the patience with which she bore many discomforts, the energy with which she met and conquered all obstacles to the fulfilment of her purpose. Unconsciously Richard did more for her than she for him: because, though unseen, his work was both more difficult and more enduring than her own. She nursed and nourished an exhausted body; he, by the influence of character, soothed and sustained an anxious soul, helped Rose to find her better self, and, through the force of a fair example, inspired her with noble emulation. They talked much, at first: Rose was the speaker, and an eloquent one; for Richard was very like his brother, as she had last seen him, and she felt the charm of that resemblance. Then, as Richard gained strength, he loved to lie conversing upon many themes, too happy in her presence to remember the sad past, or to cherish a fear for the unknown future. Having lived a deep and earnest life of late, Rose found herself fitted to comprehend the deep and earnest thoughts that found expression in those confidential hours; for if ever men and women are their simplest, sincerest selves, it is when suffering softens the one, and sympathy strengthens the other.

Often Rose caught a wistful look fixed on her face, as she read or worked beside her patient, in the little room now set apart for him, and she could not but interpret it aright, since the story of the rose had given her a key to that locked heart. Poor Richard loved her still, and was beginning to hope that Juno's wish might be fulfilled, for Rose seldom spoke of Rob, had shivered and turned pale when she told his great misfortune, and, man-like, Richard believed that her love had changed to pity, and might, in time, be given to Robert's unmarred counterpart. He was very slow to receive this hope, very remorseful when he thought of Rob, and very careful not to betray the troubled joy that was doing more toward his recovery than any cordial that passed his lips. But, when the time came for them to think of turning homeward, he felt that he could not meet his brother with any secret hidden in his heart; and, with the courage that was as natural to him as his patience, he ended his suspense, and manfully went to meet his fate.

Rose had been reading him to sleep one night, and fancying, from his stillness, that she had succeeded, she closed her book, and sat watching the thin face that looked so pale and peaceful in the shaded light that filled the room. Not long did she study it, for suddenly the clear eyes opened, and, as if some persistent thought found utterance, almost against his will, he asked, —

"Rose, why did you come to find me?"

She divined the true meaning of the look, the words, with a woman's instinct, and answered both with the perfect truth which they deserved.

"Because your brother wanted you."

"For his sake you came for me?"

"Yes, Richard."

"Then, Rose, you — you love him still?"

"How can I help it, when he needs me more than ever?"

For a moment Richard's face changed terribly; then something seemed to gush warm across his heart, sending a generous glow to cheek and forehead, banishing the despair from his eyes, and lending to his voice a heartiness unheard before.

"Forgive me, Rose; you are a nobler woman than I thought you. He does need you more than ever; give him your whole heart, and help me to make his hard life happy."

"I will — God bless my brother Rick!" and, bending, Rose kissed him softly on the forehead, the only token that ever betrayed her knowledge of his love, the only atonement she had it in her power to make him for his loss.

Richard held the beautiful, beloved face close to his own an instant, then turned his head away, and Rose heard one strong, deep sob, but never any word of lamentation or reproach. Too much moved to speak, yet too full of sympathy to leave him, she leaned her head upon the arm of the cushioned chair in which she sat, and soon forgot the lapse of time in thoughts both sweet and bitter. A light rustle and a faint perfume recalled her to the present; and looking, without moving, she saw Richard's almost transparent hand hold the dead rose in the flame of the lamp until its ashes fluttered to the ground; she saw him watch the last spark fade, and shiver as he glanced drearily about the room, as if all the warmth and beauty had died out of his life, leaving it very desolate and dark; she saw him turn toward her while his face grew clear and calm again, and, believing himself unseen, he lifted a little fold of her dress to his lips, as if he bade the woman whom he loved a long farewell; then he lay down like one spent with some sore struggle, which, though hardly fought, had been wholly won.

At that sight Rose's tears fell fast; and, long after Richard slept the sleep of utter weariness, she still sat there, with her head pillowed on her arms, keeping a vigil in which she consecrated her whole life to the service of that cause which, through many trials, had taught her a truer loyalty, a purer love.

In the ruddy glow of an October sunset, Rose led Richard across the threshold of the dear old home, and gave him to his mother's arms. At first, a joyful tumult reigned; then, as the wonder, gratitude, and joy subsided, all turned to Rose. She stood apart, silently receiving her reward; and, though worn and weary with her long labor, never had she seemed so beautiful as then; for the once proud eyes were grown sweetly humble, the serenity of a great content shone in her face, and a fine blending of gentleness and strength gave the crowning grace to one who was now, in truth, a "right noble woman."

The mother and her sons regarded her in silence for a moment, and silently she looked back at them with a glance, a gesture that said more eloquently than any words: "Forgive me, love me, and forget the past." Mrs. Stirling opened her arms, and Rose clung to that motherly bosom, feeling that no daughter could be dearer than she was now, that all her pain and penitence was known, and her reward secure at last.

"Rose, I have but one thing precious enough to give you in return for the great service you have so beautifully conferred upon me. If I read your heart aright, this is the prize for which you have striven and suffered; and, loving you the dearer for your constancy, I freely give one-half my treasure to your keeping, sure that you will find life richer, happier, and better for your devotion to the man you love."

Rose understood her,—felt that the mother wished to prove the woman's pride, the lover's truth,—and well she stood the test; for going straight to Robert, who had scarcely spoken, but whose eye had never left her since she came, she said, clearly and steadily,—too earnest for maiden shame, too humble for false pride, too hopeful for any fear, —

"Robert, you once said you would never ask either pity or love of me. Will you accept both when I offer them humbly, heartily, and tell you that all my happiness, my hopes, my peace, are now bound up in you?"

Poor Rob! he had no arms in which to receive her, no words wherewith to welcome her, for speech failed him when those tender eyes looked up into his own, and she so generously gave him the desire of his life. He only bowed his head before her, deliciously oppressed with the happiness this double gift conferred. Rose read his heart, and with a loving woman's skill robbed the moment of all its bitterness and left only its sweetness; for, putting both arms about his neck, she whispered like a pleading child, —

"Dear, let me stay; I am so happy here!"

There was but one answer to that appeal; and as it was given, Mrs. Stirling turned to beckon Richard from the room, glad to have him all her own again. He had already stolen out, and standing in the autumn sunshine, looked across the quiet river with a countenance as cheerful as the sunshine, as tranquil as the stream. His mother scanned his face with a searching yet sorrowful eye, that dimmed with sudden dew as, reading its signficance, her son met it with a glance that set her anxiety at rest.

"Have no fears for me, mother; I have fought my double fight, and am freed from my double captivity. The lost love is not dead, but sleeping, never to waken in this world, and its grave is growing green."

"Ah, my good son, the world will see Rob's sacrifice,

and honor him for it, but yours is the greater one, for through many temptations you have been loyal, both to your country and yourself. God and your mother love and honor you for that, although to other eyes you seem to stand forgotten and alone."

But Richard drew the gray head tenderly, reverently down upon his breast, and answered, with the cheerful smile unchanged, —

"Never alone while I have you, mother."

A MODERN CINDERELLA;

OR, THE LITTLE OLD SHOE.

HOW IT WAS LOST.

AMONG green New-England hills stood an ancient house, many-gabled, mossy-roofed, and quaintly built, but picturesque and pleasant to the eye; for a brook ran babbling through the orchard that encompassed it about, a garden-plot stretched upward to the whispering birches on the slope, and patriarchal elms stood sentinel upon the lawn, as they had stood almost a century ago, when the Revolution rolled that way and found them young.

One summer morning, when the air was full of country sounds,—of mowers in the meadow, blackbirds by the brook, and the low of cattle on the hill-side, the old house wore its cheeriest aspect, and a certain humble history began.

"Nan!"

"Yes, Di."

And a head, brown-locked, blue-eyed, soft-featured, looked in at the open door in answer to the call.

"Just bring me the third volume of 'Wilhelm Meister,' there's a dear. It's hardly worth while to rouse such a restless ghost as I, when I'm once fairly laid."

As she spoke, Di pushed up her black braids, thumped the pillow of the couch where she was lying, and with eager eyes went down the last page of her book.

"Nan!"

"Yes, Laura," replied the girl, coming back with the third volume for the literary cormorant, who took it with a nod, still too intent upon the "Confessions of a Fair Saint" to remember the failings of a certain plain sinner.

"Don't forget the Italian cream for dinner. I depend upon it; for it's the only thing fit for me this hot weather."

And Laura, the cool blonde, disposed the folds of her white gown more gracefully about her, and touched up the eyebrow of the Minerva she was drawing.

"Little daughter!"

"Yes, father."

"Let me have plenty of clean collars in my bag, for I must go at three; and some of you bring me a glass of cider in about an hour, — I shall be in the lower garden."

The old man went away into his imaginary paradise; and Nan into that domestic purgatory on a summer day, — the kitchen. There were vines about the windows, sunshine on the floor, and order everywhere; but it was haunted by a cooking-stove, that family altar whence such varied incense rises to appease the appetite of household gods, before which such dire incantations are pronounced to ease the wrath and woe of the priestess of the fire, and about which often linger saddest memories of wasted temper, time, and toil.

Nan was tired, having risen with the birds, hurried, having many cares those happy little housewives never know, and disappointed in a hope that hourly "dwindled, peaked, and pined." She was too young to make the anxious lines upon her forehead seem at home there, too patient to be burdened with the labor others should have shared, too light of heart to be pent up when earth and sky were keeping a blithe holiday. But she was one of that meek sisterhood who, thinking humbly of themselves, believe they are honored by being spent in the service of less conscientious souls, whose careless thanks seem quite reward enough.

To and fro she went, silent and diligent, giving the grace of willingness to every humble or distasteful task the day had brought her; but some malignant sprite seemed to have taken possession of her kingdom, for rebellion broke out everywhere. The kettles would boil over most obstreperously,—the mutton refused to cook with the meek alacrity to be expected from the nature of a sheep,—the stove, with unnecessary warmth of temper, would glow like a fiery furnace,—the irons would scorch,—the linens would dry,—and spirits would fail, though patience never.

Nan tugged on, growing hotter and wearier, more hurried and more hopeless, till at last the crisis came; for in one fell moment she tore her gown, burnt her hand, and smutched the collar she was preparing to finish in the most unexceptionable style. Then, if she had been a nervous woman, she would have scolded; being a gentle girl, she only "lifted up her voice and wept."

"Behold, she watereth her linen with salt tears, and bewaileth herself because of much tribulation. But, lo! help cometh from afar: a strong man bringeth lettuce wherewith to stay her, plucketh berries to comfort her withal, and clasheth cymbals that she may dance for joy."

The voice came from the porch, and, with her hope

fulfilled, Nan looked up to greet John Lord, the house-friend, who stood there with a basket on his arm; and as she saw his honest eyes, kind lips, and helpful hands, the girl thought this plain young man the comeliest, most welcome sight she had beheld that day.

"How good of you, to come through all this heat, and not to laugh at my despair!" she said, looking up like a grateful child, as she led him in.

"I only obeyed orders, Nan; for a certain dear old lady had a motherly presentiment that you had got into a domestic whirlpool, and sent me as a sort of life pre-server. So I took the basket of consolation, and came to fold my feet upon the carpet of contentment in the tent of friendship."

As he spoke, John gave his own gift in his mother's name, and bestowed himself in the wide window-seat, where morning-glories nodded at him, and the old butter-nut sent pleasant shadows dancing to and fro.

His advent, like that of Orpheus in Hades, seemed to soothe all unpropitious powers with a sudden spell. The fire began to slacken, the kettles began to lull, the meat began to cook, the irons began to cool, the clothes began to behave, the spirits began to rise, and the collar was finished off with most triumphant success. John watched the change, and, though a lord of creation, abased him-self to take compassion on the weaker vessel, and was seized with a great desire to lighten the homely tasks that tried her strength of body and soul. He took a com-prehensive glance about the room; then, extracting a dish from the closet, proceeded to imbrue his hands in the strawberries' blood.

"Oh, John you needn't do that; I shall have time

when I've turned the meat, made the pudding, and done these things. See, I'm getting on finely now,— you're a judge of such matters; isn't that nice?"

As she spoke, Nan offered the polished absurdity for inspection with innocent pride.

"Oh that I were a collar, to sit upon that hand!" sighed John; adding, argumentatively, "As to the berry question, I will merely say, that, as a matter of public safety, you'd better leave me alone; for such is the destructiveness of my nature, that I shall certainly eat something hurtful, break something valuable, or sit upon something crushable, unless you let me concentrate my energies by knocking off these young fellows' hats, and preparing them for their doom."

Looking at the matter in a charitable light, Nan consented, and went cheerfully on with her work, wondering how she could have thought ironing an infliction, and been so ungrateful for the blessings of her lot.

"Where's Sally?" asked John, looking vainly for the energetic functionary who usually pervaded that region like a domestic police-woman, a terror to cats, dogs, and men.

"She has gone to her cousin's funeral, and won't be back till Monday. There seems to be a great fatality among her relations, for one dies, or comes to grief in some way, about once a month. But I don't blame poor Sally for wanting to get away from this place now and then. I think I could find it in my heart to murder an imaginary friend or two, if I had to stay here long."

And Nan laughed so blithely, it was a pleasure to hear her.

"Where's Di?" asked John, seized with a most unmasculine curiosity all at once.

"She is in Germany, with 'Wilhelm Meister,' but, though 'lost to sight, to memory dear'; for I was just thinking, as I did her things, how clever she is to like all kinds of books that I don't understand at all, and to write things that make me cry with pride and delight. Yes, she's a talented dear, though she hardly knows a needle from a crow-bar, and will make herself one great blot some of these days, when the 'divine afflatus' descends upon her, I'm afraid."

And Nan rubbed away with sisterly zeal at Di's forlorn hose and inky pocket-handkerchiefs.

"Where is Laura?" proceeded the inquisitor.

"Well, I might say that *she* was in Italy; for she is copying some fine thing of Raphael's, or Michael Angelo's, or some great creature's or other; and she looks so picturesque in her pretty gown, sitting before her easel, that it's really a sight to behold, and I've peeped two or three times to see how she gets on."

And Nan bestirred herself to prepare the dish wherewith her picturesque sister desired to prolong her artistic existence.

"Where is your father?" John asked again, checking off each answer with a nod and a little frown.

"He is down in the garden, deep in some plan about melons, the beginning of which seems to consist in stamping the first proposition in Euclid all over the bed, and then poking a few seeds into the middle of each. Why, bless the dear man! I forgot it was time for the cider. Wouldn't you like to take it to him, John? He'd love to consult you; and the lane is so cool, it does one's heart good to look at it."

John glanced from the steamy kitchen to the shadowy

path, and answered, with a sudden assumption of immense industry, —

"I couldn't possibly go, Nan, I've so much on my hands. You'll have to do it yourself. 'Mr. Robert of Lincoln' has something for your private ear; and the lane is so cool, it will do one's heart good to see you in it. Give my regards to your father, and, in the words of 'Little Mabel's' mother, with slight variations, —

> 'Tell the dear old body
> This day I cannot run,
> For the pots are boiling over
> And the mutton isn't done.'"

"I will; but please, John, go in to the girls and be comfortable; for I don't like to leave you here," said Nan.

"You insinuate that I should pick at the pudding or skim the cream, do you? Ungrateful girl, leave me!" And, with melodramatic sternness, John extinguished her in his broad-brimmed hat, and offered the glass like a poisoned goblet.

Nan took it, and went smiling away. But the lane might have been the Desert of Sahara, for all she knew of it; and she would have passed her father as unconcernedly as if he had been an apple-tree, had he not called out, —

"Stand and deliver, little woman!"

She obeyed the venerable highwayman, and followed him to and fro, listening to his plans and directions with a mute attention that quite won his heart.

"That hop-pole is really an ornament now, Nan; this sage-bed needs weeding, — that's good work for you girls;

and, now I think of it, you'd better water the lettuce in the cool of the evening, after I'm gone."

To all of which remarks Nan gave her assent; though the hop-pole took the likeness of a tall figure she had seen in the porch, the sage-bed, curiously enough, suggested a strawberry ditto, the lettuce vividly reminded her of certain vegetable productions a basket had brought, and the bobolink only sung in his cheeriest voice, "Go home, go home! he is there!"

She found John, — having made a Freemason of himself, by assuming her little apron, — meditating over the partially spread table, lost in amaze at its desolate appearance; one-half its proper paraphernalia having been forgotten, and the other half put on awry. Nan laughed till the tears ran over her cheeks, and John was gratified at the efficacy of his treatment; for her face had brought a whole harvest of sunshine from the garden, and all her cares seemed to have been lost in the windings of the lane.

"Nan, are you in hysterics?" cried Di, appearing, book in hand. "John, you absurd man, what are you doing?"

"I'm helpin' the maid-of-all-work, please marm." And John dropped a courtesy with his limited apron.

Di looked ruffled, for the merry words were a covert reproach; and with her usual energy of manner and freedom of speech she tossed "Wilhelm" out of the window, exclaiming, irefully, —

"That's always the way; I'm never where I ought to be, and never think of anything till it's too late; but it's all Goethe's fault. What does he write books full of smart 'Phillinas' and interesting 'Meisters' for? How can I be expected to remember that Sally's away, and people must eat, when I'm hearing the 'Harper' and Little 'Mignon'? John, how dare you come here and do my work, instead of shaking me and telling me to do it myself? Take that toasted child away, and fan her like a Chinese mandarin, while I dish up this dreadful dinner."

John and Nan fled like chaff before the wind, while Di, full of remorseful zeal, charged at the kettles, and wrenched off the potatoes' jackets, as if she were revengefully pulling her own hair. Laura had a vague intention of going to assist; but, getting lost among the lights and shadows of Minerva's helmet, forgot to appear till dinner had been evoked from chaos, and peace was restored.

At three o'clock, Di performed the coronation ceremony with her father's best hat; Laura retied his old-fashioned neck-cloth, and arranged his white locks with an eye to saintly effect; Nan appeared with a beautifully written sermon, and suspicious ink-stains on the fingers that slipped it into his pocket; John attached himself to the bag; and the patriarch was escorted to the door of his tent with the triumphal procession which usually attended his outgoings and incomings. Having kissed the female portion of his tribe, he ascended the venerable chariot, which received him with audible lamentation, as its rheumatic joints swayed to and fro.

"Good-by, my dears! I shall be back early on Monday morning; so take care of yourselves, and be sure you all go and hear Mr. Emerboy preach to-morrow. My regards to your mother, John. Come, Solon!"

But Solon merely cocked one ear, and remained a fixed fact; for long experience had induced the philosophic beast to take for his motto the Yankee maxim, "Be sure you're right, then go ahead!" He knew things were not right; therefore he did not go ahead.

"Oh, by the way, girls, don't forget to pay Tommy Mullein for bringing up the cow; he expects it to-night. And, Di, don't sit up till daylight, nor let Laura stay out in the dew. Now, I believe, I'm off. Come, Solon!"

But Solon only cocked the other ear, gently agitated his mortified tail, as premonitory symptoms of departure, and never stirred a hoof, being well aware that it always took three "comes" to make a "go."

"Bless me! I've forgotten my spectacles. They are probably shut up in that volume of Herbert on my table. Very awkward to find myself without them ten miles away. Thank you, John. Don't neglect to water the lettuce, Nan, and don't overwork yourself, my little 'Martha.' Come——"

At this juncture Solon suddenly went off at a trot, and the benign old pastor disappeared, humming "Hebron" to the creaking accompaniment of the bulgy chaise.

Laura retired to take her *siesta;* Nan made a small *carbonaro* of herself by sharpening her sister's crayons, and Di, as a sort of penance for past sins, tried her patience over a piece of knitting, in which she soon originated a somewhat remarkable pattern, by dropping every third stitch, and seaming *ad libitum*. If John had been a gentlemanly creature, with refined tastes, he would have elevated his feet, and made a nuisance of himself by indulging in a "weed"; but being only an uncultivated youth, with a rustic regard for pure air and womankind in general, he kept his head uppermost, and talked like a man, instead of smoking like a chimney.

"It will probably be six months before I sit here again, tangling your threads and maltreating your needles, Nan. How glad you must feel to hear it!" he said, looking up from a thoughtful examination of the hard-working little citizens of the Industrial Community settled in Nan's work-basket.

"No, I'm very sorry; for I like to see you coming and going as you used to, years ago, and I miss you very much when you are gone, John," answered truthful Nan, whittling away in a sadly wasteful manner, as her thoughts flew back to the happy times when a little lad rode a little lass in the big wheelbarrow, and never spilt his load, — when two brown heads bobbed daily side by side to school, and the favorite play was "Babes in the Wood," with Di for a somewhat peckish robin to cover the small martyrs with any vegetable substance that lay at hand. Nan sighed as she thought of these things, and John regarded the battered thimble on his finger-tip with increased benignity of aspect as he heard the sound.

"When are you going to make your fortune, John, and get out of that disagreeable hardware concern?" demanded Di, pausing after an exciting "round," and looking almost as much exhausted as if it had been a veritable pugilistic encounter.

"I intend to make it by plunging still deeper into 'that disagreeable hardware concern'; for, next year, if the world keeps rolling, and John Lord is alive, he will become a partner, and then — and then ——"

The color sprang up into the young man's cheek, his eyes looked out with a sudden light, and his hand seemed involuntarily to close, as if he saw and seized some invisible delight.

"What will happen then, John?" asked Nan, with a wondering glance.

"I'll tell you in a year, Nan, — wait till then." And John's strong hand unclosed, as if the desired good were not to be his yet.

Di looked at him, with a knitting-needle stuck into her hair, saying, like a sarcastic unicorn, —

"I really thought you had a soul above pots and kettles, but I see you haven't; and I beg your pardon for the injustice I have done you."

Not a whit disturbed, John smiled, as if at some mighty pleasant fancy of his own, as he replied, —

"Thank you, Di; and as a further proof of the utter depravity of my nature, let me tell you that I have the greatest possible respect for those articles of ironmongery. Some of the happiest hours of my life have been spent in their society; some of my pleasantest associations are connected with them; some of my best lessons have come to me from among them; and when my fortune is made, I intend to show my gratitude by taking three flat-irons rampant for my coat-of-arms."

Nan laughed merrily, as she looked at the burns on her hand; but Di elevated the most prominent feature of her brown countenance, and sighed despondingly, —

"Dear, dear, what a disappointing world this is! I no sooner build a nice castle in Spain, and settle a smart young knight therein, than down it comes about my ears; and the ungrateful youth, who might fight dragons if he chose, insists on quenching his energies in a saucepan, and wasting his life on a series of gridirons. Ah, if *I* were a man, I would do something better than that, and prove that heroes are not all dead yet. But, instead of that, I'm only a woman, and must sit rasping my temper with absurdities like this." And Di wrestled with her knitting as if it were Fate, and she were paying off the grudge she owed it.

John leaned toward her, saying, with a look that made his plain face handsome, —

"Di, my father began the world as I begin it, and left it the richer for the useful years he spent here, — as I hope I may leave it some half-century hence. His memory makes that dingy shop a pleasant place to me; for there he made an honest name, led an honest life, and bequeathed to me his reverence for honest work. That is a sort of hardware, Di, that no rust can corrupt, and which will always prove a better fortune than any your knights can win with sword and shield. I think I am not quite a clod, or quite without some aspirations above money-getting; for I have a great ambition to become as good a man, and leave as green a memory behind me, as old John Lord."

Di winked violently, and seamed five times in perfect silence; but quiet Nan had the gift of knowing when to speak, and by a timely word saved her sister from a thunder-shower and her stocking from destruction.

"John, have you seen Philip since you wrote about your last meeting with him?"

The question was for John, but the soothing tone was for Di, who gratefully accepted it, and perked up again with speed.

"Yes; and I meant to have told you about it," answered John, plunging into the subject at once. "I saw him a few days before I came home, and found him more disconsolate than ever, — 'just ready to go to the deuce,' as he forcibly expressed himself. I consoled the poor lad as well as I could, telling him his wisest plan was to defer his proposed expedition, and go on as steadily as he had begun, — thereby proving the injustice of your father's prediction concerning his want of perseverance, and the sincerity of his affection. I told him the change in Laura's health and spirits was silently working in his favor, and that a few more months of persistent endeavor would conquer your father's prejudice against him, and make him a stronger man for the trial and the pain. I read him bits about Laura from your own and Di's letters, and he went away, at last, as patient as Jacob, ready to serve another 'seven years' for his beloved Rachel."

"God bless you for it, John!" cried a fervent voice; and, looking up, they saw the cold, listless Laura transformed into a tender girl, all aglow with love and longing, as she dropped her mask, and showed a living countenance eloquent with the first passion and softened by the first grief of her life.

John rose involuntarily in the presence of an innocent nature whose sorrow needed no interpreter to him. The girl read sympathy in his brotherly regard, and found comfort in the friendly voice that asked, half playfully, half seriously, —

"Shall I tell him that he is not forgotten, even for an Apollo? that Laura the artist has not conquered Laura the woman? and predict that the good daughter will yet prove the happy wife?"

With a gesture full of energy, Laura tore her Minerva from top to bottom, while two great tears rolled down the cheeks grown pale with hope deferred.

"Tell him I believe all things, hope all things, and that I never can forget."

Nan went to her and held her close, leaving the prints of two loving, but grimy hands upon her shoulders; Di looked on approvingly, for, though rather stony-hearted regarding the cause, she fully appreciated the effect; and John, turning to the window, received the commendations of a robin swaying on an elm-bough, with sunshine on its ruddy breast.

The clock struck five, and John declared that he must go; for, being an old-fashioned soul, he fancied that his mother had a better right to his last hour than any younger woman in the land, — always remembering that "she was a widow, and he her only son."

Nan ran away to wash her hands, and came back with the appearance of one who had washed her face also, — and so she had, but there was a difference in the water.

"Play I'm your father, girls, and remember it will be six months before 'that John' will trouble you again."

With which preface the young man kissed his former playfellows as heartily as the boy had been wont to do, when stern parents banished him to distant schools, and three little maids bemoaned his fate. But times were changed now, for Di grew alarmingly rigid during the ceremony; Laura received the salute like a grateful queen; and Nan returned it with heart and eyes and tender lips, making such an improvement on the childish fashion of the thing, that John was moved to support his paternal character by softly echoing her father's words, — "Take care of yourself, my little 'Martha.'"

Then they all streamed after him along the garden-path, with the endless messages and warnings girls are so prone to give; and the young man, with a great softness at his heart, went away, as many another John has gone, feeling better for the companionship of innocent maidenhood, and stronger to wrestle with temptation, to wait, and hope, and work.

"Let's throw a shoe after him for luck, as dear old 'Mrs. Gummidge' did after 'David' and the 'willin' Barkis!' Quick, Nan! you always have old shoes on; toss one, and shout 'Good luck!'" cried Di, with one of her eccentric inspirations.

Nan tore off her shoe, and threw it far along the dusty road, with a sudden longing to become that auspicious article of apparel, that the omen might not fail.

Looking backward from the hill-top, John answered the meek shout cheerily, and took in the group with a lingering glance: Laura in the shadow of the elms, Di perched on the fence, and Nan leaning far over the gate, with her hand above her eyes and the sunshine touching her brown hair with gold. He waved his hat and turned away; but the music seemed to die out of the blackbird's song, and in all the summer landscape his eye saw nothing but the little figure at the gate.

"Bless and save us! here's a flock of people coming! My hair is in a toss, and Nan's without her shoe; run! fly, girls! or the Philistines will be upon us!" cried Di, tumbling off her perch in sudden alarm.

Three agitated young ladies, with flying draperies and countenances of mingled mirth and dismay, might have been seen precipitating themselves into a respectable mansion with unbecoming haste; but the squirrels were the only witnesses of this "vision of sudden flight," and, being used to ground-and-lofty tumbling, didn't mind it.

When the pedestrians passed, the door was decorously closed, and no one visible but a young man, who snatched something out of the road, and marched away again, whistling with more vigor of tone than accuracy of tune, — only that, and nothing more.

HOW IT WAS FOUND.

Summer ripened into autumn, and something fairer than

> "Sweet-peas and mignonette
> In Annie's garden grew."

Her nature was the counterpart of the hill-side grove, where as a child she had read her fairy tales, and now as a woman turned the first pages of a more wondrous legend still. Lifted above the many-gabled roof, yet not cut off from the echo of human speech, the little grove seemed a green sanctuary, fringed about with violets, and full of summer melody and bloom. Gentle creatures haunted it, and there was none to make afraid; wood-pigeons cooed and crickets chirped their shrill roundelays, anemones and lady-ferns looked up from the moss that kissed the wanderer's feet. Warm airs were all afloat, full of vernal odors for the grateful sense, silvery birches shimmered like spirits of the wood, larches gave their green tassels to the wind, and pines made airy music sweet and solemn, as they stood looking heavenward through veils of summer sunshine or shrouds of wintry snow. Nan never felt alone now in this charmed wood; for, when she came into its precincts, once so full of solitude, all things seemed to wear one shape; familiar eyes looked at her from the violets in the grass, familiar words sounded in the whisper of the leaves, and she grew conscious that an unseen influence filled the air with new delights, and touched earth and sky with a beauty never seen before. Slowly these May-flowers budded in her maiden heart, rosily they bloomed, and silently they waited till some lover of such lowly herbs should catch their fresh aroma, should brush away the fallen leaves, and lift them to the sun.

Though the eldest of the three, she had long been overtopped by the more aspiring girls. But, though she meekly yielded the reins of government, whenever they chose to drive, they were soon restored to her again; for Di fell into literature, and Laura into love. Thus engrossed, these two forgot many duties which even bluestockings and *innamoratas* are expected to perform, and slowly all the homely humdrum cares that housewives know became Nan's daily life, and she accepted it without a thought of discontent. Noiseless and cheerful as the sunshine, she went to and fro, doing the tasks that mothers do, but without a mother's sweet reward, holding fast the numberless slight threads that bind a household tenderly together, and making each day a beautiful success.

Di, being tired of running, riding, climbing, and boating, decided, at last, to let her body rest, and put her equally active mind through what classical collegians term " a course of sprouts." Having undertaken to read and know *everything*, she devoted herself to the task with great energy, going from Sue to Swedenborg with perfect impartiality, and having different authors as children have sundry distempers, being fractious while they lasted, but all the better for them when once over. Carlyle appeared like scarlet-fever, and raged violently for a time; for, being anything but a "passive bucket," Di became prophetic with Mahomet, belligerent with Cromwell, and made the French Revolution a veritable Reign of Terror to her family. Goethe and Schiller alternated like fever and ague; Mephistopheles became her hero, Joan of Arc her model, and she turned her black eyes red over Egmont and Wallenstein. A mild attack of Emerson followed, during which she was lost in a fog; and her sisters rejoiced inwardly when she emerged, informing them that

"The Sphinx was drowsy,
Her wings were furled."

Poor Di was floundering slowly to her proper place, but she splashed up a good deal of foam by getting out of her depth, and rather exhausted herself by trying to drink the ocean dry.

Laura, after the "midsummer night's dream" that often comes to girls of seventeen, woke up to find that youth and love were no match for age and common sense. Philip had been flying about the world like a thistle-down for five-and-twenty years, generous-hearted, frank, and kind, but with never an idea of the serious side of life in his handsome head. Great, therefore, were the wrath and dismay of the enamored thistle-down, when the father of his love mildly objected to seeing her begin the world in a balloon, with a very tender but very inexperienced aeronaut for a guide.

"Laura is too young to 'play house' yet, and you are too unstable to assume the part of lord and master, Philip. Go and prove that you have prudence, patience, energy, and enterprise, and I will give you my girl; but not before. I must seem cruel, that I may be truly kind; believe this, and let a little pain lead you to great happiness, or show you where you would have made a blunder."

The lovers listened, owned the truth of the old man's words, bewailed their fate, and — yielded: Laura for love of her father, Philip for love of her. He went away to build a firm foundation for his castle in the air, and Laura retired into an invisible convent, where she cast off the world, and regarded her sympathizing sisters through a grate of superior knowledge and unsharable grief. Like a devout nun, she worshipped "St. Philip," and firmly believed in his miraculous powers. She fancied that her woes set her apart from common cares, and slowly fell into a dreamy state, professing no interest in any mundane matter, but the art that first attracted Philip. Crayons, bread-crusts and gray paper became glorified in Laura's eyes; and her one pleasure was to sit before her easel, day after day, filling her portfolios with the faces he had once admired. Her sisters observed that every Bacchus, Piping Faun, or Dying Gladiator bore some likeness to a comely countenance that heathen god or hero never owned; and, seeing this, they privately rejoiced that she had found such solace for her grief.

Mrs. Lord's keen eye had read a certain newly-written page in her son's heart, — his first chapter of that romance, begun in Paradise, whose interest never flags, whose beauty never fades, whose end can never come till Love lies dead. With womanly skill she divined the secret, with motherly discretion she counselled patience, and her son accepted her advice, feeling that, like many a healthful herb, its worth lay in its bitterness.

"Love like a man, John, not like a boy, and learn to know yourself before you take a woman's happiness into your keeping. You and Nan have known each other all your lives; yet, till this last visit, you never thought you loved her more than any other childish friend. It is too soon to say the words so often spoken hastily — so hard to be recalled. Go back to your work, dear, for another year; think of Nan in the light of this new hope; compare her with comelier, gayer girls; and by absence prove the truth of your belief. Then, if distance only makes her dearer, if time only strengthens your affection, and no doubt of your own worthiness disturbs you, come back and offer her what any woman should be glad to take, — my boy's true heart."

John smiled at the motherly pride of her words, but answered, with a wistful look, —

"It seems very long to wait, mother. If I could just ask her for a word of hope, I could be very patient then."

"Ah, my dear, better bear one year of impatience now than a lifetime of regret hereafter. Nan is happy; why disturb her by a word which will bring the tender cares and troubles that come soon enough to such conscientious creatures as herself? If she loves you, time will prove it; therefore, let the new affection spring and ripen as your early friendship has done, and it will be all the stronger for a summer's growth. Philip was rash, and has to bear his trial now, and Laura shares it with him. Be more generous, John; make *your* trial, bear *your* doubts alone, and give Nan the happiness without the pain. Promise me this, dear, — promise me to hope and wait."

The young man's eye kindled, and in his heart there rose a better chivalry, a truer valor, than any Di's knights had ever known.

"I'll try, mother," was all he said; but she was satisfied, for John seldom tried in vain.

"Oh, girls, how splendid you are! It does my heart good to see my handsome sisters in their best array," cried Nan, one mild October night, as she put the last touches to certain airy raiment fashioned by her own skilful hands, and then fell back to survey the grand effect.

Di and Laura were preparing to assist at an "event of the season," and Nan, with her own locks fallen on her shoulders for want of sundry combs promoted to her sisters' heads, and her dress in unwonted disorder for lack of the many pins extracted in exciting crises of the toilet, hovered like an affectionate bee about two very full-blown flowers.

"Laura looks like a cool Undine, with the ivy-wreaths in her shining hair; and Di has illuminated herself to such an extent with those scarlet leaves, that I don't know what great creature she resembles most," said Nan, beaming with sisterly admiration.

"Juno, Zenobia and Cleopatra simmered into one, with a touch of Xantippe, by way of spice. But, to my eye, the finest woman of the three is the dishevelled young person embracing the bed-post; for she stays at home herself, and gives her time and taste to making homely people fine. — which is a waste of good material, and an imposition on the public."

As Di spoke, both the fashion-plates looked affectionately at the gray-gowned figure; but, being works of art, they were obliged to nip their feelings in the bud, and reserve their caresses till they returned to common life.

"Put on your bonnet, and we'll leave you at Mrs. Lord's on our way. It will do you good, Nan; and perhaps there may be news from John," added Di, as she bore down upon the door like a man-of-war under full sail.

"Or from Philip," sighed Laura, with a wistful look.

Whereupon Nan persuaded herself that her strong inclination to sit down was owing to want of exercise, and the heaviness of her eyelids a freak of imagination; so, speedily smoothing her ruffled plumage, she ran down to tell her father of the new arrangement.

"Go, my dear, by all means. I shall be writing, and you will be lonely if you stay. But I must see my girls; for I caught glimpses of certain surprising phantoms flitting by the door."

Nan led the way, and the two pyramids revolved before him with the rigidity of lay-figures, much to the good man's edification; for with his fatherly pleasure there was mingled much mild wonderment at the amplitude of array.

"Yes, I see my geese are really swans, though there is such a cloud between us that I feel a long way off, and hardly know them. But this little daughter is always available, always my 'cricket on the hearth.'"

As he spoke, her father drew Nan closer, kissed her tranquil face, and smiled content.

"Well, if ever I see picters, I see 'em now, and I declare to goodness it's as interestin' as play-actin', every bit. Miss Di, with all them boughs in her head, looks like the Queen of Sheby, when she went a-visitin' What's-his-name, and if Miss Laura ain't as sweet as a lallybarster figger, I should like to know what is."

In her enthusiasm, Sally gambolled about the girls, flourishing her milk-pan as if about to sound her timbrel for excess of joy.

Laughing merrily, the two girls bestowed themselves in the family ark, Nan got up beside Patrick, and Solon, roused from his slumbers, morosely trundled them away. But, looking backward with a last "Good-night!" Nan saw her father still standing at the door with smiling countenance, and the moonlight falling like a benediction on his silver hair.

"Betsey shall go up the hill with you, my dear, and here's a basket of eggs for your father. Give him my love, and be sure you let me know the next time he is poorly," Mrs. Lord said, when her guest rose to depart, after an hour of pleasant chat.

But Nan never got the gift; for, to her great dismay, her hostess dropped the basket with a crash, and flew across the room to meet a tall figure pausing in the shadow of the door. There was no need to ask who the new-comer was; for, even in his mother's arms, John looked over her shoulder with an eager nod to Nan, who stood among the ruins with never a sign of weariness in her face, nor the memory of a care at her heart, — for they all went out when John came in.

"Now tell us how, and why, and when you came. Take off your coat, my dear! And here are the old slippers. Why didn't you let us know you were coming so soon? How have you been? and what makes you so late to-night? Betsey, you needn't put on your bonnet. And — oh, my dear boy, *have* you been to supper yet?"

Mrs. Lord was a quiet soul, and her flood of questions was purred softly in her son's ear; for, being a woman, she *must* talk, and, being a mother, *must* pet the one delight of her life, and make a little festival when the lord of the manor came home. A whole drove of fatted calves were metaphorically killed, and a banquet appeared with speed. John was not one of those romantic heroes who can go through three volumes of hair-breadth escapes without the faintest hint of that blessed institution, dinner; therefore, he partook copiously of everything, while the two women beamed over each mouthful with an interest that enhanced its flavor, and urged upon him cold meat and cheese, pickles and pie, as if dyspepsia and nightmare were among the lost arts.

Then he opened his budget of news and fed *them*.

"I was coming next month, according to custom; but Philip fell upon and so tempted me, that I was driven to sacrifice myself to the cause of friendship, and up we came to-night. He would not let me come here till we had seen your father, Nan; for the poor lad was pining for Laura, and hoped his good behavior for the past year would satisfy his judge and secure his recall. We had a fine talk with your father; and, upon my life, Phil seemed to have received the gift of tongues, for he made a most eloquent plea, which I've stowed away for future use, I assure you. The dear old gentleman was very kind, told Phil he was satisfied with the success of his probation, that he should see Laura when he liked, and, if all went well, should receive his reward in the spring. It must be a delightful sensation to know you have made a fellow-creature as happy as those words made Phil to-night."

John paused, and looked musingly at the matronly tea-pot, as if he saw a wondrous future in its shine.

Nan twinkled off the drops that rose at the thought of Laura's joy, and said, with grateful warmth, —

"You say nothing of your own share in the making of that happiness, John; but we know it, for Philip has told Laura in his letters all that you have been to him, and I am sure there was other eloquence beside his own before father granted all you say he has. Oh, John, I thank you very much for this!"

Mrs. Lord beamed a whole midsummer of delight upon her son, as she saw the pleasure these words gave him, though he answered simply, —

"I only tried to be a brother to him, Nan; for he has been most kind to me. Yes, I said my little say to-night, and gave my testimony in behalf of the prisoner at the bar, a most merciful judge pronounced his sentence, and he rushed straight to Mrs. Leigh's to tell Laura the blissful news. Just imagine the scene when he appears, and how Di will open her wicked eyes and enjoy the spectacle of the ardent lover, the bride-elect's tears, the stir, and the romance of the thing. She'll cry over it to-night, and caricature it to-morrow."

And John led the laugh at the picture he had conjured up, to turn the thoughts of Di's dangerous sister from himself.

At ten Nan retired into the depths of her old bonnet

with a far different face from the one she brought out of
it, and John, resuming his hat, mounted guard.

"Don't stay late, remember, John!" And in Mrs.
Lord's voice there was a warning tone that her son interpreted aright.

"I'll not forget, mother."

And he kept his word; for though Philip's happiness
floated temptingly before him, and the little figure at his
side had never seemed so dear, he ignored the bland
winds, the tender night, and set a seal upon his lips,
thinking manfully within himself, " I see many signs of
promise in her happy face; but I will wait and hope a
little longer for her sake."

"Where is father, Sally?" asked Nan, as that functionary appeared, blinking owlishly, but utterly repudiating the idea of sleep.

"He went down the garding, miss, when the gentlemen cleared, bein' a little flustered by the goin's on.
Shall I fetch him in?" asked Sally, as irreverently as if
her master were a bag of meal.

"No, we will go ourselves." And slowly the two
paced down the leaf-strewn walk.

Fields of yellow grain were waving on the hill-side,
and sere corn-blades rustled in the wind; from the orchard
came the scent of ripening fruit, and all the garden-plots
lay ready to yield up their humble offerings to their master's hand. But in the silence of the night a greater
Reaper had passed by, gathering in the harvest of a
righteous life, and leaving only tender memories for the
gleaners who had come so late.

The old man sat in the shadow of the tree his own

hands planted; its fruitful boughs shone ruddily, and its leaves still whispered the low lullaby that hushed him to his rest.

"How fast he sleeps! Poor father! I should have come before and made it pleasant for him."

As she spoke, Nan lifted up the head bent down upon his breast, and kissed his pallid cheek.

"Oh, John, this is not sleep!"

"Yes, dear, the happiest he will ever know."

For a moment the shadows flickered over three white faces, and the silence deepened solemnly. Then John reverently bore the pale shape in, and Nan dropped down beside it, saying, with a rain of grateful tears, —

"He kissed me when I went, and said a last 'good-night!'"

For an hour steps went to and fro about her, many voices whispered near her, and skilful hands touched the beloved clay she held so fast; but one by one the busy feet passed out, one by one the voices died away, and human skill proved vain. Then Mrs. Lord drew the orphan to the shelter of her arms, soothing her with the mute solace of that motherly embrace.

"Yes, we are poorer than we thought; but when everything is settled, we shall get on very well. We can let a part of this great house, and live quietly together until spring; then Laura will be married, and Di can go on their travels with them, as Philip wishes her to do. We shall be cared for; so never fear for us, John."

Nan said this, as her friend parted from her a week later, after the saddest holiday he had ever known.

"And what becomes of you, Nan?" he asked, watching the patient eyes that smiled when others would have wept.

"I shall stay in the dear old house; for no other place would seem like home to me. I shall find some little child to love and care for, and be quite happy till the girls come back and want me."

John nodded wisely, as he listened, and went away prophesying within himself, —

"She shall find something more than a child to love; and, God willing, shall be very happy till the girls come home and — cannot have her."

Nan's plan was carried into effect. Slowly the divided waters closed again, and the three fell back into their old life. But the touch of sorrow drew them closer; and, though invisible, a beloved presence still moved among them, a familiar voice still spoke to them in the silence of their softened hearts. Thus the soil was made ready, and in the depth of winter the good seed was sown, was watered with many tears, and soon sprang up green with the promise of a harvest for their after years.

Di and Laura consoled themselves with their favorite employments, unconscious that Nan was growing paler, thinner, and more silent, as the weeks went by, till one day she dropped quietly before them, and it suddenly became manifest that she was utterly worn out with many cares, and the secret suffering of a tender heart bereft of the paternal love which had been its strength and stay.

"I'm only tired, dear girls. Don't be troubled, for I

shall be up to-morrow," she said cheerily, as she looked into the anxious faces bending over her.

But the weariness was of many months' growth, and it was weeks before that "to-morrow" came.

Laura installed herself as nurse, and her devotion was repaid fourfold; for, sitting at her sister's bedside, she learned a finer art than that she had left. Her eye grew clear to see the beauty of a self-denying life, and in the depths of Nan's meek nature she found the strong, sweet virtues that made her what she was.

Then remembering that these womanly attributes were a bride's best dowry, Laura gave herself to their attainment, that she might become to another household the blessing Nan had been to her own; and turning from the worship of the goddess Beauty, she gave her hand to that humbler and more human teacher, Duty, — learning her lessons with a willing heart, for Philip's sake.

Di corked her inkstand, locked her bookcase, and went at housework as if it were a five-barred gate; of course she missed the leap, but scrambled bravely through, and appeared much sobered by the exercise. Sally had departed to sit under a vine and fig-tree of her own, so Di had undisputed sway; but if dish-pans and dusters had tongues, direful would have been the history of that crusade against frost and fire, indolence and inexperience. But they were dumb, and Di scorned to complain, though her struggles were pathetic to behold, and her sisters went through a series of messes equal to a course of "Prince Bedreddin's" peppery tarts. Reality turned Romance out of doors; for, unlike her favorite heroines in satin and tears, or helmet and shield, Di met her fate in a big checked apron and dust-cap wonderful to see;

yet she wielded her broom as stoutly as "Moll Flanders" shouldered her gun, and marched to her daily martyrdom in the kitchen with as heroic a heart as the "Maid of Orleans" took to *her* stake.

Mind won the victory over matter in the end, and Di was better all her days for the tribulations and the triumphs of that time; for she drowned her idle fancies in her wash-tub, made burnt-offerings of selfishness and pride, and learned the worth of self-denial, as she sang with happy voice among the pots and kettles of her conquered realm.

Nan thought of John; and in the stillness of her sleepless nights prayed Heaven to keep him safe, and make her worthy to receive, and strong enough to bear, the blessedness or pain of love.

Snow fell without, and keen winds howled among the leafless elms, but "herbs of grace" were blooming beautifully in the sunshine of sincere endeavor, and this dreariest season proved the most fruitful of the year; for love taught Laura, labor chastened Di, and patience fitted Nan for the blessing of her life.

Nature, that stillest yet most diligent of housewives, began at last that "spring-cleaning" which she makes so pleasant that none find the heart to grumble as they do when other matrons set their premises a-dust. Her handmaids, wind and rain and sun, swept, washed, and garnished busily, green carpets were unrolled, apple-boughs were hung with draperies of bloom, and dandelions, pet nurslings of the year, came out to play upon the sward.

From the South returned that opera troupe whose manager is never in despair, whose tenor never sulks, whose prima donna never fails, and in the orchard *bona fide matinées* were held, to which buttercups and clovers crowded in their prettiest spring hats, and verdant young blades twinkled their dewy lorgnettes, as they bowed and made way for the floral belles.

May was bidding June good-morrow, and the roses were just dreaming that it was almost time to wake, when John came again into the quiet room which now seemed the Eden that contained his Eve. Of course there was a jubilee; but something seemed to have befallen the whole group, for never had they all appeared in such odd frames of mind.

John was restless, and wore an excited look, most unlike his usual serenity of aspect. Nan the cheerful had fallen into a well of silence, and was not to be extracted by any hydraulic power, though she smiled like the June sky over her head. Di's peculiarities were out in full force, and she looked as if she would go off like a torpedo at a touch; but through all her moods there was a half-triumphant, half-remorseful expression in the glance she fixed on John. And Laura, once so silent, now sang like a blackbird, as she flitted to and fro; but her fitful song was always, "Philip, my king."

John felt that there had come a change upon the three, and silently divined whose unconscious influence had wrought the miracle. The embargo was off his tongue, and he was in a fever to ask that question which brings a flutter to the stoutest heart; but though the "man" had come, the "hour" had not. So, by way of steadying his nerves, he paced the room, pausing often to take notes of his companions, and each pause seemed to increase his wonder and content.

He looked at Nan. She was in her usual place, the shabby little chair she loved, because it once was large enough to hold a curly-headed playmate and herself. The old work-basket was at her side, and the battered thimble busily at work; but her lips wore a smile they had never worn before, the color of the unblown roses touched her cheek, and her downcast eyes were full of light.

He looked at Di. The inevitable book was on her knee, but its leaves were uncut; the strong-minded knob of hair still asserted its supremacy aloft upon her head, and the triangular jacket still adorned her shoulders in defiance of all fashions, past, present, or to come; but the expression of her brown countenance had grown softer, her tongue had found a curb, and in her hand lay a card with "Potts, Kettel & Co." inscribed thereon, which she regarded with never a scornful word for the "Co."

He looked at Laura. She was before her easel, as of old; but the pale nun had given place to a blooming girl, who sang at her work, which was no prim Pallas, but a Clytie turning her human face to meet the sun.

"John, what are you thinking of?"

He stirred as if Di's voice had disturbed his fancy at some pleasant pastime, but answered with his usual sincerity, —

"I was thinking of a certain dear old fairy tale, called 'Cinderella.'"

"Oh!" said Di; and her "Oh" was a most impressive monosyllable. "I see the meaning of your smile now; and, though the application of the story is not very complimentary to all parties concerned, it is very just and very true."

She paused a moment, then went on with softened voice and earnest face, —

"You think I am a blind and selfish creature. So I am, but not so blind and selfish as I have been; for many tears have cleared my eyes, and sincere regret has made me humbler than I was. I have found a better book than any father's library can give me, and I have read it with a love and admiration that grew stronger as I turned the leaves. Henceforth I take it for my guide and gospel, and, looking back upon the selfish and neglectful past, can only say, Heaven bless your dear heart, Nan!"

Laura echoed Di's last words; for, with eyes as full of tenderness, she looked down upon the sister she had lately learned to know, saying, warmly, —

"Yes, 'Heaven bless your dear heart, Nan!' I never can forget all you have been to me; and when I am far away with Philip, there will always be one countenance more beautiful to me than any pictured face I may discover, there will be one place more dear to me than Rome. The face will be yours, Nan, — always so patient, always so serene; and the dearer place will be this home of ours, which you have made so pleasant to me all these years by kindnesses as numberless and noiseless as the drops of dew."

"Why, girls, what have I ever done, that you should love me so?" cried Nan, with happy wonderment, as the tall heads, black and golden, bent to meet the lowly brown one; and her sisters' mute lips answered her.

Then Laura looked up, saying, playfully, —

"Here are the good and wicked sisters; where shall we find the Prince?"

"There!" cried Di, pointing to John; and then her secret went off like a rocket; for, with her old impetuosity, she said, —

"I have found you out, John, and am ashamed to look you in the face, remembering the past. Girls, you know, when father died, John sent us money, which he said Mr. Owen had long owed us, and had paid at last! It was a kind lie, John, and a generous thing to do; for we needed it, but never would have taken it as a gift. I know you meant that we should never find this out; but yesterday I met Mr. Owen returning from the West, and when I thanked him for a piece of justice we had not expected of him, he gruffly told me he had never paid the debt, never meant to pay it, for it was outlawed, and we could not claim a farthing. John, I have laughed at you, thought you stupid, treated you unkindly; but I know you now, and never shall forget the lesson you have taught me. I am proud as Lucifer, but I ask you to forgive me, and I seal my real repentance so — and so!"

With tragic countenance, Di rushed across the room, threw both arms about the astonished young man's neck, and dropped an energetic kiss upon his cheek. There was a momentary silence; for Di finely illustrated her strong-minded theories by crying like the weakest of her sex. Laura, with "the ruling passion strong in death," still tried to draw, but broke her pet crayon, and endowed her Clytie with a supplementary orb, owing to the dimness of her own. And Nan sat, with drooping eyes that shone upon her work, thinking, with tender pride, —

"They know him now, and love him for his generous heart."

Di spoke first, rallying to her colors, though a little daunted by her loss of self-control:

"Don't laugh, John — I couldn't help it; and don't think I'm not sincere, for I am, — I am! and I will prove it by growing good enough to be your friend. That debt must all be paid, and I shall do it; for I'll turn my books and pen to some account, and write stories full of dear old souls like you and Nan; and some one, I know, will like and buy them, though they are not 'works of Shakspeare.' I've thought of this before, have felt I had the power in me; *now* I have the motive, and *now* I'll do it."

If Di had proposed to translate the Koran, or build a new Saint Paul's, there would have been many chances of success; for, once moved, her will, like a battering-ram, would knock down the obstacles her wits could not surmount. John believed in her most heartily, and showed it, as he answered, looking into her resolute face, —

"I know you will, and yet make us very proud of our Di. Let the money lie, and when you have made a fortune, I'll claim it with enormous interest; but, believe me, I feel already doubly repaid by the esteem so generously confessed, so cordially bestowed, and can only say, as we used to years ago, — 'Now let's forgive and forget.'"

But proud Di would not let him add to her obligation, even by returning her impetuous salute; she slipped away, and, shaking off the last drops, answered, with a curious mixture of old freedom and new respect, —

"No more sentiment, please, John. We know each other now; and when I find a friend, I never let him go.

We have smoked the pipe of peace; so let us go back to our wigwams and bury the hatchet. Where were we when I lost my head? and what were we talking about?"

"Cinderella and the Prince."

As he spoke, John's eye kindled, and, turning, he looked down at Nan, who sat diligently ornamenting with microscopic stitches a great patch going on, the wrong side out.

"Yes,—so we were; and now, taking pussy for the godmother, the characters of the story are well personated—all but the slipper," said Di, laughing, as she thought of the many times they had played it together years ago.

A sudden warmth stirred John's heart, a sudden purpose shone in his countenance, and a sudden change befell his voice, as he said, producing from some hiding-place a little worn-out shoe,—

"I can supply the slipper;—who will try it first?"

Di's black eyes opened wide, as they fell on the familiar object; then her romance-loving nature saw the whole plot of that drama which needs but two to act it. A great delight flushed up into her face, as she promptly took her cue, saying,—

"No need for us to try it, Laura; for it wouldn't fit us, if our feet were as small as Chinese dolls';—our parts are played out; therefore, 'Exeunt wicked sisters to the music of the wedding-bells.'" And pouncing upon the dismayed artist, she swept her out, and closed the door with a triumphant bang.

John went to Nan, and, dropping on his knee as reverently as the herald of the fairy tale, he asked, still smiling, but with lips grown tremulous.—

"Will Cinderella try the little shoe, and, — if it fits, — go with the Prince?"

But Nan only covered up her face, weeping happy tears, while all the weary work strayed down upon the floor, as if it knew her holiday had come.

John drew the hidden face still closer; and, while she listened to his eager words, Nan heard the beating of the strong man's heart, and knew it spoke the truth.

"Nan, I promised mother to be silent till I was sure I loved you wholly, — sure that the knowledge would give no pain when I should tell it, as I am trying to tell it now. This little shoe has been my comforter through this long year, and I have kept it as other lovers keep their fairer favors. It has been a talisman more eloquent to me than flower or ring; for, when I saw how worn it was, I always thought of the willing feet that came and went for others' comfort all day long; when I saw the little bow you tied, I always thought of the hands so diligent in serving any one who knew a want or felt a pain; and when I recalled the gentle creature who had worn it last, I always saw her patient, tender, and devout, — and tried to grow more worthy of her, that I might one day dare to ask if she would walk beside me all my life, and be my 'angel in the house.' Will you, dear? Believe me, you shall never know a weariness or grief I have the power to shield you from."

Then Nan, as simple in her love as in her life, laid her arms about his neck, her happy face against his own, and answered softly, —

"Oh, John, I never can be sad or tired any more!"

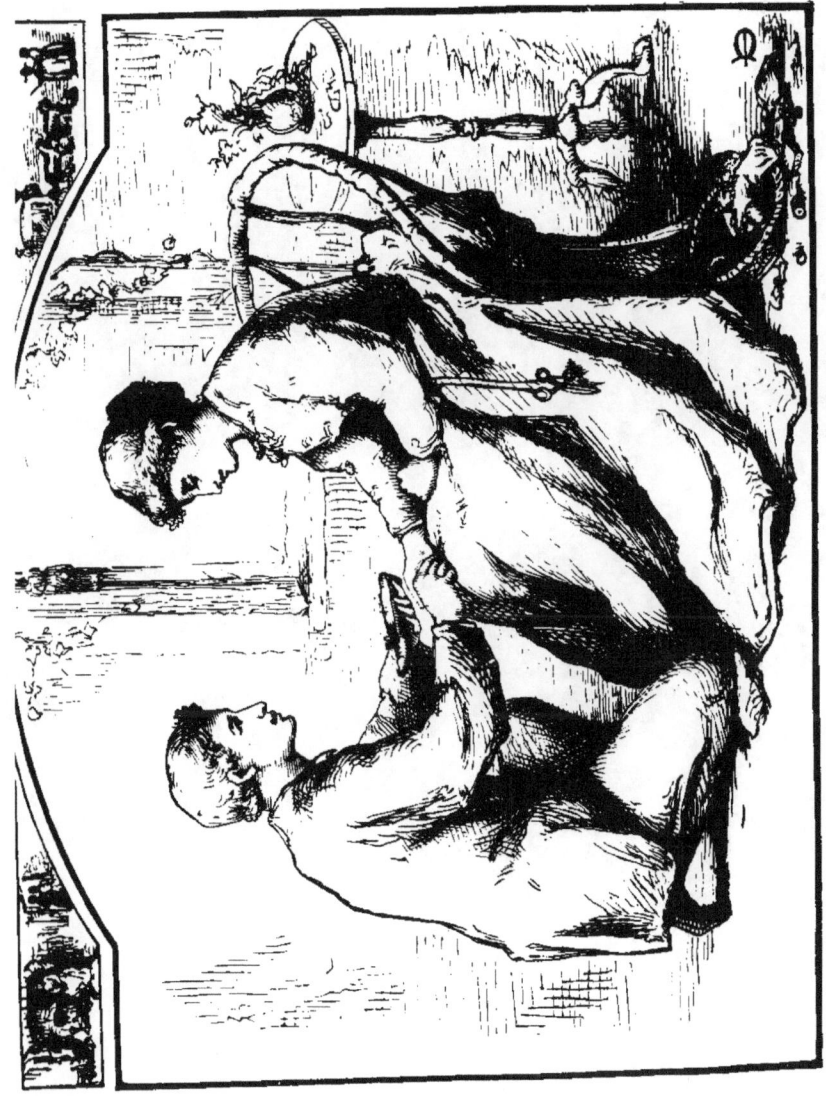

"Will Cinderella try the little shoe, and — if it fits — go with the Prince?" — PAGE 294

THE BLUE AND THE GRAY.

"DON'T bring him in here; every corner is full," said the nurse, eying with dismay the gaunt figure lying on the stretcher in the doorway.

"Where *shall* we put him, then? They can't have him in either of the other wards on this floor. He's ordered up here, and here he must stay, if he's put in the hall, poor devil!" said the foremost bearer, looking around the crowded room in despair.

The nurse's eye followed his, and both saw a thin hand beckoning from the end of the long ward.

"It's Murry; I'll see what he wants;" and Miss Mercy went to him with her quick, noiseless step, and the smile her grave face always wore for him.

"There's room here, if you turn my bed 'round, you see. Don't let them leave him in the hall," said Murry, lifting his great eyes to hers, brilliant with the fever burning his strength away, and pathetic with the silent protest of life against death.

"It's like you to think of it; he's a rebel," began Miss Mercy.

"So much more reason to take him in. I don't mind having him here; but it will distress me dreadfully to know that any poor soul was turned away, from the comfort of this ward especially."

The look he gave her made the words an eloquent compliment, and his pity for a fallen enemy reproached her for her own lack of it. Her face softened as she nodded, and glanced about the recess.

"You will have the light in your eyes, and only the little table between you and a very disagreeable neighbor," she said.

"I can shut my eyes if the light troubles them; I've nothing else to do now," he answered, with a faint laugh. "I was too comfortable before; I'd more than my share of luxuries; so bring him along, and it will be all right."

The order was given, and, after a brief bustle, the two narrow beds stood side by side in the recess under the organ-loft — for the hospital had been a church. Left alone for a moment, the two men eyed each other silently. Murry saw a tall, sallow man, with fierce black eyes, wild hair and beard, and a thin-lipped, cruel mouth. A ragged gray uniform was visible under the blanket thrown over him; and in strange contrast to the squalor of his dress, and the neglect of his person, was the diamond ring that shone on his unwounded hand. The right arm was bound up, the right leg amputated at the knee; and, though the man's face was white and haggard with suffering, not a sound escaped him as he lay with his eyes fixed half defiantly upon his neighbor.

John Clay, the new-comer, saw opposite him a small, wasted figure, and a plain face; yet both face and figure were singularly attractive, for suffering seemed to have refined away all the grosser elements, and left the spiritual very visible through that frail tenement of flesh. Pale-brown hair streaked the hollow temples and white forehead. A deep color burned in the thin cheeks still tanned by the wind and weather of a long campaign. The mouth was grave and sweet, and in the gray eyes lay an infinite patience touched with melancholy. He wore a dressing-gown, but across his feet lay a faded coat of army-blue. As the other watched him, he saw a shadow pass across his tranquil face, and for a moment he laid his wasted hand over the eyes that had been so full of pity. Then he gently pushed a mug of fresh water, and the last of a bunch of grapes, toward the exhausted rebel, saying, in a cordial tone, —

"You look faint and thirsty; have 'em."

Clay's lips were parched, and his hand went involuntarily toward the cup; but he caught it back, and, leaning forward, asked, in a shrill whisper, —

"Where are you hurt?"

"A shot in the side," answered Murry, visibly surprised at the man's manner.

"What battle?"

"The Wilderness."

"Is it bad?"

"I'm dying of wound-fever; there's no hope, they say."

That reply, so simple, so serenely given, would have touched almost any hearer; but Clay smiled grimly, and lay down as if satisfied, with his one hand clenched, and an exulting glitter in his eyes, muttering to himself, —

"The loss of my leg comes easier after hearing that."

Murry saw his lips move, but caught no sound, and asked, with friendly solicitude, —

"Do you want anything, neighbor?"

"Yes — to be let alone," was the curt reply, with a savage frown.

"That's easily done. I sha'n't trouble you very long,

any way;" and, with a sigh, Murry turned his face away, and lay silent till the surgeon came up on his morning round.

"Oh! you're here, are you? It's like Mercy Carrol to take you in," said Dr. Fitz Hugh, as he surveyed the rebel, with a slight frown; for, in spite of his benevolence and skill, he was a stanch loyalist, and hated the South just then.

"Don't praise me; he never would have been here but for Murry," answered Miss Mercy, as she approached, with her dressing-tray in her hand.

"Bless the lad! he'll give up his bed next, and feel offended if he's thanked for it. How are you, my good fellow?" and the doctor turned to press the hot hand, with a friendly face.

"Much easier and stronger, thank you, doctor," was the cheerful answer.

"Less fever, pulse better, breath freer — good symptoms. Keep on so for twenty-four hours, and, by my soul, I believe you'll have a chance for your life, Murry," cried the doctor, as his experienced eye took note of a hopeful change.

"In spite of the opinion of three good surgeons to the contrary?" asked Murry, with a wistful smile.

"Hang everybody's opinion! We are but mortal men, and the best of us make mistakes in spite of science and experience. There's Parker; we all gave him up, and the rascal is larking 'round Washington as well as ever to-day. While there's life there's hope; so cheer up my lad, and do your best for the little girl at home."

"Do you really think I may hope?" cried Murry, white with the joy of this unexpected reprieve.

"Hope is a capital medicine, and I prescribe it for a day at least. Don't build on this change too much, but if you are as well to-morrow as this morning, I give you my word I think you'll pull through."

Murry laid his hands over his face with a broken "Thank God for that!" and the doctor turned away with a sonorous "Hem!" and an air of intense satisfaction.

During this conversation Miss Mercy had been watching the rebel, who looked and listened to the others so intently that he forgot her presence. She saw an expression of rage and disappointment gather in his face as the doctor spoke; and when Murry accepted the hope held out to him, Clay set his teeth with an evil look, that would have boded ill for his neighbor had he not been helpless.

"Ungrateful traitor! I'll watch him, for he'll do mischief if he can," she thought, and reluctantly began to unbind his arm for the doctor's inspection.

"Only a flesh-wound, — no bones broken, — a good syringing, rubber cushion, plenty of water, and it will soon heal. You'll attend to that, Miss Mercy; this stump is more in my line;" and Dr. Fitz Hugh turned to the leg, leaving the arm to the nurse's skilful care.

"Evidently amputated in a hurry, and neglected since. If you're not careful, young man, you'll change places with your neighbor here."

"Damn him!" muttered Clay in his beard, with an emphasis which caused the doctor to glance at his vengeful face.

"Don't be a brute, if you can help it. But for him you'd have fared ill," began the doctor.

"But for him I never should have been here," muttered

the man, in French, with a furtive glance about the room.

"You owe this to him?" asked the doctor, touching the wound, and speaking in the same tongue.

"Yes; but he paid for it — at least, I thought he had."

"By the Lord! if you are the sneaking rascal that shot him as he lay wounded in the ambulance, I shall be tempted to leave you to your fate!" cried the doctor, with a wrathful flash in his keen eyes.

"Do it, then, for it was I," answered the man defiantly; adding, as if anxious to explain, "We had a tussle, and each got hurt in the thick of the skirmish. He was put in the ambulance afterward, and I was left to live or die, as luck would have it. I was hurt the worst; they should have taken me too; it made me mad to see him chosen, and I fired my last shot as he drove away. I didn't know whether I hit him or not; but when they told me I must lose my leg I hoped I had, and now I am satisfied."

He spoke rapidly, with clenched hand and fiery eyes, and the two listeners watched him with a sort of fascination as he hissed out the last words, glancing at the occupant of the next bed. Murry evidently did not understand French; he lay with averted face, closed eyes, and a hopeful smile still on his lips, quite unconscious of the meaning of the fierce words uttered close beside him. Dr. Fitz Hugh had laid down his instruments, and knit his black brows irefully while he listened. But as the man paused, the doctor looked at Miss Mercy, who was quietly going on with her work, though there was an expression about her handsome mouth that made her womanly face look almost grim. Taking up his tools, the doctor followed her example, saying slowly, —

"If I didn't believe Murry was mending, I'd turn you over to Roberts, whom the patients dread as they do the devil. I must do my duty, and you may thank Murry for it."

"Does he know you are the man who shot him?" asked Mercy, still in French.

"No; I shouldn't stay here long if he did," answered Clay, with a short laugh.

"Don't tell him, then — at least, till after you are moved," she said, in a tone of command.

"Where am I going?" demanded the man.

"Anywhere out of my ward," was the brief answer, with a look that made the black eyes waver and fall.

In silence nurse and doctor did their work, and passed on. In silence Murry lay hour after hour, and silently did Clay watch and wait, till, utterly exhausted by the suffering he was too proud to confess, he sank into a stupor, oblivious alike of hatred, defeat, and pain. Finding him in this pitiable condition, Mercy relented, and, womanlike, forgot her contempt in pity. He was not moved, but tended carefully all that day and night; and when he woke from a heavy sleep, the morning sun shone again on two pale faces in the beds, and flashed on the buttons of two army-coats hanging side by side on the recess wall, on loyalist and rebel, on the blue and the gray.

Dr. Fitz Hugh stood beside Murry's cot, saying cheerily, "You are doing well, my lad — better than I hoped. Keep calm and cool, and, if all goes right, we'll have little Mary here to pet you in a week."

"Who's Mary?" whispered the rebel to the attendant who was washing his face.

"His sweetheart; he left her for the war, and she's waitin' for him back — poor soul!" answered the man, with a somewhat vicious scrub across the sallow cheek he was wiping.

"So he'll get well, and go home and marry the girl he left behind him, will he?" sneered Clay, fingering a little case that hung about his neck, and was now visible as his rough valet unbuttoned his collar.

"What's that, — your sweetheart's picter?" asked Jim, the attendant, eying the gold chain anxiously.

"I've got none," was the gruff answer.

"So much the wus for you, then. Small chance of gettin' one here; our girls won't look at you, and you ain't likely to see any of your own sort for a long spell, I reckon," added Jim, working away at the rebel's long-neglected hair.

Clay lay looking at Mercy Carrol as she went to and fro among the men, leaving a smile behind her, and carrying comfort wherever she turned, — a right womanly woman, lovely and lovable, strong yet tender, patient yet decided, skilful, kind, and tireless in the discharge of duties that would have daunted most women. It was in vain she wore the plain gray gown and long apron, for neither could hide the grace of her figure. It was in vain she brushed her luxuriant hair back into a net, for the wavy locks would fall on her forehead, and stray curls would creep out or glisten like gold under the meshes meant to conceal them. Busy days and watchful nights had not faded the beautiful bloom on her cheeks, or dimmed the brightness of her hazel eyes. Always ready, fresh, and fair, Mercy Carrol was regarded as the good angel of the hospital, and not a man in it, sick or well, but was a loyal friend to her. None dared to be a lover, for her little romance was known; and, though still a maid, she was a widow in their eyes, for she had sent her lover to his death, and over the brave man's grave had said, "Well done."

Jim watched Clay as his eye followed the one female figure there, and, observing that he clutched the case still tighter, asked again, —

"What is that — a charm?"

"Yes, — against pain, captivity and shame."

"Strikes me it a'n't kep' you from any one of 'em," said Jim, with a laugh.

"I haven't tried it yet."

"How does it work?" Jim asked more respectfully, being impressed by something in the rebel's manner.

"You will see when I use it. Now let me alone;" and Clay turned impatiently away.

"You've got p'ison, or some deviltry, in that thing. If you don't let me look, I swear I'll have it took away from you;" and Jim put his big hand on the slender chain with a resolute air.

Clay smiled a scornful smile, and offered the trinket, saying coolly,—

"I only fooled you. Look as much as you like; you'll find nothing dangerous."

Jim opened the pocket, saw a lock of gray hair, and nothing more.

"Is that your mother's?"

"Yes; my dead mother's."

It was strange to see the instantaneous change that

passed over the two men as each uttered that dearest word in all tongues. Rough Jim gently reclosed and returned the case, saying kindly, —

"Keep it; I wouldn't rob you on't for no money."

Clay thrust it jealously into his breast, and the first trace of emotion he had shown softened his dark face, as he answered, with a grateful tremor in his voice, —

"Thank you. I wouldn't lose it for the world."

"May I say good-morning, neighbor?" asked a feeble voice, as Murry turned a very wan, but cheerful face toward him, when Jim moved on with his basin and towel.

"If you like," returned Clay, looking at him with those quick, suspicious eyes of his.

"Well, I do like; so I say it, and hope you are better," returned the cordial voice.

"Are you?"

"Yes, thank God!"

"Is it sure?"

"Nothing is sure, in a case like mine, till I'm on my legs again; but I'm certainly better. I don't expect *you* to be glad, but I hope you don't regret it very much."

"I don't." The smile that accompanied the words surprised Murry as much as the reply, for both seemed honest, and his kind heart warmed toward his suffering enemy.

"I hope you'll be exchanged as soon as you are able. Till then, you can go to one of the other hospitals, where there are many reb — I would say, Southerners. If you'd like, I'll speak to Dr. Fitz Hugh, and he'll see you moved," said Murry, in his friendly way.

"I'd rather stay here, thank you." Clay smiled again

as he spoke in the mild tone that surprised Murry as much as it pleased him.

"You like to be in my corner, then?" he said, with a boyish laugh.

"Very much — for a while."

"I'm very glad. Do you suffer much?"

"I shall suffer more by and by, if I go on; but I'll risk it," answered Clay, fixing his feverish eyes on Murry's placid face.

"You expect to have a hard time with your leg?" said Murry, compassionately.

"With my soul."

It was an odd answer, and given with such an odd expression, as Clay turned his face away, that Murry said no more, fancying his brain a little touched by the fever evidently coming on.

They spoke but seldom to each other that day, for Clay lay apparently asleep, with a flushed cheek and restless head, and Murry tranquilly dreamed waking dreams of home and little Mary. That night, after all was still, Miss Mercy went up into the organ-loft to get fresh rollers for the morrow, — the boxes of old linen, and such matters, being kept there. As she stood looking down on the thirty pale sleepers, she remembered that she had not played a hymn on the little organ for Murry, as she had promised that day. Stealing softly to the front, she peeped over the gallery, to see if he was asleep; if not, she would keep her word, for he was her favorite.

A screen had been drawn before the recess where the two beds stood, shutting their occupants from the sight of the other men. Murry lay sleeping, but Clay was awake, and a quick thrill tingled along the young woman's nerves as she saw his face. Leaning on one arm, he peered about the place with an eager, watchful air, and glanced up at the dark gallery, but did not see the startled face behind the central pillar. Pausing an instant, he shook his one clenched hand at the unconscious sleeper, and then threw out the locket cautiously. Two white mugs, just alike, stood on the little table between the beds, water in each. With another furtive glance about him, Clay suddenly stretched out his long arm, and dropped something from the locket into Murry's cup. An instant he remained motionless, with a sinister smile on his face; then, as Jim's step sounded beyond the screen, he threw his arm over his face, and lay, breathing heavily, as if asleep.

Mercy's first impulse was to cry out; her next, to fly down and seize the cup. No time was to be lost, for Murry might wake and drink at any moment. What was in the cup? Poison, doubtless; that was the charm Clay carried to free himself from "pain, captivity and shame," when all other hopes of escape vanished. This hidden helper he gave up to destroy his enemy, who was to outlive his shot, it seemed. Like a shadow, Mercy glided down, forming her plan as she went. A dozen mugs stood about the room, all alike in size and color; catching up one, she partly filled it, and, concealing it under the clean sheet hanging on her arm, went toward the recess, saying audibly, —

"I want some fresh water, Jim."

Thus warned of her approach, Clay lay with carefully-averted face as she came in, and never stirred as she bent over him, while she dexterously changed Murry's mug for the one she carried. Hiding the poisoned cup, she went away, saying aloud, —

"Never mind the water, now, Jim. Murry is asleep, and so is Clay; they'll not need it yet."

Straight to Dr. Fitz Hugh's room she went, and gave the cup into his keeping, with the story of what she had seen. A man was dying, and there was no time to test the water then; but putting it carefully away, he promised to set her fears at rest in the morning. To quiet her impatience, Mercy went back to watch over Murry till day dawned. As she sat down, she caught the glimmer of a satisfied smile on Clay's lips, and looking into the cup she had left, she saw that it was empty.

"He is satisfied, for he thinks his horrible revenge is secure. Sleep in peace, my poor boy! you are safe while I am here."

As she thought this, she put her hand on the broad, pale forehead of the sleeper with a motherly caress, but started to feel how damp and cold it was. Looking nearer, she saw that a change had passed over Murry, for dark shadows showed about his sunken eyes, his once quiet breath was faint and fitful now, his hand deathly cold, and a chilly dampness had gathered on his face. She looked at her watch; it was past twelve, and her heart sunk within her, for she had so often seen that solemn change come over men's faces then, that the hour was doubly weird and woful to her. Sending a message to Dr. Fitz Hugh, she waited anxiously, trying to believe that she deceived herself.

The doctor came at once, and a single look convinced him that he had left one death-bed for another.

"As I feared," he said; "that sudden rally was but

a last effort of nature. There was just one chance for him, and he has missed it. Poor lad! I can do nothing, he'll sink rapidly, and go without pain."

"Can *I* do nothing?" asked Mercy, with dim eyes as she held the cold hand close in both her own with tender pressure.

"Give him stimulants as long as he can swallow, and if he's conscious, take any messages he may have. Poor Hall is dying hard, and I can help him; I'll come again in an hour, and say good-by."

The kind doctor choked, touched the pale sleeper with a gentle caress, and went away to help Hall die.

Murry slept on for an hour, then woke, and knew without words that his brief hope was gone. He looked up wistfully, and whispered, as Mercy tried to smile with trembling lips that refused to tell the heavy truth, —

"I know — I feel it; don't grieve yourself by trying to tell me, dear friend. It's best so; I can bear it, — but I did want to live."

"Have you any word for Mary, dear?" asked Mercy, for he seemed but a boy to her since she had nursed him.

One look of sharp anguish and dark despair passed over his face, as he wrung his thin hands and shut his eyes, finding death terrible. It passed in a moment, and his pallid countenance grew beautiful with the pathetic patience of one who submits without complaint to the inevitable.

"Tell her I was ready, and the only bitterness was leaving her. I shall remember, and wait until she comes. My little Mary! O, be kind to her, for my sake, when you tell her this."

"I will, Murry, as God hears me. I will be a sister to her while I live."

As Mercy spoke, with fervent voice, he laid the hand that had ministered to him so faithfully against his cheek, and lay silent, as if content.

"What else? let me do something more. Is there no other friend to be comforted?"

"No; she is all I have in the world. I hoped to make her so happy, to be so much to her, for she's a lonely little thing; but God says 'No,' and I submit."

A long pause, as he lay breathing heavily, with eyes that were dimming fast fixed on the gentle face beside him.

"Give Jim my clothes, send Mary a bit of my hair, and — may I give you this? it's a poor thing, but all I have to leave you, best and kindest of women."

He tried to draw off a slender ring, but the strength had gone out of his wasted fingers, and she helped him, thanking him with the first tears he had seen her shed. He seemed satisfied, but suddenly turned his eyes on Clay, who lay as if asleep. A sigh broke from Murry, and Mercy caught the words, —

"How could he do it, and I so helpless!"

"Do you know him?" she whispered, eagerly, as she remembered Clay's own words.

"I knew he was the man who shot me, when he came. I forgive him; but I wish he had spared me, for Mary's sake," he answered sorrowfully, not angrily.

"Do you really pardon him?" cried Mercy, wondering, yet touched by the words.

"I do. He will be sorry one day, perhaps; at any rate, he did what he thought his duty; and war makes brutes of us all sometimes, I fear. I'd like to say goodby; but he's asleep after a weary day, so don't wake him. Tell him I'm glad *he* is to live, and that I forgive him heartily."

Although uttered between long pauses, these words seemed to have exhausted Murry, and he spoke no more till Dr. Fitz Hugh came. To him he feebly returned thanks, and whispered his farewell, then sank into a stupor, during which life ebbed fast. Both nurse and doctor forgot Clay as they hung over Murry, and neither saw the strange intentness of his face, the half awe-struck, half remorseful look he bent upon the dying man.

As the sun rose, sending its ruddy beams across the silent ward, Murry looked up and smiled, for the bright ray fell athwart the two coats hanging on the wall beside him. Some passer-by had brushed one sleeve of the blue coat across the gray, as if the inanimate things were shaking hands.

"It should be so — love our enemies; we should be brothers," he murmured faintly; and, with the last impulse of a noble nature, stretched his hand toward the man who had murdered him.

But Clay shrunk back, and covered his face without a word. When he ventured to look up, Murry was no longer there. A pale, peaceful figure lay on the narrow bed, and Mercy was smoothing the brown locks as she cut a curl for Mary and herself. Clay could not take his eyes away; as if fascinated by its serenity, he watched the dead face with gloomy eyes, till Mercy, having done her part, stooped and kissed the cold lips tenderly as she left him to his sleep. Then, as if afraid to be alone with the dead, he bid Jim put the screen between the beds, and bring him a book. His order was obeyed; but he never turned his pages, and lay, with muffled head, trying to shut out little Watts' sobs, as the wounded drummer boy mourned for Murry.

Death in an hospital makes no stir, and in an hour no trace of the departed remained but the coat upon the wall, for Jim would not take it down, though it was his now. The empty bed stood freshly made, the clean cup and worn Bible lay ready for other hands, and the card at the bed's head hung blank for a new-comer's name. In the hurry of this event, Clay's attempted crime was forgotten for a time. But that evening Dr. Fitz Hugh told Mercy that her suspicions were correct, for the water *was* poisoned.

"How horrible! what shall we do?" she cried, with a gesture full of energetic indignation.

"Leave him to remorse!" replied the doctor, sternly "I've thought over the matter, and believe this to be the only thing we can do. I fancy the man won't live a week; his leg is in a bad way, and he is such a fiery devil he gives himself no chance. Let him believe he killed poor Murry, at least for a few days. He thinks so now, and tries to rejoice; but if he has a human heart he will repent."

"But he may not. Should we not tell of this? Can he not be punished?"

"Law won't hang a dying man, and I'll not denounce him. Let remorse punish him while he lives, and God judge him when he dies. Murry pardoned him, — can we do less?"

Mercy's indignant face softened at the name, and for Murry's sake she yielded. Neither spoke of what they tried to think the act of a half-delirious man; and soon they could not refuse to pity him, for the doctor's prophecy proved true.

Clay was a haunted man, and remorse gnawed like a worm at his heart. Day and night he saw that tranquil face on the pillow opposite; day and night he saw the pale hand outstretched to him; day and night he heard the faint voice murmuring kindly, regretfully, "I forgive him; but I wish he had spared me, for Mary's sake."

As the days passed, and his strength visibly declined, he began to suspect that he must soon follow Murry. No one told him; for, though both doctor and nurse did their duty faithfully, neither lingered long at his bedside, and not one of the men showed any interest in him. No new patient occupied the other bed, and he lay alone in the recess with his own gloomy thoughts.

"It will be all up with me in a few days, won't it?" he asked, abruptly, as Jim made his toilet one morning with unusual care, and such visible pity in his rough face that Clay could not but observe it.

"I heard the doctor say you wouldn't suffer much more. Is there any one you'd like to see, or leave a message for?" answered Jim, smoothing the long lock as gently as a woman.

"There isn't a soul in the world that cares whether I live or die, except the man who wants my money," said Clay, bitterly, as his dark face grew a shade paler at this confirmation of his fear.

"Can't you head him off some way, and leave your money to some one that's been kind to you? Here's the doctor — or, better still, Miss Carrol. Neither on 'em is rich, and both on 'em has been good friends to you, or paused an instant, glanced quickly at Mercy's face, and seeing only womanly compassion there, added, with an irrepressible tremble in his voice, — "To little Mary."

If he had expected any reward for the act, any comfort for his lonely death-bed, he received both in fullest measure when he saw Mercy's beautiful face flush with surprise and pleasure, her eyes fill with sudden tears, and heard her cordial voice, as she pressed his hand warmly in her own.

"I wish I could tell you how glad I am for this! I thought you were better than you seemed; I was sure you had both heart and conscience, and that you would repent before you died."

"Repent of what?" he asked, with a startled look.

"Need I tell you?" and her eye went from the empty bed to his face.

"You mean that shot? But it was only fair, after all; we killed each other, and war is nothing but wholesale murder, any way." He spoke easily, but his eyes were full of trouble, and other words seemed to tremble on his lips.

Leaning nearer, Mercy whispered in his ear, —

"I mean the other murder, which you would have committed when you poisoned the cup of water he offered you, his enemy."

Every vestige of color faded out of Clay's thin face, and his haggard eyes seemed fascinated by some spectre opposite, as he muttered slowly, —

"How do you know?"

"I saw you;" and she told him all the truth.

A look of intense relief passed over Clay's countenance, and the remorseful shadow lifted as he murmured, brokenly, —

"Thank God I didn't kill him! Now, dying isn't so hard; now I can have a little peace."

Neither spoke for several minutes; Mercy had no words for such a time, and Clay forgot her presence as the tears dropped from between the wasted fingers spread before his face.

Presently he looked up, saying eagerly, as if his fluttering breath and rapidly failing strength warned him of approaching death, —

"Will you write down a few words for me, so Mary can have the money? She needn't know anything about me, only that I was one to whom Murry was kind, and so I gave her all I had."

"I'll get my pen and paper; rest, now, my poor fellow," said Mercy, wiping the unheeded tears away for him.

"How good it seems to hear you speak so to *me!* How can you do it?" he whispered, with such grateful wonder in his dim eyes that Mercy's heart smote her for the past.

"I do it for Murry's sake, and because I sincerely pity you."

Timidly turning his lips to that kind hand, he kissed it, and then hid his face in his pillow. When Mercy returned, she observed that there were but seven tarnished buttons where she had left eight. She guessed who had taken it, but said nothing, and endeavored to render poor Clay's last hours as happy as sympathy and care could make them. The letter and will were prepared as well as they could be, and none too soon; for, as if that secret was the burden that bound Clay's spirit to the shattered body, no sooner was it lifted off than the diviner part seemed ready to be gone.

"You'll stay with me; you'll help me die; and — oh, if I dared to ask it, I'd beg you to kiss me once when I am dead, as you did Murry. I think I could rest then, and be fitter to meet him, if the Lord lets me," he cried imploringly, as the last night gathered around him, and the coming change seemed awful to a soul that possessed no inward peace, and no firm hope to lean on through the valley of the shadow.

"I will — I will! Hold fast to me, and believe in the eternal mercy of God," whispered Miss Carrol, with her firm hand in his, her tender face bending over him as the long struggle began.

"Mercy," he murmured, catching that word, and smiling feebly as he repeated it lingeringly. "Mercy! yes, I believe in her; she'll save me, if any one can. Lord, bless and keep her forever and forever."

There was no morning sunshine to gladden his dim eyes as they looked their last, but the pale glimmer of the lamp shone full on the blue and the gray coats hanging side by side. As if the sight recalled that other death-bed, that last act of brotherly love and pardon, Clay rose up in his bed, and while one hand clutched the button hidden in his breast, the other was outstretched toward the empty bed, as his last breath parted in a cry of remorseful longing, —

"I will! I will! Forgive me, Murry, and let me say good-by!"

A HOSPITAL CHRISTMAS.

"MERRY Christmas!" "Merry Christmas!" "Merry Christmas, and lots of 'em, ma'am!" echoed from every side, as Miss Hale entered her ward in the gray December dawn. No wonder the greetings were hearty, that thin faces brightened, and eyes watched for the coming of this small luminary more eagerly than for the rising of the sun; for when they woke that morning, each man found that in the silence of the night some friendly hand had laid a little gift beside his bed. Very humble little gifts they were, but well chosen and thoughtfully bestowed by one who made the blithe anniversary pleasant even in a hospital, and sweetly taught the lesson of the hour — Peace on earth, good-will to man.

"I say, ma'am, these are just splendid. I've dreamt about such for a week, but I never thought I'd get 'em," cried one poor fellow, surveying a fine bunch of grapes with as much satisfaction as if he had found a fortune.

"Thank you kindly, Miss, for the paper and the fixings. I hated to keep borrowing, but I hadn't any money," said another, eying his gift with happy anticipations of the home letters with which the generous pages should be filled.

"They are dreadful soft and pretty, but I don't believe I'll ever wear 'em out; my legs are so wimbly there's no go in 'em," whispered a fever patient, looking sorrowfully at the swollen feet ornamented with a pair of carpet slippers gay with roses, and evidently made for his especial need.

"Please hang my posy basket on the gas-burner in the middle of the room, where all the boys can see it. It's too pretty for one alone."

"But then you can't see it yourself, Joe, and you are fonder of such things than the rest," said Miss Hale, taking both the little basket and the hand of her pet patient, a lad of twenty, dying of rapid consumption.

"That's the reason I can spare it for a while, for I shall feel 'em in the room just the same, and they'll do the boys good. You pick out the one you like best, for me to keep, and hang up the rest till by-and-by, please."

She gave him a sprig of mignonette, and he smiled as he took it, for it reminded him of her in her sad-colored gown, as quiet and unobtrusive, but as grateful to the hearts of those about her as was the fresh scent of the flower to the lonely lad who never had known womanly tenderness and care until he found them in a hospital. Joe's prediction was verified; the flowers did do the boys good, for all welcomed them with approving glances, and all felt their refining influence more or less keenly, from cheery Ben, who paused to fill the cup inside with fresher water, to surly Sam, who stopped growling as his eye rested on a geranium very like the one blooming in his sweetheart's window when they parted a long year ago.

"Now, as this is to be a merry day, let us begin to enjoy it at once. Fling up the windows, Ben, and Barney, go for breakfast while I finish washing faces and settling bed-clothes."

With which directions the little woman fell to work with such infectious energy that in fifteen minutes thirty gentlemen with spandy clean faces and hands were partaking of refreshment with as much appetite as their various conditions would permit. Meantime the sun came up, looking bigger, brighter, jollier than usual, as he is apt to do on Christmas days. Not a snow-flake chilled the air that blew in as blandly as if winter had relented, and wished the "boys" the compliments of the season in his mildest mood; while a festival smell pervaded the whole house, and appetizing rumors of turkey, mince-pie, and oysters for dinner, circulated through the wards. When breakfast was done, the wounds dressed, directions for the day delivered, and as many of the disagreeables as possible well over, the fun began. In any other place that would have been considered a very quiet morning; but to the weary invalids prisoned in that room, it was quite a whirl of excitement. None were dangerously ill but Joe, and all were easily amused, for weakness, homesickness and *ennui* made every trifle a joke or an event.

In came Ben, looking like a "Jack in the Green," with his load of hemlock and holly. Such of the men as could get about and had a hand to lend, lent it, and soon, under Miss Hale's direction, a green bough hung at the head of each bed, depended from the gas-burners, and nodded over the fireplace, while the finishing effect was given by a cross and crown at the top and bottom of the room. Great was the interest, many were the mishaps, and frequent was the laughter which attended this performance; for wounded men, when convalescent, are particularly jovial. When "Daddy Mills," as one venerable volunteer was irreverently christened, expatiated learnedly upon the difference between "sprewce, hemlock and pine," how they all listened, each thinking of some familiar wood still pleasantly haunted by boyish recollections of stolen gunnings, gum-pickings, and bird-nestings. When quiet Hayward amazed the company by coming out strong in a most unexpected direction, and telling with much effect the story of a certain "fine old gentleman" who supped on hemlock tea and died like a hero, what commendations were bestowed upon the immortal heathen in language more hearty than classical, as a twig of the historical tree was passed round like a new style of refreshment, that inquiring parties might satisfy themselves regarding the flavor of the Socratic draught. When Barney, the colored incapable, essayed a grand ornament above the door, and relying upon one insufficient nail, descended to survey his success with the proud exclamation, "Look at de neatness of dat job, gen'l'men,"—at which point the whole thing tumbled down about his ears,—how they all shouted but Pneumonia Ned, who, having lost his voice, could only make ecstatic demonstrations with his legs. When Barney cast himself and his hammer despairingly upon the floor, and Miss Hale, stepping into a chair, pounded stoutly at the traitorous nail and performed some miracle with a bit of string which made all fast, what a burst of applause arose from the beds. When gruff Dr. Bangs came in to see what all the noise was about, and the same intrepid lady not only boldly explained, but stuck a bit of holly in his button-hole, and wished him a merry Christmas with such a face full of smiles that the crabbed old doctor felt himself giving in very fast, and bolted out again, calling

Christmas a humbug, and exulting over the thirty emetics he would have to prescribe on the morrow, what indignant denials followed him. And when all was done, how everybody agreed with Joe when he said, "I think we are coming Christmas in great style; things look so green and pretty, I feel as I was settin' in a bower."

Pausing to survey her work, Miss Hale saw Sam looking as black as any thunder-cloud. He bounced over on his bed the moment he caught her eye, but she followed him up, and gently covering the cold shoulder he evidently meant to show her, peeped over it, asking, with unabated gentleness, —

"What can I do for you, Sam? I want to have all the faces in my ward bright ones to-day."

"My box ain't come; they said I should have it two, three days ago; why don't they do it, then?" growled Ursa Major.

"It is a busy time, you know, but it will come if they promised, and patience won't delay it, I assure you."

"My patience is used up, and they are a mean set of slow coaches. I'd get it fast enough if I wore shoulder straps; as I don't, I'll bet I sha'n't see it till the things ain't fit to eat; the news is old, and I don't care a hang about it."

"I'll see what I can do; perhaps before the hurry of dinner begins some one will have time to go for it."

"Nobody ever does have time here but folks who would give all they are worth to be stirring round. You can't get it, I know; it's my luck, so don't you worry, ma'am."

Miss Hale did not "worry," but worked, and in time a messenger was found, provided with the necessary money, pass and directions, and despatched to hunt up the missing Christmas-box. Then she paused to see what came next, not that it was necessary to look for a task, but to decide which, out of many, was most important to do first.

"Why, Turner, crying again so soon? What is it now? the light head or the heavy feet?"

"It's my bones, ma'am. They ache so I can't lay easy any way, and I'm so tired I just wish I could die and be out of this misery," sobbed the poor ghost of a once strong and cheery fellow, as the kind hand wiped his tears away, and gently rubbed the weary shoulders.

"Don't wish that Turner, for the worst is over now, and all you need is to get your strength again. Make an effort to sit up a little; it is quite time you tried; a change of posture will help the ache wonderfully; and make this 'dreadful bed,' as you call it, seem very comfortable when you come back to it."

"I can't, ma'am, my legs ain't a bit of use, and I ain't strong enough even to try."

"You never will be if you don't try. Never mind the poor legs, Ben will carry you. I've got the matron's easy-chair all ready, and can make you very cosy by the fire. It's Christmas-day, you know; why not celebrate it by overcoming the despondency which retards your recovery, and prove that illness has not taken all the manhood out of you?"

"It has, though, I'll never be the man I was, and may as well lay here till spring, for I shall be no use if I do get up."

If Sam was a growler this man was a whiner, and few hospital wards are without both. But knowing that much suffering had soured the former and pitifully weakened the latter, their nurse had patience with them, and still hoped to bring them round again. As Turner whimpered out his last dismal speech she bethought herself of something which, in the hurry of the morning, had slipped her mind till now.

"By the way, I've got another present for you. The doctor thought I'd better not give it yet, lest it should excite you too much; but I think you need excitement to make you forget yourself, and that when you find how many blessings you have to be grateful for, you will make an effort to enjoy them."

"Blessings, ma'am? I don't see 'em."

"Don't you see one now?" and drawing a letter from her pocket she held it before his eyes. His listless face brightened a little as he took it, but gloomed over again as he said fretfully, —

"It's from wife, I guess. I like to get her letters, but they are always full of grievings and groanings over me, so they don't do me much good."

"She does not grieve and groan in this one. She is too happy to do that, and so will you be when you read it."

"I don't see why, — hey? — why you don't mean — "

"Yes I do!" cried the little woman, clapping her hands, and laughing so delightedly that the Knight of the Rueful Countenance was betrayed into a broad smile for the first time in many weeks. "Is not a splendid little daughter a present to rejoice over and be grateful for?"

"Hooray! hold on a bit, — it's all right, — I'll be out again in a minute."

After which remarkably spirited burst, Turner vanished under the bed-clothes, letter and all. Whether he read, laughed or cried, in the seclusion of that cotton grotto, was unknown; but his nurse suspected that he did all three, for when he reappeared he looked as if during that pause he had dived into his "sea of troubles," and fished up his old self again.

"What *will* I name her?" was his first remark, delivered with such vivacity that his neighbors began to think he was getting delirious again.

"What is your wife's name?" asked Miss Hale, gladly entering into the domesticities which were producing such a salutary effect.

"Her name's Ann, but neither of us like it. I'd fixed on George, for I wanted my boy called after me; and now you see I ain't a bit prepared for this young woman." Very proud of the young woman he seemed, nevertheless, and perfectly resigned to the loss of the expected son and heir.

"Why not call her Georgiana then? That combines both her parents' names, and is not a bad one in itself."

"Now that's just the brightest thing I ever heard in my life!" cried Turner, sitting bolt upright in his excitement, though half an hour before he would have considered it an utterly impossible feat. "Georgiana Butterfield Turner, — it's a tip-top name, ma'am, and we can call her Georgie just the same. Ann will like that, it's so genteel. Bless 'em both! don't I wish I was at home." And down he lay again, despairing.

"You can be before long, if you choose. Get your strength up, and off you go. Come, begin at once, — drink your beef-tea, and sit up for a few minutes, just in honor of the good news, you know."

"I will, by George! — no, by Georgiana! That's a

good one, ain't it?" and the whole ward was electrified by hearing a genuine giggle from the "Blueing-bag."

Down went the detested beef-tea, and up scrambled the determined drinker with many groans, and a curious jumble of chuckles, staggers, and fragmentary repetitions of his first, last, and only joke. But when fairly settled in the great rocking-chair, with the gray flannel gown comfortably on, and the new slippers getting their inaugural scorch, Turner forgot his bones, and swung to and fro before the fire, feeling amazingly well, and looking very like a trussed fowl being roasted in the primitive fashion. The languid importance of the man, and the irrepressible satisfaction of the parent, were both laughable and touching things to see, for the happy soul could not keep the glad tidings to himself. A hospital ward is often a small republic, beautifully governed by pity, patience, and the mutual sympathy which lessens mutual suffering. Turner was no favorite; but more than one honest fellow felt his heart warm towards him as they saw his dismal face kindle with fatherly pride, and heard the querulous quaver of his voice soften with fatherly affection, as he said, " My little Georgie, sir."

"He'll do now, ma'am; this has given him the boost he needed, and in a week or two he'll be off our hands."

Big Ben made the remark with a beaming countenance, and Big Ben deserves a word of praise, because he never said one for himself. An ex-patient, promoted to an attendant's place, which he filled so well that he was regarded as a model for all the rest to copy. Patient, strong, and tender, he seemed to combine many of the best traits of both man and woman; for he appeared to know by instinct where the soft spot was to be found in every heart, and how best to help sick body or sad soul. No one would have guessed this to have seen him lounging in the hall during one of the short rests he allowed himself. A brawny, six-foot fellow, in red shirt, blue trousers tucked into his boots, an old cap, visor always up, and under it a roughly-bearded, coarsely-featured face, whose prevailing expression was one of great gravity and kindliness, though a humorous twinkle of the eye at times betrayed the man, whose droll sayings often set the boys in a roar. "A good-natured, clumsy body" would have been the verdict passed upon him by a casual observer; but watch him in his ward, and see how great a wrong that hasty judgment would have done him.

Unlike his predecessor, who helped himself generously when the meals came up, and carelessly served out rations for the rest, leaving even the most helpless to bungle for themselves or wait till he was done, shut himself into his pantry, and there, — to borrow a hospital phrase, — gormed, Ben often left nothing for himself, or took cheerfully such cold bits as remained when all the rest were served; so patiently feeding the weak, being hands and feet to the maimed, and a pleasant provider for all that, as one of the boys said, — "It gives a relish to the vittles to have Ben fetch 'em." If one were restless, Ben carried him in his strong arms; if one were undergoing the sharp torture of the surgeon's knife, Ben held him with a touch as firm as kind; if one were homesick, Ben wrote letters for him with great hearty blots and dashes under all the affectionate or important words. More than one poor fellow read his fate in Ben's pitiful eyes, and breathed his last breath away on Ben's broad breast,—always a quiet pillow till its work was done, then it would heave with genuine grief, as his big hand softly closed the tired eyes, and made another comrade ready for the last review. The war shows us many Bens, — for the same power of human pity which makes women brave also makes men tender; and each is the womanlier, the manlier, for these revelations of unsuspected strength and sympathies.

At twelve o'clock dinner was the prevailing idea in ward No. 3, and when the door opened every man sniffed, for savory odors broke loose from the kitchens and went roaming about the house. Now this Christmas dinner had been much talked of; for certain charitable and patriotic persons had endeavored to provide every hospital in Washington with materials for this time-honored feast. Some mistake in the list sent to head-quarters, some unpardonable neglect of orders, or some premeditated robbery, caused the long-expected dinner in the —— Hospital to prove a dead failure; but to which of these causes it was attributable was never known, for the deepest mystery enveloped that sad transaction. The full weight of the dire disappointment was mercifully lightened by premonitions of the impending blow. Barney was often missing; for the attendants were to dine *en masse* after the patients were done, therefore a speedy banquet for the latter parties was ardently desired, and he probably devoted his energies to goading on the cooks. From time to time he appeared in the doorway, flushed and breathless, made some thrilling announcement, and vanished, leaving ever-increasing appetite, impatience and expectation, behind him.

Dinner was to be served at one; at half-past twelve

Barney proclaimed, "Dere ain't no vegetables but squash and pitaters." A universal groan arose; and several indignant parties on a short allowance of meat consigned the defaulting cook to a warmer climate than the tropical one he was then enjoying. At twenty minutes to one, Barney increased the excitement by whispering, ominously, "I say, de puddins isn't plummy ones."

"Fling a piller at him and shut the door, Ben," roared one irascible being, while several others *not* fond of puddings received the fact with equanimity. At quarter to one Barney piled up the agony by adding the bitter information, "Dere isn't but two turkeys for dis ward, and dey's little fellers."

Anxiety instantly appeared in every countenance, and intricate calculations were made as to how far the two fowls would go when divided among thirty men; also friendly warnings were administered to several of the feebler gentlemen not to indulge too freely, if at all, for fear of relapses. Once more did the bird of evil omen return, for at ten minutes to one Barney croaked through the key-hole, "Only jes half ob de pies has come, gen'l'men." That capped the climax, for the masculine palate has a predilection for pastry, and mince-pie was the sheet-anchor to which all had clung when other hopes went down. Even Ben looked dismayed; not that he expected anything but the perfume and pickings for his share, but he had set his heart on having the dinner an honor to the institution and a memorable feast for the men, so far away from home, and all that usually makes the day a festival among the poorest. He looked pathetically grave as Turner began to fret, Sam began to swear under his breath, Hayward to sigh, Joe to wish it was all over, and the rest began to vent their emotions with a freedom which was anything but inspiring. At that moment Miss Hale came in with a great basket of apples and oranges in one hand, and several convivial-looking bottles in the other.

"Here is our dessert, boys! A kind friend remembered us, and we will drink her health in her own currant wine."

A feeble smile circulated round the room, and in some sanguine bosoms hope revived again. Ben briskly emptied the basket, while Miss Hale whispered to Joe, —

"I know you would be glad to get away from the confusion of this next hour, to enjoy a breath of fresh air, and dine quietly with Mrs. Burton round the corner, wouldn't you?"

"Oh, ma'am, so much! the noise, the smells, the fret and flurry, make me sick just to think of! But how can I go? that dreadful ambulance 'most killed me last time, and I'm weaker now."

"My dear boy, I have no thought of trying that again till our ambulances are made fit for the use of weak and wounded men. Mrs. Burton's carriage is at the door, with her motherly self inside, and all you have got to do is to let me bundle you up, and Ben carry you out."

With a long sigh of relief Joe submited to both these processes, and when his nurse watched his happy face as the carriage slowly rolled away, she felt well repaid for the little sacrifice of rest and pleasure so quietly made; for Mrs. Burton came to carry her, not Joe, away.

"Now, Ben, help me to make this unfortunate dinner go off as well as we can," she whispered. "On many accounts it is a mercy that the men are spared the temptations of a more generous meal; pray don't tell them so, but make the best of it, as you know very well how to do."

"I'll try my best, Miss Hale, but I'm no less disappointed, for some of 'em, being no better than children, have been living on the thoughts of it for a week, and it comes hard to give it up."

If Ben had been an old-time patriarch, and the thirty boys his sons, he could not have spoken with a more paternal regret, or gone to work with a better will. Putting several small tables together in the middle of the room, he left Miss Hale to make a judicious display of plates, knives and forks, while he departed for the banquet. Presently he returned, bearing the youthful turkeys and the vegetables in his tray, followed by Barney, looking unutterable things at a plum-pudding baked in a milk-pan, and six very small pies. Miss Hale played a lively tattoo as the procession approached, and, when the viands were arranged, with the red and yellow fruit prettily heaped up in the middle, it really did look like a dinner.

"Here's richness! here's the delicacies of the season and the comforts of life!" said Ben, falling back to survey the table with as much apparent satisfaction as if it had been a lord mayor's feast.

"Come, hurry up, and give us our dinner, what there is of it!" grumbled Sam.

"Boys," continued Ben, beginning to cut up the turkeys, "these noble birds have been sacrificed for the defenders of their country; they will go as far as ever they can, and, when they can't go any farther, we shall endeavor to supply their deficiencies with soup or ham, oysters having given out unexpectedly. Put it to vote;

both have been provided on this joyful occasion, and a word will fetch either."

"Ham! ham!" resounded from all sides. Soup was an every-day affair, and therefore repudiated with scorn; but ham, being a rarity, was accepted as a proper reward of merit and a tacit acknowledgment of their wrongs.

The "noble birds" did go as far as possible, and were handsomely assisted by their fellow martyr. The pudding was not as plummy as could have been desired, but a slight exertion of fancy made the crusty knobs do duty for raisins. The pies were small, yet a laugh added flavor to the mouthful apiece, for, when Miss Hale asked Ben to cut them up, that individual regarded her with an inquiring aspect as he said, in his drollest tone, —

"I wouldn't wish to appear stupid, ma'am, but, when you mention 'pies,' I presume you allude to these trifles. 'Tarts,' or 'patties,' would meet my views better, in speaking of the third course of this lavish dinner. As such I will do my duty by 'em, hoping that the appetites is to match."

Carefully dividing the six pies into twenty-nine diminutive wedges, he placed each in the middle of a large clean plate, and handed them about with the gravity of an undertaker. Dinner had restored good humor to many; this hit at the pies put the finishing touch to it, and from that moment an atmosphere of jollity prevailed. Healths were drunk in currant wine, apples and oranges flew about as an impromptu game of ball was got up, Miss Hale sang a Christmas carol, and Ben gambolled like a sportive giant as he cleared away. Pausing in one of his prances to and fro, he beckoned the nurse out, and, when she followed, handed her a plate heaped up with good things from a better table than she ever sat at now.

"From the matron, ma'am. Come right in here and eat it while it's hot; they are most through in the dining-room, and you'll get nothing half so nice," said Ben, leading the way into his pantry and pointing to a sunny window-seat.

"Are you sure she meant it for me, and not for yourself, Ben?"

"Of course she did! Why, what should I do with it, when I've just been feastin' sumptuous in this very room?"

"I don't exactly see what you have been feasting on," said Miss Hale, glancing round the tidy pantry as she sat down.

"Havin' eat up the food and washed up the dishes, it naturally follows that you don't see, ma'am. But if I go off in a fit by-and-by you'll know what it's owin' to," answered Ben, vainly endeavoring to look like a man suffering from repletion.

"Such kind fibs are not set down against one, Ben, so I will eat your dinner, for if I don't I know you will throw it out of the window to prove that you can't eat it."

"Thankee ma'am, I'm afraid I should; for, at the rate he's going on, Barney wouldn't be equal to it," said Ben, looking very much relieved, as he polished his last pewter fork and hung his towels up to dry.

A pretty general siesta followed the excitement of dinner, but by three o'clock the public mind was ready for amusement, and the arrival of Sam's box provided it. He was asleep when it was brought in and quietly deposited at his bed's foot, ready to surprise him on awaking. The advent of a box was a great event, for the fortunate receiver seldom failed to " stand treat," and next best to getting things from one's own home was the getting them from some other boy's home. This was an unusually large box, and all felt impatient to have it opened, though Sam's exceeding crustiness prevented the indulgence of great expectations. Presently he roused, and the first thing his eye fell upon was the box, with his own name sprawling over it in big black letters. As if it were merely the continuance of his dream, he stared stupidly at it for a moment, then rubbed his eyes and sat up, exclaiming, —

"Hullo! that's mine!"

"Ah! who said it wouldn't come? who hadn't the faith of a grasshopper? and who don't half deserve it for being a Barker by nater as by name?" cried Ben, emphasizing each question with a bang on the box, as he waited, hammer in hand, for the arrival of the wardmaster, whose duty it was to oversee the opening of such matters, lest contraband articles should do mischief to the owner or his neighbors.

"Ain't it a jolly big one? Knock it open, and don't wait for anybody or anything!" cried Sam, tumbling off his bed and beating impatiently on the lid with his one hand.

In came the ward-master, off came the cover, and out came a motley collection of apples, socks, dough-nuts, paper, pickles, photographs, pocket-handkerchiefs, gingerbread, letters, jelly, newspapers, tobacco, and cologne. "All right, glad it's come, — don't kill yourself," said the ward-master, as he took a hasty survey and walked off again. Drawing the box nearer the bed, Ben delicately followed, and Sam was left to brood over his treasures in peace.

At first all the others, following Ben's example, made elaborate pretences of going to sleep, being absorbed in books, or utterly uninterested in the outer world. But very soon curiosity got the better of politeness, and one by one they all turned round and stared. They might have done so from the first, for Sam was perfectly unconscious of everything but his own affairs, and, having read the letters, looked at the pictures, unfolded the bundles, turned everything inside out and upside down, tasted all the eatables and made a spectacle of himself with jelly, he paused to get his breath and find his way out of the confusion he had created. Presently he called out, —

"Miss Hale, will you come and right up my duds for me?" adding, as her woman's hands began to bring matters straight, "I don't know what to do with 'em all, for some won't keep long, and it will take pretty steady eating to get through 'em in time, supposin' appetite holds out."

"How do the others manage with their things?"

"You know they give 'em away; but I'll be hanged if I do, for they are always callin' names and pokin' fun at me. Guess they won't get anything out of me now."

The old morose look came back as he spoke, for it had disappeared while reading the home letters, touching the home gifts. Still busily folding and arranging, Miss Hale asked, —

"You know the story of the Three Cakes; which are you going to be — Harry, Peter, or Billy?"

Sam began to laugh at this sudden application of the

nursery legend; and, seeing her advantage, Miss Hale pursued it:

"We all know how much you have suffered, and all respect you for the courage with which you have borne your long confinement and your loss; but don't you think you have given the boys some cause for making fun of you, as you say? You used to be a favorite, and can be again, if you will only put off these crusty ways, which will grow upon you faster than you think. Better lose both arms than cheerfulness and self-control, Sam."

Pausing to see how her little lecture was received, she saw that Sam's better self was waking up, and added yet another word, hoping to help a mental ailment as she had done so many physical ones. Looking up at him with her kind eyes, she said, in a lowered voice, —

"This day, on which the most perfect life began, is a good day for all of us to set about making ourselves readier to follow that divine example. Troubles are helpers if we take them kindly, and the bitterest may sweeten us for all our lives. Believe and try this, Sam, and when you go away from us let those who love you find that two battles have been fought, two victories won."

Sam made no answer, but sat thoughtfully picking at the half-eaten cookey in his hand. Presently he stole a glance about the room, and, as if all helps were waiting for him, his eye met Joe's. From his solitary corner by the fire and the bed he would seldom leave again until he went into his grave, the boy smiled back at him so heartily, so happily, that something gushed warm across Sam's heart as he looked down upon the faces of mother, sister, sweetheart, scattered round him, and remembered how poor his comrade was in all such tender ties, and yet how rich in that beautiful content, which, "having nothing, yet hath all." The man had no words in which to express this feeling, but it came to him and did him good, as he proved in his own way. "Miss Hale," he said, a little awkwardly, "I wish you'd pick out what you think each would like, and give 'em to the boys."

He got a smile in answer that drove him to his cookey as a refuge, for his lips would tremble, and he felt half proud, half ashamed to have earned such bright approval.

"Let Ben help you, — he knows better than I. But you must give them all yourself, it will so surprise and please the boys; and then to-morrow we will write a capital letter home, telling what a jubilee we made over their fine box."

At this proposal Sam half repented; but, as Ben came lumbering up at Miss Hale's summons, he laid hold of his new resolution as if it was a sort of shower-bath and he held the string, one pull of which would finish the baptism. Dividing his most cherished possession, which (alas for romance!) was the tobacco, he bundled the larger half into a paper, whispering to Miss Hale, —

"Ben ain't exactly what you'd call a ministerin' angel to look at, but he is amazin' near one in his ways, so I'm goin' to begin with him."

Up came the "ministering angel," in red flannel and cow-hide boots; and Sam tucked the little parcel into his pocket, saying, as he began to rummage violently in the box, —

"Now jest hold your tongue, and lend a hand here about these things."

Ben was so taken aback by this proceeding that he

stared blankly, till a look from Miss Hale enlightened him; and, taking his cue, he played his part as well as could be expected on so short a notice. Clapping Sam on the shoulder, — not the bad one, Ben was always thoughtful of those things, — he exclaimed heartily, —

"I always said you'd come round when this poor arm of yours got a good start, and here you are jollier'n ever. Lend a hand! so I will, a pair of 'em. What's to do? Pack these traps up again?"

"No; I want you to tell what *you'd* do with 'em if they were yours. Free, you know, — as free as if they really was."

Ben held on to the box a minute as if this second surprise rather took him off his legs; but another look from the prime mover in this resolution steadied him, and he fell to work as if Sam had been in the habit of being "free."

"Well, let's see. I think I'd put the clothes and sich into this smaller box that the bottles come in, and stan' it under the table, handy. Here's newspapers — pictures in 'em, too! I should make a circulatin' lib'ry of them; they'll be a real treat. Pickles — well, I guess I should keep them on the winder here as a kind of a relish dinnertimes, or to pass along to them as longs for 'em. Cologne — that's a dreadful handsome bottle, ain't it? That, now, would be fust-rate to give away to somebody as was very fond of it, — a kind of a delicate attention, you know, — if you happen to meet such a person anywheres."

Ben nodded towards Miss Hale, who was absorbed in folding pocket-handkerchiefs. Sam winked expressively, and patted the bottle as if congratulating himself that it **was** handsome, and that he *did* know what to do with it.

The pantomime was not elegant, but as much real affection and respect went into it as if he had made a set speech, and presented the gift upon his knees.

"The letters and photographs I should probably keep under my piller for a spell; the jelly I'd give to Miss Hale, to use for the sick ones; the cake-stuff and that pot of jam, that's gettin' ready to work, I'd stand treat with for tea, as dinner wasn't all we could have wished. The apples I'd keep to eat, and fling at Joe when he was too bashful to ask for one, and the *tobaccer* I would *not* go lavishin' on folks that have no business to be enjoyin' luxuries when many a poor feller is dyin' of want down to Charlestown. There, sir! that's what *I'd* do if any one was so clever as to send me a jolly box like this."

Sam was enjoying the full glow of his shower-bath by this time. As Ben designated the various articles, he set them apart; and when the inventory ended, he marched away with the first instalment: two of the biggest, rosiest apples for Joe, and all the pictorial papers. Pickles are not usually regarded as tokens of regard, but as Sam dealt them out one at a time, — for he would let nobody help him, and his single hand being the left, was as awkward as it was willing, — the boys' faces brightened; for a friendly word accompanied each, which made the sour gherkins as welcome as sweetmeats. With every trip the donor's spirits rose; for Ben circulated freely between whiles, and, thanks to him, not an allusion to the past marred the satisfaction of the present. Jam, soda-biscuits, and cake, were such welcome additions to the usual bill of fare, that when supper was over a vote of thanks was passed, and speeches were made; for, being true Americans, the ruling passion found vent in the usual "Fellow-citizens!" and allusions to the "Star-spangled Banner." After which Sam subsided, feeling himself a public benefactor, and a man of mark.

A perfectly easy, pleasant day throughout would be almost an impossibility in any hospital, and this one was no exception to the general rule; for, at the usual time, Dr. Bangs went his rounds, leaving the customary amount of discomfort, discontent and dismay behind him. A skilful surgeon and an excellent man was Dr. Bangs, but not a sanguine or conciliatory individual; many cares and crosses caused him to regard the world as one large hospital, and his fellow-beings all more or less dangerously wounded patients in it. He saw life through the bluest of blue spectacles, and seemed to think that the sooner people quitted it the happier for them. He did his duty by the men, but if they recovered he looked half disappointed, and congratulated them with cheerful prophecies that there would come a time when they would wish they hadn't. If one died he seemed relieved, and surveyed him with pensive satisfaction, saying heartily, —

"He's comfortable, now, poor soul, and well out of this miserable world, thank God!"

But for Ben the sanitary influences of the doctor's ward would have been small, and Dante's doleful line might have been written on the threshold of the door, —

"Who enters here leaves hope behind."

Ben and the doctor perfectly understood and liked each other, but never agreed, and always skirmished over the boys as if manful cheerfulness and medical despair were fighting for the soul and body of each one.

"Well," began the doctor, looking at Sam's arm, or, rather, all that was left of that member after two amputations, "we shall be ready for another turn at this in a day or two if it don't mend faster. Tetanus sometimes follows such cases, but that is soon over, and I should not object to a case of it, by way of variety." Sam's hopeful face fell, and he set his teeth as if the fatal symptoms were already felt.

"If one kind of lockjaw was more prevailing than 'tis, it wouldn't be a bad thing for some folks I could mention," observed Ben, covering the well-healed stump as carefully as if it were a sleeping baby; adding, as the doctor walked away, "There's a sanguinary old sawbones for you! Why, bless your buttons, Sam, you are doing splendid, and he goes on that way because there's no chance of his having another cut at you! Now he's squenchin' Turner, jest as we've blowed a spark of spirit into him. If ever there was a born extinguisher its Bangs!"

Ben rushed to the rescue, and not a minute too soon; for Turner, who now labored under the delusion that his recovery depended solely upon his getting out of bed every fifteen minutes, was sitting by the fire, looking up at the doctor, who pleasantly observed, while feeling his pulse, —

"So you are getting ready for another fever, are you? Well, we've grown rather fond of you, and will keep you six weeks longer if you have set your heart on it."

Turner looked nervous, for the doctor's jokes were always grim ones; but Ben took the other hand in his, and gently rocked the chair as he replied, with great politeness, —

"This robust convalescent of ourn would be happy to oblige you, sir, but he has a pressin' engagement up to Jersey for next week, and couldn't stop on no account. You see Miss Turner wants a careful nuss for little Georgie, and he's a goin' to take the place."

Feeling himself on the brink of a laugh as Turner simpered with a ludicrous mixture of pride in his baby and fear for himself, Dr. Bangs said, with unusual sternness and a glance at Ben, —

"You take the responsibility of this step upon yourself, do you? Very well; then I wash my hands of Turner; only, if that bed is empty in a week, don't lay the blame of it at my door."

"Nothing shall induce me to do it, sir," briskly responded Ben. "Now then, turn in my boy, and sleep your prettiest for I wouldn't but disappoint that cheerfulest of men for a month's wages; and that's liberal, as I ain't likely to get it."

"How is this young man after the rash dissipations of the day?" asked the doctor, pausing at the bed in the corner, after he had made a lively progress down the room, hotly followed by Ben.

"I'm first-rate, sir," panted Joe, who always said so, though each day found him feebler than the last. Every one was kind to Joe, even the gruff doctor, whose manner softened, and who was forced to frown heavily to hide the pity in his eyes

"How's the cough?"

"Better, sir; being weaker, I can't fight against it as I used to do, so it comes rather easier."

"Sleep any last night?"

"Not much; but it's very pleasant laying here when

the room is still, and no light but the fire. Ben keeps it bright; and, when I fret, he talks to me, and makes the time go telling stories till he gets so sleepy he can hardly speak. Dear old Ben! I hope he'll have some one as kind to him, when he needs it as I do now."

"He will get what he deserves by-and-by, you may be sure of that," said the doctor, as severely as if Ben merited eternal condemnation.

A great drop splashed down upon the hearth as Joe spoke; but Ben put his foot on it, and turned about as if defying any one to say he shed it.

"Of all the perverse and reckless women whom I have known in the course of a forty years' practice, this one is the most perverse and reckless," said the doctor, abruptly addressing Miss Hale, who just then appeared, bringing Joe's "posy-basket" back. "You will oblige me, ma'am, by sitting in this chair with your hands folded for twenty minutes; the clock will then strike nine, and you will go straight up to your bed."

Miss Hale demurely sat down, and the doctor ponderously departed, sighing regretfully as he went through the room, as if disappointed that the whole thirty were not lying at death's door; but on the threshold he turned about, exclaimed "Good-night, boys! God bless you!" and vanished as precipitately as if a trap-door had swallowed him up.

Miss Hale was a perverse woman in some things; for, instead of folding her tired hands, she took a rusty-covered volume from the mantle-piece, and, sitting by Joe's bed, began to read aloud. One by one all other sounds grew still; one by one the men composed themselves to listen; and one by one the words of the sweet old Christmas story came to them, as the woman's quiet voice went reading on. If any wounded spirit needed balm, if any hungry heart asked food, if any upright purpose, new-born aspiration, or sincere repentance wavered for want of human strength, all found help, hope, and consolation in the beautiful and blessed influences of the book, the reader, and the hour.

The bells rung nine, the lights grew dim, the day's work was done; but Miss Hale lingered beside Joe's bed, for his face wore a wistful look, and he seemed loath to have her go.

"What is it, dear?" she said; "what can I do for you before I leave you to Ben's care?"

He drew her nearer, and whispered earnestly, —

"It's something that I know you'll do for me, because I can't do it for myself, not as I want it done, and you can. I'm going pretty fast now, ma'am; and when — when some one else is laying here, I want you to tell the boys, — every one, from Ben to Barney, — how much I thanked 'em, how much I loved 'em, and how glad I was that I had known 'em, even for such a little while."

"Yes, Joe, I'll tell them all. What else can I do, my boy?"

"Only let me say to you what no one else must say for me, that all I want to live for is to try and do something in my poor way to show you how I thank you, ma'am. It isn't what you've said to me, it isn't what you've done for me alone, that makes me grateful; it's because you've learned me many things without knowing it, showed me what I ought to have been before, if I'd had any one to tell me how, and made this such a happy, home-like place, I shall be sorry when I have to go."

Poor Joe! it must have fared hardly with him all those twenty years, if a hospital seemed home-like, and a little sympathy, a little care, could fill him with such earnest gratitude. He stopped a moment to lay his cheek upon the hand he held in both of his, then hurried on as if he felt his breath beginning to give out:

"I dare say many boys have said this to you, ma'am, better than I can, for I don't say half I feel; but I know that none of 'em ever thanked you as I thank you in my heart, or ever loved you as I'll love you all my life. To-day I hadn't anything to give you, I'm so poor; but I wanted to tell you this, on the last Christmas I shall ever see."

It was a very humble kiss he gave that hand; but the fervor of a first love warmed it, and the sincerity of a great gratitude made it both a precious and pathetic gift to one who, half unconsciously, had made this brief and barren life so rich and happy at its close. Always womanly and tender, Miss Hale's face was doubly so as she leaned over him, whispering,—

"I have had my present, now. Good-night, Joe."

AN HOUR.

THE clock struck eleven.

"Look again, Gabriel; is there no light coming?"

"Not a ray, mother, and the night seems to darken every instant."

"Surely, half an hour is time enough to reach the main land and find Dr. Firth."

"Ample time; but Alec probably found the doctor absent, and is waiting for him."

"But I bade the boy leave my message, and return at once. Every moment is precious; what can we do?"

"Nothing but wait."

An impatient sigh was the only answer vouchsafed to the unpalatable advice, and silence fell again upon the anxious watchers in the room. Still leaning in the deep recess of the window, the young man looked out into the murky night, listened to the flow of the great river rolling to the sea, and let the unquiet current of his thoughts drift him whithersoever it would. His imaginative temperament found a sad similitude between the night and his own mood, for neither his physical nor mental eye could see what lay before him, and in his life there seemed to have come an hour as full of suspense, as prophetic of storm, as that which now oppressed the earth and lowered in the sky.

Every instant that brought the peace of death nearer to the father, also brought the cares of life nearer to the son, and their grim aspect daunted him. The child of a Northern mother, bred at the North by her dying desire, he had been summoned home to take the old man's place, and receive a slave-cursed inheritance into his keeping. Had he stood alone, his task would have been an easy one; for an upright nature, an enthusiastic spirit, would have found more sweetness than bitterness in a sacrifice made for conscience sake, more pride than pain in a just deed generously performed. But a step-mother and her daughters were dependent on him now, for the old man's sudden seizure left him no time to make provision for them; and the son found a double burden laid upon his shoulders when he returned to what for years had been a loveless home to him. To reduce three delicately nurtured women to indigence seemed a cruel and Quixotic act to others, a very hard, though righteous one to him; for poverty looked less terrible than affluence founded upon human blood and tears. He had resolved to set aside all private ambitions and aspirations that he might dedicate his life to his kindred; had manfully withstood their ridicule and reproaches, and only faltered when, in their hour of bereavement, they appealed to him with tears and prayers. Then pity threatened to conquer principle, for Gabriel's heart was as gentle as it was generous. Three days of sorrowful suspense and inward strife had passed; now death seemed about to set its seal upon one life, and irresolution to mar another, for Gabriel still wavered between duty and desire, crying within himself, "Lord, help me! I see the right, but I am not strong enough to do it; let it be decided for me."

It was — suddenly, entirely, and forever!

The tinkle of a bell roused him from his moody reverie, and, without quitting the shadow of the half-drawn curtain, he watched the scene before him with the interest of one in whom both soul and sense were alert to interpret and accept the divine decree which he had asked, in whatever guise it came.

The bell summoned a person whose entrance seemed to bring warmth, vitality and light into that gloomy room, although she was only a servant, with the blood of a despised race in her veins. More beautiful than either of her young mistresses, she looked like some brilliant flower of the tropics beside two pale exotics, and the unavoidable consciousness of this showed itself in the skill with which she made her simple dress a foil to her beauty, in the carriage of her graceful head and the sad pride of her eyes, as if, being denied all the other rights of womanhood, the slave clung to and cherished the one possession which those happier women lacked. As she entered, noiselessly, she gave one keen, comprehensive glance about the room, — a glance that took in the gray head and pallid face upon the pillow, the languid lady sitting at the bedside, the young sisters spent with weeping and watching, half asleep in either corner of a couch, and the man's glove that lay beside a brace of pistols on a distant table. Then her eyes fell, all expression faded from her face, and she stood before her mistress with a meek air, curiously at variance with the animated aspect she had worn on entering.

"Milly, are you sure you gave Alec my message correctly?" asked Mrs. Butler, imperiously, with a look of unconcealed dislike.

"Yes, missis, I gave it word for word."

The voice that answered would have gone straight to a stranger's heart and made it ache, for a world of hopeless patience rendered its music pathetic, and dignified the little speech, as if the woman's spirit uttered a protest in every word that passed her lips.

"He has been gone nearly an hour. I can wait no longer. Tell Andy to go at once and see what keeps him."

"Andy's down at the landing, seeing to the boats before the storm, missis."

"Let Tony do that, and send Andy off at once."

"Tony's too cut up with his last whipping to stir."

"How very tiresome! Where is overseer Neal?"

"Sick, missis."

"Sick! I saw him two hours ago, and he was perfectly well then."

"He was taken very suddenly, but he'll be out of pain by morning."

As Milly spoke, with a slight motion of the lips that would have been a scornful smile had she not checked it, a faint, far-off cry came on the wind; a cry of mortal fear or pain it seemed, and so full of ominous suggestion that, though inured to sounds of suffering, Mrs. Butler involuntarily exclaimed, —

"What is that?"

"It's only Rachel screaming for her baby; the last thing old master did was to sell it, and she's been crazy ever since," answered Milly, with a peculiar quickening of the breath and a sidelong glance.

"Foolish creature! but never mind her now: tell me who is about that I can send for Dr. Firth."

"There's no one in the house but blind Sandra and me.'

"What do you mean? Who gave the people leave to go?"

"I did."

Hitherto the girl had spoken in the subdued tone of a well-trained servant, though there was no trace of her race in her speech but a word or two here and there; for Milly's beauty had secured for her all the advantages which would increase her value as a chattel. But in the utterance of the last two words her voice rose with a sudden ring that arrested Mrs. Butler's attention, and caused her to glance sharply at the girl. Milly stood before her meek and motionless, and not an eyelash stirred during that brief scrutiny. Her mistress could not see the mingled triumph and abhorrence burning in those averted eyes, did not observe the close clenching of the hand that hung at her side, nor guess what a sea of black and bitter memories was surging in her comely handmaid's heart.

"How dared you send the servants away without my orders?" demanded Mrs. Butler, in an irritated and irritating voice.

"Master Gabriel said the house must be kept very quiet on old master's account; I couldn't make the boys mind, so I sent them to the quarters."

"This is not the first time you have presumed upon my son's favor. and exceeded my orders. You have been spoiled by indulgence, but that shall be altered soon."

"Yes, missis, — it shall;" and as the girl added the latter words below her breath, there was a glitter as of white teeth firmly set lest some impetuous speech should break loose in spite of her. Her mistress did not mark that little demonstration, for her mind was occupied with its one care, as she said, half aloud, half to herself, —

"What shall I do? The night is passing, your master needs help, and Alec has evidently forgotten, or never received, my message."

For the first time an expression of anxiety was visible on Milly's face, and there was more eagerness than deference in her suggestion:

"Master Gabriel might go; it would save time and make the matter sure, as missis doubts my word."

"It is impossible; his father might rouse and ask for him, and I will not be left alone. It is not his place to carry messages, nor yours to propose it. Quick! lift your master's head, and chafe his hands. God help us all!"

A low sigh from the bed caused the sudden change from displeasure to distress, as Mrs. Butler bent over her husband, forgetful of all else. What a strange smile flashed across Milly's face, and kindled the dark fire of her eyes, as she looked down upon the master and mistress, whose helplessness and grief touched no chord of pity or sympathy in her heart! Only an instant did she stand so, but in that instant the expression of her face was fully revealed, not to the drowsy sisters, but to Gabriel in his covert. He saw it, but before he could fathom its significance it was hidden from him; and when his mother looked up there was nothing to be seen but the handsome head bending over the pale hand that Milly was assiduously chafing. Something in the touch of those warm palms seemed to rouse in the old man a momentary flicker of memory and strength, for the last thought that that had disturbed his failing consciousness found utterance in broken words:

"I promised her her liberty, — she shall have it; wait a little, Milly, — wait till I am better."

"Yes, master, I can wait now;" and the girl's eye turned toward the clock with an impatient glance.

The old man did not hear her, for, with an incoherent murmur, he seemed to sink into a deeper lethargy than before. His wife believed him dying; and cried, as she wrung her hands in a paroxysm of despairing helplessness, —

"Look out, Milly, look out! and if no one is coming, run to the quarters and send off the first boy you meet."

Milly moved deliberately toward the window, but paused half-way to ask, with the same shade of anxiety flitting over her face, —

"Where is Master Gabriel? shouldn't he be called?"

"He was here a moment ago, and has gone to the landing, doubtless; you can call him as you go."

With sudden eagerness the girl glided to the window, now too intent upon some purpose of her own to see the dark outline of a figure half concealed in the deep folds of the curtain; and, leaning far out, she peered into the gloom with an intentness that sharpened every feature.

"There is no one coming, missis," she said, raising her voice unnecessarily, as one listener thought, unless the momentary stillness made any sound seem unusually loud. As the words left her lips, from below there came a soft chirp as of some restless bird; it was twice repeated, then came a pause, and in it, with a rapid, noiseless gesture, Milly drew a handkerchief from her pocket and dropped it from the window. It fluttered whitely for a moment, and as it disappeared an acute ear might have caught the sound of footsteps stealing stealthily away. Milly evidently heard them, for an expression of relief began to dawn upon her face. Suddenly it changed to one of terror, as, in the act of withdrawing her arm, a strong hand grasped it, and Gabriel's voice demanded,—

"What does this mean, Milly?"

For a moment she struggled like some wild creature caught in a net, then steadied herself by a desperate effort, exclaiming, breathlessly,—

"Oh, Master Gabriel, how you frightened me!"

"I meant to. Now tell what all this means, at once and truly," he said, in a tone intended to be stern, but which was only serious and troubled.

"All what means, sir?" she answered, feigning innocent surprise, though her eye never met his, and she still trembled in his hold.

"You know; the signals, the dropping of the handkerchief, the steps below there, and the figure creeping through the grass."

"Master must have quick eyes and ears to see and hear all that in such a minute. I only saw my handkerchief drop by accident; I only heard a bird chirp, and one of the dogs creep round the house;" but as she spoke she cast an uneasy glance over her shoulder into the night without.

"Why lie to me, Milly? I have watched you ever since you came in, and you are not yourself to-night. Something is wrong; I've felt it all day, but thought it was anxiety for my poor father. Why are all the people sent off to the quarters? Why is Andy meddling with the boats without my orders? and why do you look, speak, and act in this inexplicable manner?"

"If master gets worried and imagines mischief when there is none, I can't help it," she said, doggedly.

Both while speaking and listening Gabriel had scrutinized her closely, and all he saw confirmed his suspicion that something serious was amiss. In the slender wrist he held the pulse thrilled quick and strong; he heard the rapid beating of her heart, the flutter of the breath upon her lips; saw that her face was colorless, her eyes both restless and elusive. He was sure that no transient fear agitated her, but felt that some unwonted excitement possessed her, threatenening to break out in spite of the self-control which years of servitude had taught her. What he had just seen and heard alarmed him; for his father had been a hard master, the island was governed by fear alone, and he never trod the dykes that bounded the long, low rice-fields without feeling as if he walked upon a crater-crust which might crack and spew fire any day. Many small omens of evil had occurred of late, which now returned to his recollection with sinister significance; and the vague disquiet that had haunted him all day now seemed an instinctive premonition of impending danger. Many fears flashed through his mind, and one resolution was firmly fixed. His face grew stern, his voice commanding, and his hand tightened its hold as he said, —

"Speak, Milly, or I shall be tempted to use my authority as a master, and that I never wish to do. If there is any deviltry afloat I must know it; and if you will not tell it me I shall search the island till I find it for myself."

She looked at him for the first time, as he spoke, with a curious blending of defiance for the master and admiration for the man. His last words changed it to one of fear; and her free hand was extended as if to bar his way, while she said, below her breath, and with another glance into the outer gloom, —

"You are safe here, but if you leave the house it will cost you your life."

"Then it must; for if you will not show me the peril, I swear I'll go to meet it blindly."

"No, no, wait a little; I dare not tell!"

"You shall tell. I am the mistress here, and have borne enough. Speak, girl, at once, or this proud spirit of yours shall be broken till you do."

Mrs. Butler had heard all that passed, had approached them, and being a woman who was by turns imperious, peevish, and passionate, she yielded to the latter impulse as she spoke, and gave the girl's shoulder an impatient shake, as if to force the truth out of her. The touch, the tone, were like sparks to powder; for the smouldering fire blazed up as Milly flung her off, wrenched herself free from Gabriel, and turned on his mother with a look that sent her back to her husband trembling and dismayed.

"Yes, I will speak, though it is too soon!" cried Milly, with a short, sharp laugh. "They may kill me for telling before the time; I can't help it; I must have one hour of freedom, if I die the next. There *is* deviltry afloat to-night, and it is yourselves you may blame for it. We can't bear any more, and before a new master comes to torment us like the old one, we've determined to try for liberty, though there'll be bloody work before we get it. The boys are not at the quarters, but fifty are waiting at the rice-mill till midnight, and then they'll come up here to do as they've been done by. While they wait they're beginning with overseer Neal; whipping, burning, torturing him, for all I know, as other men, and women too, have been whipped, burnt and tortured there. That was his scream you heard. Alec never went for the doctor; Andy's guarding the boats till we want them; big Mose is watching round the house; the alarm bell's down; I've cleared the house of arms, and spoilt the pistols that I dared not take; Master Gabriel's the only white man on the island, and there's no help for you unless the Lord turns against us. Who is the mistress now?"

The girl paused there, breathless but exultant, for the words had poured from her lips as if the pent-up degradation, wrath and wrong of nineteen years had broken bounds at last and must overflow, even though they wrecked her by their vehemence. Some spirit stronger than herself seemed to possess and speak out of her, making her look like an embodied passion, beautiful, yet terrible, as she glanced from face to face, seeing how pale and panic-stricken each became, as her rapid words made visible the retribution that hung over them. Gabriel stood aghast at the swift and awful answer given to his prayer; the daughters fled to their mother's arms for shelter; the wife clung to her husband for the protection which he could no longer give, and, as if dragged back to life by the weight of a woe, such as he had himself inflicted upon others, the old man rose up in his bed, speechless, helpless, yet conscious of the dangers of the hour, and doubly daunted by death's terrors, because so powerless to succor those for whom he had periled his own soul. A bitter cry broke from him as his last look showed him the impending doom which all his impotent remorse could not avert, and in that cry the old man's spirit passed, to find that, even for such as he, Infinite justice was tempered by Infinite mercy.

During the few moments in which the wife and daughters forgot fear in sorrow, and the son took hurried counsel with himself how best to meet the coming danger, Milly was learning that the bitter far exceeds the sweet in human vengeance. The slave exulted in the freedom so dearly purchased, but the woman felt that in avenging them her wrongs had lost their dignity, and though she had changed places with her mistress, she found that power did not bring her peace. She had no skill to analyze the feeling, no words in which to express it, even to herself, but she was so strongly conscious of it, that its mysterious power marred the joy she thought to feel, and forced her to confess that in the hour of expected triumph she was baffled and defeated by her own conscience. With women doomed to a fate like hers, the higher the order of intelligence the deeper the sense of degradation, the more intense the yearning for liberty at any price. Milly had always rebelled against her lot, although, compared with that of her class, it had not been a hard one till the elder Butler bought her, that his son, seeing slavery in such a lovely form, might learn to love it. But Gabriel, in his brief visits, soon convinced his father that no temptation could undermine his sturdy Northern sense of right and justice, and though he might easily learn to love the beautiful woman, he could not learn to oppress the slave whose utter helplessness appealed to all that was manliest in him.

Milly felt this deeply, and knew that the few black drops in her veins parted herself and Gabriel more hopelessly than the widest seas that ever rolled between two lovers. This inexorable fact made all the world look dark to her; life became a burden, and one purpose alone sustained her,— the resolution to achieve her own liberty, to enjoy a brief triumph over those who had wronged her, then to die, and find compensation for a hapless human love in the fatherly tenderness of a Divine one. She had prayed, worked and waited for this hour, with all the ardor, energy and patience of her nature. Yet when it came she was not satisfied; a sense of guilt oppressed her, and the loss seemed greater than the gain. Gabriel had given her a look which wounded more deeply than the sharpest reproach; and the knowledge that she had forfeited the confidence he had always shown her, now made her gloomy when she would have been glad, humble when she thought to have been proudest. Gabriel saw and understood her mood, felt that their only hope of deliverance lay in her, and while his mother and sisters lamented for the dead, he bestirred himself to save the living.

"Milly," he began, with sad seriousness, "we deserve no mercy, and I ask none for myself; I only implore you to spare the women and give me time to atone for the weak, the wicked hesitation which has brought us to this pass. I meant to free you all as soon as you were legally mine, as it was too late for my father to endear his memory by one just act. But it was hard to make my mother and my sisters poor, and so I waited, hoping to be shown some way by which I could be just and generous both to you and them."

"Three women were more precious than two hundred helpless creatures in the eyes of a Christian gentleman from the free North! I'm glad you told me this;" and there was something like contempt in the look she gave her master.

There was no answer to that, for it was true; and in the remorseful shame that sent the blood to Gabriel's forehead, he confessed the fact which he was too honest to deny. Still looking at her, with eyes that pleaded for him better than his words, he said, with a humility that conquered her disdain, —

"I shall expiate that sin if I die to-night; and I will give myself up to be dealt with as you please, if you will save my mother and my sisters, and let them free you in my name. Before God and my dead father I promise this, upon my honor!"

"There are no witnesses to that but those whom I'll not trust; honor means nothing to us who are not allowed to keep our own," said Milly, looking moodily upon the ground, as if she feared to look up lest she should relent, for excitement was ebbing fast, and a flood of regretful recollections rising in her heart.

"I did not expect that reproach from you," Gabriel answered, taking courage from the signs he saw. "Do you remember, when my father gave you to me, how indignantly I rejected the gift, and promised that in my eyes you should be as sacred as either of those poor girls? Have I not kept my word, Milly?"

"Yes! O yes!" she said, with trembling lips, and eyes she dared not lift, they were so full of grateful tears. Carefully steadying her traitorous voice, she added, earnestly, "Master Gabriel! I *do* remember, and I've tried all day to save you, but you wouldn't go. I will trust your word, and do my best to help the ladies, if they'll promise to free us all to-morrow, and you will leave the island at once. Mose will let you pass; for that handkerchief was dropped to tell him that you were abroad, and were to be got off against your will, if you wouldn't go quietly. Both he and Andy will save you for my sake; the others won't, because they don't know you as we do. Please go, Master Gabriel, before it is too late."

"No, I shall stay. What would you think of me, if I deserted these helpless women in such danger, to save myself at their expense? I cannot quite trust you, Milly, after treachery like this."

"Who taught us to be treacherous, and left us nothing but our own cunning to help ourselves with?"

The first part of Gabriel's speech made the last less hard to bear; and Milly's question was put in a tone that was more apologetic than accusatory, for Gabriel cared what she thought of him, and that speech comforted her.

"Not I, Milly; but let the sins of the dead rest, and tell me if you will not help my mother and Grace and Clara off, instead of me? The promise will be all the sooner and the better kept, or, if it comes too late, I shall be the only and the fittest person to pay the penalty."

Milly's face darkened, and she turned away with an expression of keen disappointment. Mrs. Butler and her daughters had restrained their lamentations to listen; but at the sound of Gabriel's proposal, the sisters ran to Milly, and, clinging about her knees, implored her to pity, forgive, and save them. Well for them that they did so; for Milly felt as if many degradations were cancelled by that act, and, as she saw her young mistresses at her feet, the sense of power soothed her sore heart.

and added the grace of generosity to the duty of forgiveness. She did not speak, yet she did not deny their prayer, and stood wavering between doubt and desire as the fateful moments rapidly flew by; Gabriel remembered that, and, taking her hand, said, in a voice whose earnestness was perilously persuasive to the poor girl's ear, —

"Milly, you said there was no hope for us unless God turned against you. I think He has, and, speaking through that generous heart of yours, pleads for us better than we can plead for ourselves. It is so beautiful to pity, so magnanimous to forgive; and the greater the wrong, the more pardon humbles the transgressor and ennobles the bestower. Dear Milly, spare these poor girls as you have been spared; prove yourself the truer woman, the nobler mistress; teach them a lesson which they never can forget, and sweeten your liberty with the memory of this act."

Milly listened still with downcast eyes and averted face, but every word went straight to her heart, soothing, strengthening, inspiring all that was best and bravest in that poor heart, so passionate, and yet so warm and womanly withal. No man had ever spoken to her before of magnanimity, of proving herself superior to those who had shown no mercy to her faults, accorded no praise to her virtues, nor lightened a hard servitude with any touch of friendliness. No man had ever looked into her face before with eyes in which admiration for her beauty was mingled with pity for her helpless womanhood; and, better than all, no man, old or young, had ever until now recognized in her a fellow-creature, born to the same rights, gifted with the same powers, and capable of the same sufferings and sacrifices as himself.

That touched and won her; that appealed to the spirit which lives through all oppression in the lowest of God's children; and through all her frame there went a glow of warmth and joy, as if some strong, kind hand had lifted her from the gloom of a desolate despair into the sunshine of a happier world. Her eye wandered toward the faces of dead master, conquered mistress, and darkened as it looked; passed to the pale girls still clinging to her skirts, and softened visibly; was lifted to Gabriel, and kindled with the new-born desire to prove herself worthy of the confidence which would be her best reward. A smile broke beautifully across her face, and her lips were parted to reply, when Mrs. Butler, who sat trembling behind her, cried, in a shrill, imploring whisper,—

"Remember all I've done for you, Milly, all I still have it in my power to do. I promise to free you, if you will only save us now. Be merciful, for your old master's sake, if not for mine."

The sound of that querulous voice seemed to sting Milly like a lash, threatening to undo all Gabriel's work. Her eye grew fiery again, her mouth hard, her face bitterly scornful, as she said, with a glance which her mistress never forgot,—

"I'm not likely to forget all you've done for me; I would not accept my liberty from you if you could give it; and if a word of mine could save you, I'd not say it for old master's sake, much less for yours."

With a warning gesture to his mother, Gabriel turned that defiant face toward himself, and holding it firmly yet gently between his hands, bent on it a look that allayed the rising storm by the magic of a power which the young man had never used till now, though conscious of possessing it, — for Milly's tell-tale countenance had betrayed her secret long ago. As he looked deep into her eyes, with a glance which was both commanding and compassionate, they first fell with sudden shame, then, as if controlled by the power of those other eyes, they rose again and met them with a sad sincerity that made their beauty tragical, as they filled slowly till two great tears rolled down her cheeks, wetting the hands that touched them; and when Gabriel said, softly, "For my sake you will save us?" she straightway answered, "Yes."

"God bless you, Milly! Now tell me how I am to help you, for time is going, and lives hang on the minutes."

He released her as he spoke; and, though she still looked at him as if he were the one saving power of her thwarted life, she answered, pleadingly, —

"Hush, Master Gabriel! please don't speak to me, for then I only feel, — now I must think."

How still the room grew as they waited! The presence of death was less solemn than that of fear, for the dead seemed forgotten, and the living all unconscious of the awesome contrast between the pale expectancy of their panic-stricken faces and the repose of that one untroubled countenance. How suddenly the night grew full of ominous sounds! How intently all eyes were fixed upon the beautiful woman who stood among them holding their lives in her hands, and how they started, when, through the hush, came a soft chime as the half-hour struck! Milly heard and answered that silvery sound as the anxious watchers would have had her:

"It can be done," she said, in a tone which carried hope to every heart "It can be done, but I must do it alone, for I can pass Mose and get Andy across the river without their suspecting that I'm going for help. You must stay here and do your best to guard the ladies, Master Gabriel; it won't be safe for any of you to go now."

"But, Milly, the boys may not wait till twelve, or you may be delayed, and then we are lost."

"I have thought of that; and as I go out I'll take old Sandra with me; she'll understand in a minute. She'll go down to the mill and talk to them and keep them, if anything can do it, for they love and fear her more than any one on the island. Be quiet, trust to me, and I'll save you, Master Gabriel."

He silently held out his hand, as if pledging his word to obey and trust. With the warmth and grace of her impulsive temperament, Milly bent her head, laid her cheek against that friendly hand, wet it with grateful tears, kissed it with loving lips, and went her way, feeling as if all things were possible to her for Gabriel's sake.

Listening breathlessly, they heard her foot-falls die away, heard Sandra's voice below, a short parley with Mose, then watched the old woman and the young depart in opposite directions, leaving them to feel the bitterness of dependence in a strange, stern fashion, which they had never thought to know. Man-like, Gabriel could not long stand idle while danger menaced and women faced it for him. Anxious to take such precautions as might hold the expected assailants at bay, even for a moment, he bade his mother and sisters remain quiet, that no suspicion might be excited, and crept down to test the capabilities of the house to withstand a short siege, if other hopes failed. The slight, many-doored and windowed mansion, built for a brief occupancy when the winter months rendered the region habitable for whites, was but ill-prepared to repel any attack; and a hasty survey convinced Gabriel that it was both hazardous and vain to attempt a barricade which a few strong arms could instantly destroy. As he stood disheartened, unarmed, and alone in the long hall, dimly lighted by the lamp he carried, a sense of utter desolation came over him, dampening his courage, and oppressing his mind with the dreariest forebodings. Thinking of the many true hearts and stout arms far away there at the North, which would have come to his aid so readily could his need have been known, he yearned for a single friend, a single weapon, that he might conquer or die like a man. And both were given him.

Pausing before a door that opened out upon the rear of the house, his eye caught sight of a heavy whip, whose loaded handle had felled men before now, and might easily do so again, if wielded by a strong arm. He took it down, saying to himself, "It is the first time I ever touched the accursed thing; God grant that it may be the last." A low sound behind him caused the blood to chill an instant in his veins, then to rush on with a quicker flow, as, poising the weapon in one hand, he lifted the lamp above his head, and searched the gloom. Far at the other end of the long hall a dark figure crept along, and a pair of glittering eyes were fixed upon his own. "Come on; I'm ready," he said, steadily, and was answered by the patter of rapid steps, the sight of an unexpected ally, as a great black hound came leaping upon him in a rapture of canine delight. Old Mort had been the fiercest, most efficient blood-hound on the island; and still, in spite of age, was a formidable beast, ready to track or assault a negro, and pull him down or throttle him, at word of command. He had been his possessor's favorite till Gabriel came; then he deserted the old master for the young, and was always left at large when he was at home. Mort had been missing all day, and now the rope trailing behind him was sufficient evidence that he had been decoyed away, lest his vigilance should warn his master, and that, having freed himself, he had stolen home, to lie concealed till night and his master's presence reassured him.

As the great creature reared himself before the young man, with a paw on either shoulder, and looked into his face with eyes that seemed almost human in their intelligent affection, Gabriel dropped the whip, put down the lamp, and caressed the hound with an almost boyish gratitude and fondness; for, with the sense of security this powerful ally brought, there came a remorseful memory, that, though the possessor of two hundred human beings, he had no friend but a dog. At this point Mort suddenly pricked up his ears, slipped from his master's hold, and snuffed suspiciously at the closed door. Some one was evidently without, and the creature's keen scent detected the unseen listener. With a noiseless command to the dog to keep quiet, Gabriel caught up his only weapon, and stood waiting for whatever demonstration should follow. None came; and presently Mort returned to him with a sagacious glance and a sleepy yawn, sure evidences that Mose had paused a moment in his round, and had gone on again. Big Mose was, with one exception, the strongest, most rebellious slave on the place; and though Gabriel had longed to rush out and attack him, he had not dared to try it, for his strength was as a child's compared to the stalwart slave's. Now, with Mort to help him, the thing was possible; and as he stood there, with only a door between him and the man who had sworn to take his life, a strange consciousness of power came to him; his muscles seemed to grow firm as iron, his blood flowed calm and cool, and in his mind there rose a purpose, desperately simple, yet wise, despite its seeming rashness. He would master Mose, and, leaving Mort to guard him, would go down to the mill, and, if both Sandra's and his own appeals and promises proved unavailing, would give himself up, hoping that his death or torture would delay the doom of those defenceless women, and give Milly time to bring them better help than any he could give. Some atonement must be made, he thought, and perhaps innocent blood would wash the black stain from his father's memory better than the deed he had hoped to do in that father's name on the morrow. He had held a precious opportunity in his hands, had delayed through a mistaken kindness; now it was lost, perhaps forever, and he must pay the costly price which God exacts of those who palter with their consciences. As the thought came, and the purpose grew, it brought with it that high courage, that entire self-abnegation which we call heroism; and that fateful moment made Gabriel a man.

A word, a gesture, put the dog upon his mettle; then cutting away the long rope, Gabriel threw it over his arm, unbarred the door, set it ajar, and, standing behind it, with the hound under his hand, he waited for Mose to make his round. Soon Mort's restless ears gave token of his approach; and, as the stealthy steps came stealing on, he was with difficulty restrained; for now instinct showed him danger, and he was as eager as his master to be up and doing. The streak of light attracted the man's eye. He paused, drew nearer, listened; then softly pushed the door open, and leaned in to reconnoitre. That instant Mort was on him, a heavy blow half stunned him, and, before his scattered wits could be collected, he was down, his hands fast bound, and both master and dog standing over him panting, but unhurt.

"Now, Mose, if you want to save your life, be still, and answer my questions truly," said Gabriel, with one hand on the man's throat, the other holding back Mort, whose tawny eye was savage now. "I know your plot, and have found means to spoil it. How do you think I'm going to punish you all?"

"Dun'no, massa," muttered Mose, with a grim resignation to any fate.

"I'm going to free every man, woman, and child on the island, and fling that devilish thing into the river," he said, as he spurned the whip with his foot.

An incredulous look and derisive grin was the only thanks and answer he received.

"You don't believe it? Well, who can blame you, poor soul? Not I. Now tell me how many men are on the watch between here and the rice-mill?" Gabriel spoke with a flash of the eye and a sudden deepening of the voice; for both indignation and excitement stirred him. The look, the tone, did more to convince Mose than a flood of words; for he had learned to try men by tests of his own, and had more faith in the promises of their faces than those of their tongues. More respectfully, he said, —

"No one, 'sides me, massa. Andy's at de landin', and de rest at de mill 'ceptin' dem as isn't in de secret."

"Mind, no lies, Mose, or your free papers will be the last I sign to-morrow. Get up, and come quietly with me; for if you try to run, Mort will pin you. I'm going to the mill, and want you safely under lock and key first."

"Is massa gwine alone?" asked Mose, glancing about him, for Gabriel spoke as if he had a score of men at his command.

"Yes, I'm going alone; why not?"

"Massa knows dere's fifty of de boys dar sworn to kill him, if Milly don't git him 'way 'fore dey comes up?"

"I know, and Milly's done her best to get me off, but I'd rather stay; I'm not afraid."

Gabriel's blood was up now: danger had no terrors for him; and, beyond the excitement of the moment, his purpose lent him a calm courage which impressed the slave as something superhuman. Like one in a maze of doubt and fear, he obediently followed his master to an out-house, where, binding feet as well as hands, Gabriel left him with the promise and the warning, —

"Sit here till I come to let you out a free man, if I live to do it. Don't stir nor call, for Mort will be at the door to silence you and howl for me, if you try any tricks. I'll not keep you long, if I can help it."

The slave only stared dumbly at him, incapable of receiving the vast idea of liberty, pardon, and kindness all at once; and bidding Mort guard both prisoner and house, Gabriel stole along the path that wound away through grove and garden to the rice-mill, where so many fates were soon to be decided. As he went he glanced from earth to sky, and found propitious omens everywhere. No flowery thicket concealed a lurking foe to clutch at him in the dark; but the fragrance of trodden grass, the dewy touch of leaves against his cheek, the peaceful night-sounds that surrounded him, gave him strange comfort and encouragement; for when his fellow-creatures had deserted, Nature took him to her motherly heart. From above, fitful glimpses of the moon guided him on his perilous way; for the wind had changed, the black clouds were driving seaward, and the storm was passing without either thunderbolt or hurricane. Coming, at length, within sight of the half-ruined mill, he paused to reconnoitre. Through chinks in the rude walls a dim light shone, muffled voices rose and fell; and once there was a hoarse sound, as of a half-uttered shout. Creeping warily to a dark nook among the ruins, Gabriel made his way to a crevice in an inner wall, and, looking through it, saw a sight little fitted to reassure him, either as a master or a man.

The long, low-raftered portion of the mill, which once had been the threshing-floor, was now lighted by the red glare of several torches, which filled the place with weird shadows, and sudden glimpses of objects that seemed the more mysterious or terrible for being but half seen. In one corner, under a coarse covering, something lay stark and still; a clenched hand was visible, and several locks of light hair dabbled with blood, but nothing more. Fifty men, old and young, of all shades of color, all types of their unhappy race, stood or sat about three, who evidently were the leaders of the league. One, a young man, so fair that the red lines across his shoulders looked doubly barbarous there, was half-kneeling, and steadily filing at a chain that held his feet together as his hands had been held till some patient friend had freed them, and left him to finish the slow task. He worked so eagerly that the drops stood thick upon his haggard face, and his scarred chest heaved with his painful breath; for this was the Tony who was too much cut up with his last whipping to run on Mrs. Butler's errand, but not too feeble to strike a blow for liberty. The second man was as near an animal as a human creature could become, and yet be recognized as such. A burly, brutal-looking negro, maimed and distorted by every cruelty that could be invented or inflicted, he was a sight to daunt the stoutest heart, as he sat sharpening the knife which had often threatened him in the overseer's hand, and was still red with the overseer's blood.

Standing erect between the two, and in striking contrast to them, was a gigantic man, with a fine, dark face, a noble head, and the limbs of an ebony Hercules. A native African, from one of those tribes whose wills are never broken, — who can be subdued by kindness, but who often kill themselves rather than suffer the degradation of the lash. No one had dared to subject him to that chastisement, as was proved by the unmarred smoothness of the muscular body, bare to the waist; but round his neck was riveted an iron collar, with four curved spikes. It was a shameful badge of serfdom; it prevented him from lying down, it galled him with its ceaseless chafing, yet he wore it with an air which would have made the hideous necklace seem some barbaric ornament, if that had been possible; and faced the excited crowd with a native dignity which nothing could destroy, and which proved him their master in intelligence, as well as strength and courage.

Before them all, yet lifted a little above them by her position on a fallen fragment of the roof, stood old Cassandra. A tall, gaunt woman, with a countenance which age, in making venerable, had not robbed of its vigor; her sightless eyes were wide open with a weird effect of seeing without sight, and her high white turban, her long staff, and the involuntary tremor of her shrivelled hands, gave her the air of some ancient sorceress or priestess, bearing her part in some heathen rite. The majestic-looking slave with the collar had apparently been speaking, for his face was turned toward her, and his dark features were still alive with the emotions which had just found vent in words. As Gabriel looked, old Sandra struck the floor with her staff, as if commanding silence; and, as the stir of some momentary outbreak subsided, she said, in a strong voice, which rose and fell in a sort of solemn chant as her earnestness increased and her listeners grew obedient to its spell, —

"Chil'en, I'se heerd yer plans, — now I wants ter len' a han' and help you in dis hour of tribbleation. You's killed oberseer Neal, and d'rectly you's all gwine up ter de house to kill massa, missis and de young folks. Now what's you gwine to do dat fer? and what's dey eber done bad nuf ter make you willin' ter fro 'way yer souls dis night?"

"Kase we can't b'ar no more." "Old massa hunted my boy wid hounds and dey tore him ter def." "He sold my chil'en and drove Rachel crazy wid de partin'." 'Old missis had my pore girl whipped kase she was too sick ter stan' and dress her." "Massa Gabriel may be harder dan de ole one, and we's tired ob hell."

These, and many another short, stern answer, came to Sandra's question; she expected them, was ready to meet them, and knew how best to reach the outraged hearts now hungering for vengeance. Her well-known afflictions, her patience, her piety, gave a certain sanctity to her presence, great weight to her words, and an almost marvellous power to her influence over her own people, who believed her to be half saint, half seer. She felt her power, and, guided by an instinct that seldom failed, she used it wisely in this perilous hour, remembering that her listeners, though men in their passions, were children in their feelings.

"You pore boys, I knows de troof ob all dat, and I'se had my trubbles hard and heavy as you has, but I'se learnt to fergib 'em, and dey don't hurt now. Ole massa bought me thirty year' ago 'way from all I keered fer, and I'se slaved fer him widout no t'anks, no wages, eber since; but I'se fergived him dat. He sole my chil'en, all ten; my boys up de riber, my perty little girls down to Orleans, and bringed up his chil'en on de money; dat come bery hard, but de Lord helped me, and I fergived him dat. He shot my ole Ben kase he couldn't whip me hisself, nor stan' by and see it done; dat mos' broke my heart, but in de end I foun' I could fergib him one time more. He made me nuss him when de fever come and every one was 'fraid ob him; de long watchin', de hard work and de cryin' fer my chil'en made me bline at last; but I fergived him dat right hearty, fer though dey took my eyes away dey couldn't bline my soul, and in de darkness I hab seen de Lord."

The truth, the pathos, the devout assurance of her words, impressed and controlled the sympathetic creatures to whom she spoke, as no reproach or denunciation would have done. A murmur went through the crowd, and more than one savage face lost something of its brutality, gained something of its former sad patience, as the old woman touched, with wondrous skill, the chords that still made music in these tried and tempted hearts.

"Yes, chil'en, I hab seen de Lord, and He has made de night into day fer me, has held me up in all my trubbles, tole me to hole fas' by Him, and promised He would bring me safe ter glory. I'se faith ter feel He will, and while I wait, I'se savin' up my soul fer Him. Boys, He says de same to you froo me; He says hole fas', b'ar all dat's sent, beleebe in Him, and wait the coming ob de Lord."

"We's done tired a-waitin', de Lord's so bery long a comin', Sandra."

It was a weary, hopeless voice that answered, as an old man shook his white head and lifted up the dim eyes that for eighty years had watched in vain.

"It's you dat's long a-comin' ter Him, Uncle Dave, but He ain't tired ob waitin' for yer. De places dar in heaven is all ready, de shinin' gowns, de harps ob gole, de eberlastin' glory, and de peace. No rice-swamps dar, no sugar-mills, no cotton-fields, no houn's, no oberseer, no massa but de blessed Lord. Dar's yer chil'en, Uncle Dave, growed beautiful white angels, and a-waitin' till yer comes. Dar's yer wife, Pete, wid no lashes on her back, no sobbin' in her heart, a-waiting fer yer, anxious. Dar's yer fader, Jake; he don't need no proppin' now, and he'll run to meet yer when yer comes. Dar's yer pore sister Rachel, Ned; she ain't crying fer baby now, de Lord's got her in de holler ob His han', and she's a-waitin' fer de little one and you to come. Dar's my Ben, my chil'en all saved up for me, and when I comes I'll see 'em waitin' fer me at de door. But, best ob all, dar's de dear Lord waitin' fer us; He's holdin' out his arms, He's beckonin' all de while, He's sayin', in dat lovin' voice ob His, 'I sees yer sorrows, my pore chil'en, I hears yer sobbin' and yer prayers, I fergives yer sins, I knows yer won't 'spoint me ob dese yere fifty precious souls, and I'se a-waitin', waitin', waitin' fer yer all.' "

Strange fervor was in the woman's darkened face, strange eloquence in her aged voice, strange power in the persuasive gestures of her withered hands outstretched above them, warning, pleading, beckoning, as if, in truth, the Lord spoke through her, illuminating that poor place with the light of His divine compassion, the promises of His divine salvation. A dead silence followed as the last yearning cadence of the one voice rose, fell, and died away. Sandra let the strong contrast between the here and the hereafter make its due impression, then broke the silence, saying briefly, solemnly, —

"Boys, de Lord has spared yer one great sin dis night; ole massa's dead."

"Glory be to God, amen!" "Halleluyer! dat I'se libed ter see dis happy day!" "De Debble's got him, shore!" "Don't give up de chance, boys; young massa and de missis is lef' for us."

Such exclamations of gratitude, joy, and revenge, were the only demonstration which the news produced, and, mingling with them, a gust of wind came sweeping through the mill, as if nature gave a long sigh of relief that another tyrant had ceased to blight and burden her fair domain. Sandra's quick ear caught the last words, and a deep oath or two, as several men rose with the fierce fire rekindling in their eyes.

"Yes!" she cried, in a tone that held them even against their will, — "yes, young massa's lef'; but not to die, for if yer gives up your chance of damnation dis night, you'll all be free to-morrer. He's promised it; he'll do it, and dere'll be no blood but dat bad man's yonder, to cry from de groun', and b'ar witness 'ginst yer at de Judgment-Day."

"Free! to-morrer! Who's gwine to b'lieve dat, Sandra? We's been tole such stories often; but de morrer's never come, and now we's gwine to bring one for ourselves."

The gigantic man with the spiked collar on his neck said that, with a smile of grim determination, as he took up the iron bar, which in his desperate hands became a terribly formidable weapon.

A low growl, as of muttering thunder, answered him, and Sandra's heart sunk within her. But one hope remained; and, desperately clinging to it, she found that even in these betrayed, benighted creatures there still lived a sense of honor, a loyalty to truth, born of the manhood God had given them, the gratitude which one man had inspired.

"Hear me, jes once more, 'fore yer goes, boys. Tell me, what has young massa done ter make yer want his blood? Has he ever lashed yer, kicked, and cussed yer? Has he sole yer chil'ren, 'bused yer wives, or took yer ole folks from yer? Has he done anything but try to make ole massa kinder, to do his best fer us while he's here; and when he can't do nor b'ar no more, don't he go 'way to pray de Lord ter help us fer His sake?"

Not a voice answered; not one complaint, accusation, or reproach was made, and Prince, the fierce leader of the insurrection, paused, with his foot upon the threshold of the door; for a grateful memory confronted and arrested him. One little daughter, the last of many children, had been taken from him to be sold, when Gabriel, moved by his despair, had bought and freed and given her back to him, with the promise that she never should be torn from him again. For an instant the clasp of little clinging arms seemed to make the sore chafing of the iron ring unfelt; the touch of the hand that gave the precious gift now made that rude weapon weigh heavily in his own, and from the darkness which lay between him and the doomed home there seemed to rise the shadow of the face which once had looked compassionately into his and recognized him as a man. He turned, and, standing with his magnificent yet mournful figure fully revealed by the red flicker of the torches, put out one hand as if to withhold the desperate crowd before him, and asked, with an air of authority which well became a prince by birth as well as name, —

"Sandra, who tole you massa meant ter free us right away? You has blessed dreams sometimes, and maybe dis is one ob 'em. It's too good to be de troof."

"It is de troof, de livin' troof, and no dream ob mine was eber half so blessed as dis yere will be, if we has faith. Milly tole me jes now dat Massa Gabriel swore before de Lord and his dead father dat he'd free us all ter-morrer; and I come here ter save yer from de sin dat won't help, but hinder yer awful in dis world and de next. Dere's more good news 'sides dat. I heerd 'em talkin' 'bout de Norf. It's risin', boys, it's risin'! — de tings we's heerd is shore, and de day ob jubilee is comin' fas'."

It was well she added that last hope, for its effect was wonderful. Men lifted up their heads, hope quenched hatred in eyes that grew joyfully expectant, and for a moment the black sky seemed to glimmer with the first rays of the North star which should lead them up from that Dismal Swamp to a goodly land. Sandra felt the change, knew that only one more effective touch was needed to secure the victory, and, like the pious soul she was, turned in her hour of need to the only Friend who never had deserted her. Painfully bending her stiff knees, she knelt down before them, folded her hard hands, lifted her sightless eyes, and cried, in an agony of supplication, —

"Dear Lord, speak to dese yere pore chil'en, fer I'se done my bes'! Help 'em, save 'em, don't let 'em spile de freedom dat's comin' by a sin like dis to-night, but let 'em take it sweet and clean from Thy han' in de mornin'. Stan' by young massa, hole him up, don't let him 'spoint us, fer we'se ben bery patient, Lord; and help us to wait one night more, shore dat he'll keep de promise fer Thy blessed sake."

"I will!"

The voice rang through the place like a voice from heaven; and out from the darkness Gabriel came among them. To their startled, superstitious eyes he seemed no mortal man, but a beautiful, benignant angel, bringing tidings of great joy, as he stood there, armed with no weapon but a righteous purpose, gifted with no eloquence but the truth, stirred to his heart's core by strong emotion, and lifted above himself by the high mood born of that memorable hour

"My people! mine only while I speak; break up your league, lay down your arms, dry your tears, and forgive as you are forgiven, for this island no longer holds a master or a slave; but all are free forever and forever."

An awful silence fell upon the place, unbroken till old Sandra cried, with a glad, triumphant voice, —

"Chil'en! de Lord hab heerd, de Lord hab answered! Bless de Lord! O bless de Lord!"

Then, as a strong wind bows a field of grain, the breath of liberty swept over fifty souls, and down upon their knees fell fifty free men, while a great cry went up to heaven. Shouts, sobs, prayers and praises; the clash of falling arms; the rattle of fetters wrenched away; the rush of men gathered to each other's breasts, — all added to the wild abandonment of a happiness too mighty for adequate expression, as that wave of gratitude and love rolled up and broke at Gabriel's feet. With face hidden in his hands he stood; and while his heart sung for joy, tears from the deepest fountains of a man's repentant spirit fitly baptized the freedmen, who, clinging to his garments, kissing his feet and pouring blessings on his head, bestowed upon him a far nobler inheritance than that which he had lost.

"Hark!"

The word, and Sandra's uplifted hand, hushed the tumultuous thanksgiving, as if she were in truth the magician they believed her. A far-off murmur of many voices, the tramp of many feet was heard; all knew what it portended, yet none trembled, none fled; for a mightier power than either force or fear had conquered, and the victory was already won.

Through widening rifts in the stormy sky the moon broke clear and calm, gliding, like a visible benediction, from the young man's bent head to the dusky faces lifted toward the promised light; and in that momentary hush, solemn and sweet, across the river a distant clock struck twelve.

BOOK JUNGLE

Bringing Classics to Life

www.bookjungle.com   email: sales@bookjungle.com   fax: 630-214-0564   mail: Book Jungle PO Box 2226 Champaign, IL 61825

The Two Babylons
Alexander Hislop

You may be surprised to learn that many traditions of Roman Catholicism in fact don't come from Christ's teachings but from an ancient Babylonian "Mystery" religion that was centered on Nimrod, his wife Semiramis, and a child Tammuz. This book shows how this ancient religion transformed itself as it incorporated Christ into its teachings...

Religion/History Pages:358
ISBN: *1-59462-010-5*   MSRP *$22.95* QTY

The Go-Getter
Kyne B. Peter

The Go Getter is the story of William Peck. He was a war veteran and amputee who will not be refused what he wants. Peck not only fights to find employment but continually proves himself more than competent at the many difficult test that are throw his way in the course of his early days with the Ricks Lumber Company...

Business/Self Help/Inspirational Pages:68
ISBN: *1-59462-186-1*   MSRP *$8.95* QTY

The Power Of Concentration
Theron Q. Dumont

It is of the utmost value to learn how to concentrate. To make the greatest success of anything you must be able to concentrate your entire thought upon the idea you are working on. The person that is able to concentrate utilizes all constructive thoughts and shuts out all destructive ones...

Self Help/Inspirational Pages:196
ISBN: *1-59462-141-1*   MSRP *$14.95*

Self Mastery
Emile Coue

Emile Coue came up with novel way to improve the lives of people. He was a pharmacist by trade and often saw ailing people. This lead him to develop autosuggestion, a form of self-hypnosis. At the time his theories weren't popular but over the years evidence is mounting that he was indeed right all along...

New Age/Self Help Pages:98
ISBN: *1-59462-189-6*   MSRP *$7.95*

Rightly Dividing The Word
Clarence Larkin

The "Fundamental Doctrines" of the Christian Faith are clearly outlined in numerous books on Theology, but they are not available to the average reader and were mainly written for students. The Author has made it the work of his ministry to preach the "Fundamental Doctrines." To this end he has aimed to express them in the simplest and clearest manner...

Religion Pages:352
ISBN: *1-59462-334-1*   MSRP *$23.45*

The Awful Disclosures Of Maria Monk

"I cannot banish the scenes and characters of this book from my memory. To me it can never appear like an amusing fable, or lose its interest and importance. The story is one which is continually before me, and must return fresh to my mind with painful emotions as long as I live..."

Religion Pages:232
ISBN: *1-59462-160-8*   MSRP *$17.95*

The Law of Psychic Phenomena
Thomson Jay Hudson

"I do not expect this book to stand upon its literary merits; for if it is unsound in principle, felicity of diction cannot save it, and if sound, homeliness of expression cannot destroy it. My primary object in offering it to the public is to assist in bringing Psychology within the domain of the exact sciences. That this has never been accomplished..."

New Age Pages:420
ISBN: *1-59462-124-1*   MSRP *$29.95*

As a Man Thinketh
James Allen

"This little volume (the result of meditation and experience) is not intended as an exhaustive treatise on the much-written-upon subject of the power of thought. It is suggestive rather than explanatory, its object being to stimulate men and women to the discovery and perception of the truth that by virtue of the thoughts which they choose and encourage..."

Inspirational/Self Help Pages:80
ISBN: *1-59462-231-0*   MSRP *$9.45*

Beautiful Joe
Marshall Saunders

When Marshall visited the Moore family in 1892, she discovered Joe, a dog that had nursed back to health from his previous abusive home to live a happy life. So moved was she, that she wrote this classic masterpiece which won accolades and was recognized as a heartwarming symbol for humane animal treatment...

Fiction Pages:256
ISBN: *1-59462-261-2*   MSRP *$18.45*

The Enchanted April
Elizabeth Von Arnim

It began in a woman's club in London on a February afternoon, an uncomfortable club, and a miserable afternoon, when Mrs. Wilkins, who had come down from Hampstead to shop and had lunched at her club, took up The Times from the table in the smoking-room...

Fiction Pages:368
ISBN: *1-59462-150-0*   MSRP *$23.45*

The Codes Of Hammurabi And Moses - W. W. Davies

The discovery of the Hammurabi Code is one of the greatest achievements of archaeology, and is of paramount interest, not only to the student of the Bible, but also to all those interested in ancient history...

Religion Pages:132
ISBN: *1-59462-338-4*   MSRP *$12.95*

Holland - The History Of Netherlands
Thomas Colley Grattan

Thomas Grattan was a prestigious writer from Dublin who served as British Consul to the US. Among his works is an authoritative look at the history of Holland. A colorful and interesting look at history....

History/Politics Pages:408
ISBN: *1-59462-137-3*   MSRP *$26.95*

The Thirty-Six Dramatic Situations
Georges Polti

An incredibly useful guide for aspiring authors and playwrights. This volume categorizes every dramatic situation which could occur in a story and describes them in a list of 36 situations. A great aid to help inspire or formalize the creative writing process...

Self Help/Reference Pages:204
ISBN: *1-59462-134-9*   MSRP *$15.95*

A Concise Dictionary of Middle English
A. L. Mayhew
Walter W. Skeat

The present work is intended to meet, in some measure, the requirements of those who wish to make some study of Middle-English, and who find a difficulty in obtaining such assistance as will enable them to find out the meanings and etymologies of the words most essential to their purpose...

Reference/History Pages:332
ISBN: *1-59462-119-5*   MSRP *$29.95*

BOOK JUNGLE

Bringing Classics to Life

www.bookjungle.com email: sales@bookjungle.com fax: 630-214-0564 mail: Book Jungle PO Box 2226 Champaign, IL 61825

The Witch-Cult in Western Europe
Margaret Murray
The mass of existing material on this subject is so great that I have not attempted to make a survey of the whole of European "Witchcraft" but have confined myself to an intensive study of the cult in Great Britain. In order, however, to obtain a clearer understanding of the ritual and beliefs I have had recourse to French and Flemish sources...

Occult   Pages:308
ISBN: *1-59462-126-8*   MSRP *$22.45*

QTY

Philosophy Of Natural Therapeutics
Henry Lindlahr
We invite the earnest cooperation in this great work of all those who have awakened to the necessity for more rational living and for radical reform in healing methods...

Health/Philosophy/Self Help   Pages:552
ISBN: *1-59462-132-2*   MSRP *$34.95*

QTY

The Science Of Psychic Healing
Yogi Ramacharaka
This book is not a book of theories it deals with facts. Its author regards the best of theories as but working hypotheses to be used only until better ones present themselves. The "fact" is the principal thing the essential thing to uncover which the tool, theory, is used...

New Age/Health   Pages:180
ISBN: *1-59462-140-3*   MSRP *$13.95*

A Message to Garcia
Elbert Hubbard
This literary trifle, A Message to Garcia, was written one evening after supper, in a single hour. It was on the Twenty-second of February, Eighteen Hundred Ninety-nine, Washington's Birthday, and we were just going to press with the March Philistine...

New Age/Fiction   Pages:92
ISBN: *1-59462-144-6*   MSRP *$9.95*

Bible Myths
Thomas Doane
In pursuing the study of the Bible Myths, facts pertaining thereto, in a condensed form, seemed to be greatly needed, and nowhere to be found. Widely scattered through hundreds of ancient and modern volumes, most of the contents of this book may indeed be found; but any previous attempt to trace exclusively the myths and legends...

Religion/History   Pages:644
ISBN: *1-59462-163-2*   MSRP *$38.95*

The Book of Jasher
Alcuinus Flaccus Albinus
The Book of Jasher is an historical religious volume that many consider as a missing holy book from the Old Testament. Particularly studied by the Church of Later Day Saints and historians, it covers the history of the world from creation until the period of Judges in Israel. It's authenticity is bolstered due to a reference to the Book of Jasher in the Bible in Joshua 10:13

Religion/History   Pages:276
ISBN: *1-59462-197-7*   MSRP *$18.95*

Tertium Organum
P. D. Ouspensky
A truly mind expanding writing that combines science with mysticism with unprecedented elegance. He presents the world we live in as a multi dimensional world and time as a motion through this world. But this isn't a cold and purely analytical explanation but a masterful presentation filled with similes and analogies...

New Age   Pages:356
ISBN: *1-59462-205-1*   MSRP *$23.95*

The Titan
Theodore Dreiser
"When Frank Algernon Cowperwood emerged from the Eastern District Penitentiary, in Philadelphia he realized that the old life he had lived in that city since boyhood was ended. His youth was gone, and with it had been lost the great business prospects of his earlier manhood. He must begin again..."

Fiction   Pages:564
ISBN: *1-59462-220-5*   MSRP *$33.95*

Advance Course in Yogi Philosophy
Yogi Ramacharaka
"The twelve lessons forming this volume were originally issued in the shape of monthly lessons, known as "The Advanced Course in Yogi Philosophy and Oriental Occultism" during a period of twelve months beginning with October, 1904, and ending September, 1905."

Philosophy/Inspirational/Self Help   Pages:340
ISBN: *1-59462-229-9*   MSRP *$22.95*

Biblical Essays
J. B. Lightfoot
About one-third of the present volume has already seen the light. The opening essay "On the Internal Evidence for the Authenticity and Genuineness of St John's Gospel" was published in the "Expositor" in the early months of 1890, and has been reprinted since...

Religion/History   Pages:480
ISBN: *1-59462-238-8*   MSRP *$30.95*

Ambassador Morgenthau's Story
Henry Morgenthau
"By this time the American people have probably become convinced that the Germans deliberately planned the conquest of the world. Yet they hesitate to convict on circumstantial evidence and for this reason all eye witnesses to this, the greatest crime in modern history, should volunteer their testimony..."

History   Pages:472
ISBN: *1-59462-244-2*   MSRP *$29.95*

The Settlement Cook Book
Simon Kander
A legacy from the civil war, this book is a classic "American charity cookbook," which was used for fundraisers starting in Milwaukee. While it has transformed over the years, this printing provides great recipes from American history. Over two million copies have been sold. This volume contains a rich collection of recipes from noted chefs and hostesses of the turn of the century...

How-to   Pages:472
ISBN: *1-59462-256-6*   MSRP *$29.95*

The Aquarian Gospel of Jesus the Christ
Levi Dowling
A retelling of Jesus' story which tells us what happened during the twenty year gap left by the Bible's New Testament. It tells of his travels to the far-east where he studied with the masters and fought against the rigid caste system. This book has enjoyed a resurgence in modern America and provides spiritual insight with charm. Its influences can be seen throughout the Age of Aquarius.

Religion   Pages:264
ISBN: *1-59462-321-X*   MSRP *$18.95*

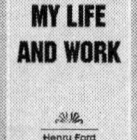

My Life and Work
Henry Ford
Henry Ford revolutionized the world with his implementation of mass production for the Model T automobile. Gain valuable business insight into his life and work with his own auto-biography... "We have only started on our development of our country we have not as yet, with all our talk of wonderful progress, done more than scratch the surface. The progress has been wonderful enough but..."

Biographies/History/Business   Pages:300
ISBN: *1-59462-198-5*   MSRP *$21.95*

BOOK JUNGLE

Bringing Classics to Life

www.bookjungle.com email: sales@bookjungle.com fax: 630-214-0564 mail: Book Jungle PO Box 2226 Champaign, IL 61825

QTY

- [ ] **The Rosicrucian Cosmo-Conception Mystic Christianity** by *Max Heindel* ISBN: *1-59462-188-8* **$38.95**
  The Rosicrucian Cosmo-conception is not dogmatic, neither does it appeal to any other authority than the reason of the student. It is: not controversial, but is: sent forth in the, hope that it may help to clear... *New Age/Religion Pages 646*

- [ ] **Abandonment To Divine Providence** by *Jean-Pierre de Caussade* ISBN: *1-59462-228-0* **$25.95**
  "The Rev. Jean Pierre de Caussade was one of the most remarkable spiritual writers of the Society of Jesus in France in the 18th Century. His death took place at Toulouse in 1751. His works have gone through many editions and have been republished... *Inspirational/Religion Pages 400*

- [ ] **Mental Chemistry** by *Charles Haanel* ISBN: *1-59462-192-6* **$23.95**
  Mental Chemistry allows the change of material conditions by combining and appropriately utilizing the power of the mind. Much like applied chemistry creates something new and unique out of careful combinations of chemicals the mastery of mental chemistry... *New Age Pages 354*

- [ ] **The Letters of Robert Browning and Elizabeth Barret Barrett 1845-1846 vol II** ISBN: *1-59462-193-4* **$35.95**
  by *Robert Browning* and *Elizabeth Barrett* *Biographies Pages 596*

- [ ] **Gleanings In Genesis (volume I)** by *Arthur W. Pink* ISBN: *1-59462-130-6* **$27.45**
  Appropriately has Genesis been termed "the seed plot of the Bible" for in it we have, in germ form, almost all of the great doctrines which are afterwards fully developed in the books of Scripture which follow... *Religion Inspirational Pages 420*

- [ ] **The Master Key** by *L. W. de Laurence* ISBN: *1-59462-001-6* **$30.95**
  In no branch of human knowledge has there been a more lively increase of the spirit of research during the past few years than in the study of Psychology, Concentration and Mental Discipline. The requests for authentic lessons in Thought Control, Mental Discipline and... *New Age/Business Pages 422*

- [ ] **The Lesser Key Of Solomon Goetia** by *L. W. de Laurence* ISBN: *1-59462-092-X* **$9.95**
  This translation of the first book of the "Lemegton" which is now for the first time made accessible to students of Talismanic Magic was done, after careful collation and edition, from numerous Ancient Manuscripts in Hebrew, Latin, and French... *New Age Occult Pages 92*

- [ ] **Rubaiyat Of Omar Khayyam** by *Edward Fitzgerald* ISBN: *1-59462-332-5* **$13.95**
  Edward Fitzgerald, whom the world has already learned, in spite of his own efforts to remain within the shadow of anonymity, to look upon as one of the rarest poets of the century, was born at Bredfield, in Suffolk, on the 31st of March, 1809. He was the third son of John Purcell... *Music Pages 172*

- [ ] **Ancient Law** by *Henry Maine* ISBN: *1-59462-128-4* **$29.95**
  The chief object of the following pages is to indicate some of the earliest ideas of mankind, as they are reflected in Ancient Law, and to point out the relation of those ideas to modern thought. *Religion History Pages 452*

- [ ] **Far-Away Stories** by *William J. Locke* ISBN: *1-59462-129-2* **$19.45**
  "Good wine needs no bush, but a collection of mixed vintages does. And this book is just such a collection. Some of the stories I do not want to remain buried for ever in the museum files of dead magazine-numbers an author's not unpardonable vanity..." *Fiction Pages 272*

- [ ] **Life of David Crockett** by *David Crockett* ISBN: *1-59462-250-7* **$27.45**
  "Colonel David Crockett was one of the most remarkable men of the times in which he lived. Born in humble life, but gifted with a strong will, an indomitable courage, and unremitting perseverance... *Biographies/New Age Pages 424*

- [ ] **Lip-Reading** by *Edward Nitchie* ISBN: *1-59462-206-X* **$25.95**
  Edward B. Nitchie, founder of the New York School for the Hard of Hearing, now the Nitchie School of Lip-Reading, Inc, wrote "LIP-READING Principles and Practice". The development and perfecting of this meritorious work on lip-reading was an undertaking... *How-to Pages 400*

- [ ] **A Handbook of Suggestive Therapeutics, Applied Hypnotism, Psychic Science** ISBN: *1-59462-214-0* **$24.95**
  by *Henry Munro* *Health/New Age Health/Self-help Pages 376*

- [ ] **A Doll's House: and Two Other Plays** by *Henrik Ibsen* ISBN: *1-59462-112-8* **$19.95**
  Henrik Ibsen created this classic when in revolutionary 1848 Rome. Introducing some striking concepts in playwriting for the realist genre, this play has been studied the world over. *Fiction/Classics/Plays 308*

- [ ] **The Light of Asia** by *sir Edwin Arnold* ISBN: *1-59462-204-3* **$13.95**
  In this poetic masterpiece, Edwin Arnold describes the life and teachings of Buddha. The man who was to become known as Buddha to the world was born as Prince Gautama of India but he rejected the worldly riches and abandoned the reigns of power when... *Religion/History/Biographies Pages 170*

- [ ] **The Complete Works of Guy de Maupassant** by *Guy de Maupassant* ISBN: *1-59462-157-8* **$16.95**
  "For days and days, nights and nights, I had dreamed of that first kiss which was to consecrate our engagement, and I knew not on what spot I should put my lips..." *Fiction/Classics Pages 240*

- [ ] **The Art of Cross-Examination** by *Francis L. Wellman* ISBN: *1-59462-309-0* **$26.95**
  Written by a renowned trial lawyer, Wellman imparts his experience and uses case studies to explain how to use psychology to extract desired information through questioning. *How-to/Science/Reference Pages 408*

- [ ] **Answered or Unanswered?** by *Louisa Vaughan* ISBN: *1-59462-248-5* **$10.95**
  Miracles of Faith in China *Religion Pages 112*

- [ ] **The Edinburgh Lectures on Mental Science (1909)** by *Thomas* ISBN: *1-59462-008-3* **$11.95**
  This book contains the substance of a course of lectures recently given by the writer in the Queen Street Hall, Edinburgh. Its purpose is to indicate the Natural Principles governing the relation between Mental Action and Material Conditions... *New Age/Psychology Pages 148*

- [ ] **Ayesha** by *H. Rider Haggard* ISBN: *1-59462-301-5* **$24.95**
  Verily and indeed it is the unexpected that happens! Probably if there was one person upon the earth from whom the Editor of this, and of a certain previous history, did not expect to hear again... *Classics Pages 380*

- [ ] **Ayala's Angel** by *Anthony Trollope* ISBN: *1-59462-352-X* **$29.95**
  The two girls were both pretty, but Lucy who was twenty-one who supposed to be simple and comparatively unattractive, whereas Ayala was credited, as her Bombwhat romantic name might show, with poetic charm and a taste for romance. Ayala when her father died was nineteen... *Fiction Pages 484*

- [ ] **The American Commonwealth** by *James Bryce* ISBN: *1-59462-286-8* **$34.45**
  An interpretation of American democratic political theory. It examines political mechanics and society from the perspective of Scotsman James Bryce *Politics Pages 572*

- [ ] **Stories of the Pilgrims** by *Margaret P. Pumphrey* ISBN: *1-59462-116-0* **$17.95**
  This book explores pilgrims religious oppression in England as well as their escape to Holland and eventual crossing to America on the Mayflower, and their early days in New England... *History Pages 268*

BOOK JUNGLE

Bringing Classics to Life

www.bookjungle.com email: sales@bookjungle.com fax: 630-214-0564 mail: Book Jungle PO Box 2226 Champaign, IL 61825

QTY

The Fasting Cure *by Sinclair Upton* ISBN: *1-59462-222-1* **$13.95**
In the Cosmopolitan Magazine for May, 1910, and in the Contemporary Review (London) for April, 1910, I published an article dealing with my experiences in fasting. I have written a great many magazine articles, but never one which attracted so much attention... *New Age/Self Help/Health Pages 164*

Hebrew Astrology *by Sepharial* ISBN: *1-59462-308-2* **$13.45**
In these days of advanced thinking it is a matter of common observation that we have left many of the old landmarks behind and that we are now pressing forward to greater heights and to a wider horizon than that which represented the mind-content of our progenitors... *Astrology Pages 144*

Thought Vibration or The Law of Attraction in the Thought World ISBN: *1-59462-127-6* **$12.95**
by William Walker Atkinson *Psychology/Religion Pages 144*

Optimism *by Helen Keller* ISBN: *1-59462-108-X* **$15.95**
Helen Keller was blind, deaf, and mute since 19 months old, yet famously learned how to overcome these handicaps, communicate with the world, and spread her lectures promoting optimism. An inspiring read for everyone... *Biographies/Inspirational Pages 84*

Sara Crewe *by Frances Burnett* ISBN: *1-59462-360-0* **$9.45**
In the first place, Miss Minchin lived in London. Her home was a large, dull, tall one, in a large, dull square, where all the houses were alike, and all the sparrows were alike, and where all the door-knockers made the same heavy sound... *Childrens/Classic Pages 88*

The Autobiography of Benjamin Franklin *by Benjamin Franklin* ISBN: *1-59462-135-7* **$24.95**
The Autobiography of Benjamin Franklin has probably been more extensively read than any other American historical work, and no other book of its kind has had such ups and downs of fortune. Franklin lived for many years in England, where he was agent... *Biographies/History Pages 332*

Name	
Email	
Telephone	
Address	
City, State ZIP	

☐ Credit Card   ☐ Check / Money Order

Credit Card Number	
Expiration Date	
Signature	

Please Mail to: Book Jungle
PO Box 2226
Champaign, IL 61825
or Fax to: 630-214-0564

ORDERING INFORMATION

web: www.bookjungle.com
email: sales@bookjungle.com
fax: 630-214-0564
mail: Book Jungle PO Box 2226 Champaign, IL 61825
or PayPal to sales@bookjungle.com

Please contact us for bulk discounts

DIRECT-ORDER TERMS

20% Discount if You Order Two or More Books
Free Domestic Shipping!
Accepted: Master Card, Visa, Discover, American Express

www.ingramcontent.com/pod-product-compliance
Lightning Source LLC
Chambersburg PA
CBHW082105230426
43671CB00015B/2610